Critical Survey of Poetry
Latin American Poets

Editor

Rosemary M. Canfield Reisman
Charleston Southern University

SALEM PRESS
A Division of EBSCO Publishing, Ipswich, Massachusetts

Cover photo:
Octavio Paz (© William Coupon/CORBIS)

Copyright © 2012, by Salem Press, A Division of EBSCO Publishing, Inc. All rights in this book are reserved. No part of this work may be used or reproduced in any manner whatsoever or transmitted in any form or by any means, electronic or mechanical, including photocopy, recording, or any information storage and retrieval system, without written permission from the copyright owner except in the case of brief quotations embodied in critical articles and reviews or in the copying of images deemed to be freely licensed or in the public domain. For information address the publisher, Salem Press, at csr@salempress.com.

ISBN: 978-1-42983-664-7

CONTENTS

Contributors iv

Latin American Poetry 1

Claribel Alegría 9
Jorge Luis Borges 17
Ernesto Cardenal 24
Sor Juana Inés de la Cruz 31
Rubén Darío 40
Carlos Drummond de Andrade 48
Enrique González Martínez 60
José Hernández 70
Gabriela Mistral 76
Pablo Neruda 85
Nicanor Parra 99
Octavio Paz 107
Alfonso Reyes 118
César Vallejo 126
Daisy Zamora 139

Checklist for Explicating a Poem 145
Bibliography 148
Guide to Online Resources 153
Geographical Index 156
Category Index 157
Subject Index 159

CONTRIBUTORS

Carole A. Champagne
University of Maryland-Eastern Shore

Rogelio A. de la Torre
Indiana University at South Bend

Lee Hunt Dowling
University of Houston

Desiree Dreeuws
Sunland, California

William L. Felker
Yellow Springs, Ohio

Robert Hauptman
St. Cloud State University

Alfred W. Jensen
University of Idaho-Moscow

Rebecca Kuzins
Pasadena, California

Linda Ledford-Miller
University of Scranton

David Nerkle
Washington, D.C.

Caryn E. Neumann
Miami University of Ohio

Charles A. Perrone
University of Florida

Jack Shreve
Allegany Community College

Paul Siegrist
Fort Hays State University

Kenneth A. Stackhouse
Virginia Commonwealth University

James Whitlark
Texas Tech University

LATIN AMERICAN POETRY

The panorama of Latin American poetry spans five hundred years, from the sixteenth to the twenty-first centuries. The first "Renaissance" in the New World (1492-1556) was the era of discovery, exploration, conquest, and colonization under the reign of the Spanish monarchs Ferdinand and Isabela and later Carlos V. The origins of Latin American literature are found in the chronicles of these events, narrated by Spanish soldiers or missionaries. The era of colonization during the reign of Philip II (1556-1598) was a second Renaissance and the period of the Counter-Reformation. During this time, Alonso de Ercilla y Zúñiga (1533-1594) wrote the first epic poem, *La Araucana* (1569-1589). The native saga narrated the wars between the Spanish conquistadors and the Araucano Indians of Chile. This is the first truly poetic literary work with an American theme.

Sor Juana Inés de la Cruz

During the period of the Austrian Habsburg kings (1598-1701), this Renaissance was gradually replaced by the Baroque era. While the Golden Age of Spanish letters was declining in the Old World, Sor Juana Inés de la Cruz (1648-1695) reigned supreme as the queen of colonial letters. She was the major poet during the colonial era. The autodidactic nun, who wrote plays and prose as well as poetry, was known as the tenth muse, *la décima musa*. Her poetic masterpiece, the autobiographical "Primero sueño," combines Baroque elements with a mastery of Spanish and classical languages and her unique style. Her shorter poems, with their lyrical verse phrasing and native themes, capture popular Mexican culture. Some of her most famous sonnets are "Este que ves, engaño colorido" (what you see [is] dark deception), "¿En perseguirme, mundo, qué interesas?" (in pursuing me, world, what interests you?), "Détente, sombra de mi bien esquivo" (stop, shadow of my elusive love), and "Esta tarde, mi bien, cuando te hablaba" (this afternoon, love, when I spoke to you). Her most recognized *redondillas* (or "roundelays," stanzas of four octosyllabic lines rhyming *abba*) are "Este amoroso tormento" (this tormented love) and "Hombres necios" ("Foolish Men"). Her charm and brilliance won her many wealthy and royal patrons. While she initially accepted their admiration, she died a recluse after rejecting her literary career and denouncing her precocious fame and vain pursuits.

Neoclassicism

During the Wars of Independence (1808-1826), Neoclassicism and other French influences dominated literary production. Andrés Bello (1781-1865) is better known for his prose, but he was also a prolific verse writer who followed the European neoclassical movement. He wrote the poems "Alocución a la poesía" and "La agricultura en la zona tórida" with American themes and European style. José Maria Heredia (1803-1839) was a Cuban exiled in Mexico and the United States who wrote about the beauty of the countries that adopted him. Romanticism characterized his poems about Niagara Falls, "Niágara," Aztec ruins, "En el Teocalli de Cholula," and other wonders such as a storm in "En una tempestad." His ode "Himno a un desterrado" relates his experience as an exile in adopted nations.

Gertrudis Gómez de Avellaneda (1814-1873) left Cuba to write in Spain because of the greater freedom she could enjoy there as a female poet. Romanticism influenced her poems about love, God, and her homeland, such as "Noche de insomnio y el alba" (night of insomnia and dawn), "Al partir" (upon leaving), and "Amor y orgullo" (love and pride).

José Hernández (1834-1886) wrote about the Argentinean gauchos in *El Gaucho Martín Fierro* (1872; *The Gaucho Martin Fierro*, 1935) and *La vuelta de Martín Fierro* (1879; *The Return of Martin Fierro*, 1935; included in *The Gaucho Martin Fierro*, 1935). His Romantic verses followed the structures and lyrical rhythms of popular songs that romanticized the gauchos as a dying breed in the wake of industrialization.

Modernismo

By 1875, the roots of a poetic movement had grown into a new poetic era. The Latin American *Modernistas* were innovators and critics of the conservative thematic and stylistic structures that persisted from the colonial period. In Latin American society, global industrialization, capitalism, North American cultural and economic imperialism, and Spain's loss of all its colonies had a significant impact on artistic development.

A definitive moment in the progress of the movement resulted from José Martí's publication of *Ismaelillo* in 1882. The poet and hero, who died fighting for Cuban independence (1853-1895), published *Versos libres* that same year, a collection that followed *Versos sencillos*, published in 1881. All three collections characterized the existential angst of the era as they experimented with new lyrical forms and themes. Martí approached language as a sculptor approaches clay and molded words into new forms. His innovations have allowed him to be considered the first great visionary Latin American poet as he sought to define *Nuestra América*, a Latin American identity struggling for artistic as well as political and economic independence. Throughout the movement, the anguish, emptiness, and uncertainty of modernity provided a unifying thread for poets seeking innovation.

The Mexican modernist Manuel Gutierrez Nájera (1859-1895) was a journalist renowned for his prose writings in his own time. He founded *La Revista Azul*, a literary review that promoted *Modernismo* throughout Latin America. His contemporary Rubén Darío (1867-1916), however, defined the *Modernista* poetic. Darío's poetry was a reaction to the decadence of Romanticism in which he sought a unique voice while reinvigorating the Spanish language. He led a movement that borrowed themes popularized by the European Romantics and stylistic models of the French Parnassian movement. Darío not only was an instigator and initiator of the vindication of his language, but also served as a bridge to the second stage of *Modernismo*. His *Azul* (1888; blue) and *Cantos de vida y esperanza, Los cisnes, y otros poemas* (1905; songs of life and hope, the swans, and other poems) represent Darío's dynamic style, respect for beauty, search for harmonious words, and celebration of pleasure. Despite the Decadence of his later poetry collections, Darío maintained confidence in the saving power of art and its use to protest against social and historical injustices and resolve existential enigmas. The *Modernistas* defended humanism in the face of economic progress and international imperialism, which devaluated art. They elevated art as an end in itself.

Leopoldo Lugones (1874-1938) was the major Argentinean *Modernista* poet. His poems "Delectación morosa," "Emoción aldeana," and "Divagación lunar" lament ephemeral beauty captured and immortalized by perfectly placed words. Alfonsina Storni (1892-1938) was influenced by postmodernist tendencies. Her intense verse experimented with Symbolism and other twentieth century innovations. Her vivid sensual poems include "Tú me quieres blanca," "Epitafio para mi tumba," "Voy a dormir," "Hombre pequeñito," and "Fiera de amor." The Uruguayan Delmira Agustini (1886-1914) wrote intensely emotional and erotic poems that highlighted the dualities of human nature. Pleasure and pain, good and evil, love and death create and maintain verbal tension. These opposites struggle for dominance in poems such as "La musa," "Explosión," and "El vampiro."

All of these individual elements come together in these poets' faith in the artistic power of the word. This autonomous aesthetic power opposed the *fin de siglo* (turn of the century) angst resulting from industrialism, positivism, and competing ideologies. While reflecting on their predecessors, the *Modernistas* created original verse with unique usage of sometimes archaic or exotic words. The language was sometimes luxurious and sensual, adapting classical and Baroque usage, from elements of the Parnassians to those of the Pre-Raphaelites to the Art Nouveau and European Symbolist movements and tendencies of decadent Romanticism. The symbolic impact of words characterized the movement as a whole. This all-encompassing factor defines the movement and its existential nature. This poetry is the living expression of an era of spiritual crises, personal and societal anguish, and uncertainty about the future of art as well as humanity's direction as it embarked upon the twentieth century.

Postmodernism and the Vanguard

No exact date marks the transition from Latin American modernism to postmodernism or to a vanguard movement. A combination of historical and societal factors influenced the artistic development of individual Latin American countries. In the first two decades of the twentieth century, World War I and the Mexican Revolution interrupted artistic and literary exchange between the Old World models and the New World innovators. The urban bourgeoisie, who were patrons of the arts, were displaced. The United States had gradually replaced the European masters in science and industry as well as politics, and its dominance permeated all levels of Latin American society.

Altazor (wr. 1919, pb. 1931), by Chilean Vicente Huidobro (1893-1948), marks a break with the past. Huidobro originated stylistic practices never seen before in Latin American poetry. In *creacionismo*, his personal version of creationism, he sought to create a poem the way nature made a tree. His words, invested with autonomous linguistic and symbolic significance, reinvent themselves by creating a world apart from other words. They are antilyrical, intellectual, and disconnected from emotional and spiritual experience. Nevertheless, Huidobro's world, created by his unique use of words, was a human creation because in it the poet experiences alienation and existential angst. Huidobro's poems "Arte poética," "Depart," and "Marino" voice his despair in isolation.

Huidobro had a significant influence on younger poets, particularly in his development of a school of thought that centered on the theory of *Ultraísmo*, which attempted to construct alternative linguistic choices to those offered by the external world. *Ultraísmo* synthesized Latin American with Spanish and European tendencies.

Among those influenced by *Ultraísmo* were Jorge Luis Borges (1899-1986), and in fact, Borges became its main proponent. While his short stories have repeatedly caused him to be nominated for the Nobel Prize in Literature, his poetry reveals a linguistic expertise and lyrical genius unparalleled by his contemporaries. He believed that lyricism and metaphysics united to justify the means of the poetic process. This fusion provides the genesis of his most representative poems, "Everything and Nothing," "Everness," "Laberinto," "Dreamtigers," and "Borges y yo."

The Peruvian César Vallejo (1892-1938) developed a unique and distinctive poetic voice. His *Los heraldos negros* (1918; *The Black Heralds*, 1990), *Trilce* (1922; English translation, 1973), and *Poemas humanos* (1939; *Human Poems*, 1968) demonstrate the impossibility of mutual communication and comprehension, the absurdity of the human condition, and the inevitability of death.

In 1945, Gabriela Mistral (1889-1957) was the first Latin American writer to receive the Nobel Prize in Literature. Her verses echo the folksongs and traditional ballads of her native Chile, the Caribbean, and Mexico. They naturally blend native dialects with Castilian in a lyrical fusion. Some of her best poems include "Sonetos a la muerte," "Todos íbamos a ser reinas," "Pan," and "Cosas."

Mistral's countryman Pablo Neruda (1904-1973) also won the Nobel Prize in Literature, in 1971. During his formative years he was influenced by *Modernismo*, experimenting with various styles while serving as an international diplomat. The last stage of his poetry was marked by didacticism and political themes, and he was exiled for his activity in the Communist Party. Neruda sought to create a forum for "impure" poetry that encompassed all experience. His *Canto general* (1950; partial translation in *Let the Rail Splitter Awake, and Other Poems*, 1951; full translation as *Canto General*, 1991) voiced his solidarity with humanity in his political and poetic conversion. *Odas elementales* (1954; *The Elemental Odes*, 1961) continued his mission of solidarity with the humblest members of creation. Other landmark collections include *Los versos del capitán* (1952; *The Captain's Verses*, 1972) and *Cien sonetos de amor* (1959; *One Hundred Love Sonnets*, 1986). Neruda believed that America and clarity should be one and the same.

The Mexican literary generation known as the *Taller* was led by Octavio Paz (1914-1998). He was awarded the Nobel Prize in Literature in 1990 for his brilliant prose and poetry that defined the Mexican culture and connected its isolation and universality to other cultures. His landmark analysis of poetic theory is proposed in *El arco y la lira* (1956; *The Bow and the Lyre*, 1973). The poetic evolution of linguistic progression considered "signs in rotation" culminated in *Piedra de sol* (1957; *Sun Stone*, 1963) and synthesized all twentieth century poetic theories into a highly original yet distinctly Mexican work. Representative poems include "Himno entre ruinas," "Viento entero," and "La poesía."

The Chilean poet Nicanor Parra (born 1914) developed a unique yet popular style. He called his poems *antipoemas* for their super-realism, sarcasm, self-criticism, and humor. Parra's poetry speaks to the masses and rejects pretension, as the poet revitalizes language and innovates with words in action. His masterwork, *Poemas y antipoemas* (1954; *Poems and Antipoems*, 1967), epitomizes antirhetorical and antimetaphorical free verse. "Soliloquio del individuo" and "Recuerdos de juventud" are representative.

The work of Sara de Ibañez (1910-1981) represents the antithesis of fellow Uruguayan Agustini. Her intellectual and metaphysical themes and neoclassical style allude to the poetry of Sor Juana and Golden Age masters such as Spain's Luis de Góngora y Argote. Love and death are analyzed in "Isla en la tierra," "Isla en la luz," "Liras," and "Soliloquios del Soldado."

The "impure" poetry of Ernesto Cardenal (born 1925) unites political ugliness and the beauty of the imagination. It is characterized by *exteriorismo*, a technique that incorporates propaganda, sound bites, advertisements, and fragments of popular culture into poetry that seeks to convert and enlighten. The aesthetic value of these poems is not overshadowed by their political and spiritual message. Representative collections include *La hora O* (1960), *Salmos* (1967; *The Psalms of Struggle and Liberation*, 1971), *Oración por Marilyn Monroe, y otros poemas* (1965; *Marilyn Monroe, and Other Poems*, 1975), and *Cántico cósmico* (1989; *The Music of the Spheres*, 1990; also known as *Cosmic Canticle*).

Rosario Castellanos (1925-1974) is best known for her novels and essays about social injustice in her native Chiapas. Because she focused on the status of women within the Mayan culture and within Mexican society as a whole, she was considered a feminist. Her poetry and prose are concerned with the human condition, not only with the plight of women. Her most representative poems are "Autorretrato," "Entrevista de Prensa," and "Se habla de Gabriel."

Thematically and stylistically more militant and radical, Rosario Ferré (born 1938) writes overtly feminist poetry using elements of symbolism and irony. Her poems include "Pretalamio," "Negativo," "La prisionera," and "Epitalamio." As editor of a literary journal, Ferré introduced feminist criticism to Latin American literature.

Movements on a smaller national scale characterize present-day poetry. They are characterized by experimental and politically and socially conscious efforts. The twenty-first century heralds the work of *los nuevos*, the new poets whose work is linked to national as well as international issues.

Individual postvanguard poets do not identify with particular ideologies. The poetry of Argentineans Mario Benedetti (1920-2009) and Juan Gelman (born 1930) deals with personal exile as well as the universal experience of exile. Since the 1980's, women have emerged with empowered poetry that serves as liberation from oppression. Poets including Alejandra Pizarnik (1936-1972), Rosario Murillo (born 1951), Giaconda Belli (born 1948), Claribel Alegría (born 1924), Juana de Ibarbourou (1895-1979), and Ana Istarú (born 1960) have given voice to the silent struggles of women striving to realize their potential in a male-dominated society.

Poetry written since the 1980's has focused on oppression and exile. The focus on the withdrawal from history as a condition for the poetry of Paz has shifted to the poet belonging in the historical moment so that poetry has a public place and common concern. Contemporary Latin American poetry has become the process of naming the word and rewriting history in a lived world. The making of that world is the creative act that celebrates the word.

BIBLIOGRAPHY

Agosín, Marjorie, ed. and trans. *These Are Not Sweet Girls: Latin American Women Poets*. Fredonia, N.Y.: White Pine Press, 1994. Bilingual edition. Agosín is a prolific and influential poet as well as a distinguished professor and literary critic. This volume from the Secret Weavers series focuses on the poetic production of Hispanic women since the advent of feminism as expressed through their work, written predominantly during the last thirty years of the twentieth century.

Agosín, Marjorie, and Roberta Gordenstein, eds. *Miriam's Daughters: Jewish Latin American Women Poets*. Foreword by Agosín. Santa Fe, N.Mex.: Sherman Asher, 2001. Twenty-eight poets are represented in this anthology, which includes the Spanish or Portuguese texts, along with English translations. Author biographies.

Gonzalez, Mike, and David Treece. *The Gathering of Voices: The Twentieth Century Poetry of Latin America*. New York: Verso, 1992. This study addresses a wide range of topics. The contradictions of Latin American *Modernismo* are explored, including its elements of shock and despair that distinguished it from its predecessors. The roots of the vanguard movement are examined, and the enduring poetry of Neruda is discussed in detail. Special topics are discussed, such as Brazilian *Modernismo* and the Guerrilla Poets of Cuba. The work concludes with studies of Postmodernism in Brazil and Spanish-language poets in exile.

Green, Roland Arthur. *Unrequited Conquests: Love and Empire in the Colonial Americas*. Chicago: University of Chicago Press, 1999. This volume offers insight into Spanish colonialism, European imperialism, and their influences upon literature. Colonial love poetry is analyzed within its sociopolitical and historical contexts. Chapters are devoted to Sor Juana's fascinating life and works. Illustrated. Bibliography.

Rowe, William. *Poets of Contemporary Latin America: History and Inner Life*. New York: Oxford University Press, 2000. This study discusses contemporary Latin American poets who bridge the centuries, including Nicanor Parra, Carmen Ollé, and Ernesto Cardenal. Williams explores two major influences on late twentieth century and early twenty-first century poetry: the avant-garde movement and politically motivated poetic writing. He examines these roots from contextual and historical perspectives.

Smith, Verity. *Encyclopedia of Latin American Literature*. Chicago: Fitzroy Dearborn, 1996. This reference of nearly one thousand pages contains essays of at least fifteen hundred words on major poets, novelists, dramatists, other writers, movements, concepts, and other topics relating to South American, Central American, and Caribbean (including Spanish, French, and English) literatures. Overview essays cover literatures of individual countries, eras, and themes (such as science fiction, children's literature, and indigenous literatures), as well as the literatures of the major U.S. Latino communities: Cuban, Mexican, and Puerto Rican.

Sonntag Blay, Iliana L. *Twentieth-Century Poetry from Spanish America: An Index to Spanish Language Poetry and Bilingual Anthologies*. Lanham, Md.: Scarecrow Press, 1998. Three indexes provide access to more than twelve thousand Latin American poems from seventy-two anthologies: an author index, a title index, and an index of first lines. An important reference for serious scholars.

Tapscott, Stephen, ed. *Twentieth-Century Latin American Poetry: A Bilingual Anthology*. Austin: University of Texas Press, 1996. This is the first bilingual collection of the most important Latin American poets. Portuguese as well as Spanish poems are translated, and the selections cover the full range of the century, from the *Modernistas* to the postmoderns, the vanguardists, and contemporary political and experimental poetry. Tapscott provides background material and introductions to eighty-five poets in a well-organized volume with excellent translations.

Vicuña, Cecilia, and Ernesto Livon-Grosman, eds. *The Oxford Book of Latin American Poetry: A Bilingual Anthology*. New York: Oxford University Press, 2009. This impressive anthology contains poems by more than 120 poets. Includes such often overlooked traditions as native chants, mestizo poetry, and invented languages. Excellent introduction by the editors. Biographical notes and bibliography.

Washburne, Kelly, ed. *An Anthology of Spanish American Modernismo: In English Translation, with Spanish Text.* Translated by Washbourne with Sergio Waisman. New York: Modern Language Association of America, 2007. Superb translations of poems by eighteen *Modernista* poets from Argentina, Bolivia, Colombia, Cuba, Mexico, Nicaragua, Peru, and Uruguay. Introduction, suggestions for further reading, and bibliography.

Carole A. Champagne

CLARIBEL ALEGRÍA

Born: Estelí, Nicaragua; May 12, 1924

PRINCIPAL POETRY
Anillo de silencio, 1948
Suite de amor, angustia y soledad, 1951
Vigilias, 1953
Acuario, 1955
Huésped de mi tiempo, 1961
Vía ánica, 1965
Aprendizaje, 1970
Pagaré a cobrar y otros poemas, 1973
Sobrevivo, 1978
Suma y sigue, 1981
Flores del volcán/Flowers from the Volcano, 1982 (Carolyn Forché, translator)
Luisa en el país de la realidad, 1987 (*Luisa in Realityland*, 1987)
La mujer del rio Sumpul, 1987 (*Woman of the River*, 1989)
Y este poema-río, 1988
Fugues, 1993 (Darwin J. Flakoll, translator)
Variaciones en clave de mí, 1993
Umbrales = Thresholds, 1996 (Flakoll, translator)
Saudade = Sorrow, 1999 (Forché, translator)
Soltando Amarras = Casting Off, 2003 (Margaret Sayers Peden, translator)
Esto soy: Antologia de Claribel Alegría, 2004

OTHER LITERARY FORMS

Though primarily known as a poet, the prolific Claribel Alegría (ahl-ay-GREE-ah) has published in a range of genres, sometimes in collaboration with her husband and principal translator, Darwin "Bud" J. Flakoll. Alegría and Flakoll collaborated on the novel *Cenizas de Izalco* (1966; *Ashes of Izalco*, 1989), on a translation of the poems of Robert Graves (1981), on the anthology *New Voices of Hispanic America* (1962), and on the testimonials *Nicaragua: La revolución sandinista, una crónica política, 1855-1979* (1982; Nicaragua: the Sandinista revolution, a political chronicle, 1855-1979), *Para romper el silencio: Resistencia y lucha en las cárceles salvadoreñas* (1984; to break the silence: resistance and struggle in Salvadoran prisons), and *Fuga de Canto Grande* (1992; *Tunnel to Canto Grande*, 1996). Alegría also has published novellas, three of which are collected in *Album familiar* (1982, 1986; *Family Album: Three Novellas*, 1991), as well as essays and children's literature. She has also edited poetry collections.

Achievements

Claribel Alegría's *Ashes of Izalco*, a novel about the 1932 massacre known as the Matanza, was a finalist in 1964 in the Biblioteca Breve contest, sponsored by the Spanish publishing house Seix Barral. In 1978, she won Cuba's prestigious Casa de las Américas Prize for her volume of poetry *Sobrevivo* (I survive). In 2006, Alegría capped her career with the Neustadt International Prize for Literature. Perhaps most important, Alegría brought Central American literature, especially women's writing, to the attention of readers in the United States, and with it she brought a concern for the political situation in El Salvador and Nicaragua in particular. Her works have been translated into more than ten languages.

Biography

Clara Isabel Alegría Vides was born in Estelí, Nicaragua, to a Salvadoran mother and a Nicaraguan father, but her family soon moved to Santa Ana, El Salvador, because of the political problems her father suffered as a Sandino sympathizer. In 1932, she witnessed the Matanza, in which more than thirty thousand peasants were slaughtered by government troops after a peaceful protest against the military dictatorship.

Alegría published her first poems in 1941. In 1943, she went to the United States to attend a girls' school near New Orleans, Louisiana. She next attended George Washington University, where she met her husband, Flakoll, an American journalist from South Dakota who was studying for his master of arts degree. They married in December, 1947. In 1948, Alegría graduated with a bachelor's degree in philosophy and letters. Later that same year, her first book of poetry, *Anillo de silencio* (ring of silence), was published in Mexico. She gave birth to a daughter, Maya, in Washington, D.C., in 1949, and twin daughters, Patricia and Karen, in Alexandria, Virginia, in 1950. In 1951, the family visited El Salvador briefly before moving to Mexico, where their circle included various writers and intellectuals, some living in exile like Alegría.

In 1953, the family moved to Santiago, Chile, where they lived for almost three years, to work on an anthology (and translation) of Latin American writers and poets, *New Voices of Hispanic America*, which introduced writers such as Juan Rulfo and Julio Cortázar, who would later be part of the "boom" in Latin American literature. Her son Erik was born in Santiago in 1954. In 1956, the family returned to the United States, where Flakoll applied to the U.S. Foreign Service. In 1958, he was appointed second secretary to the U.S. Embassy in Montevideo, Uruguay, and two years later, he was posted to Argentina. However, Flakoll, disillusioned by the world of politics, resigned from the Foreign Service. In 1962, Alegría and Flakoll moved to Paris, where they met many Latin American writers living in exile, including Carlos Fuentes, Mario Benedetti, and Mario Vargas Llosa. Alegría and Flakoll and worked on the first of many subsequent collaborations, producing her first novel, *Ashes of Izalco*, whose publication in Spain was delayed by censorship. In 1966, the family moved to Mallorca, where they lived for many years.

In 1979, after the Sandinistas overthrew the dictatorship of Anastasio Somosa in Nicaragua, Alegría and her husband went to Nicaragua to do research for a testimonial on the revolution. In 1980, a right-wing group assassinated outspoken human rights advocate and Roman Catholic archbishop Oscar Romero in El Salvador. Alegría gave a poetic eulogy for Romero at the Sorbonne in Paris. Her public criticism of Salvadoran government atrocities earned her a spot on a death list and made her a political exile from her adopted homeland. In 1983, Alegría and Flakoll moved permanently to Nicaragua. Flakoll died in 1995. Alegría remained in Nicaragua and has mentored numerous poets, including Gioconda Belli and Daisy Zamora.

Analysis

Claribel Alegría has often spoken in interviews of the writer's role as the voice of the voiceless, of poetry as a weapon against repression, oppression, exploitation, and injustice. She considers herself a feminist, which she defines as wanting equality for women and men, and she both writes about women and promotes the work of women writers. Her poetry reflects her experience of exile, loss, and absence, often with a sense of nostalgia, or of longing for a happier, more innocent past. Much of her work is at least partially autobiographical, and memory serves as a powerful means of preserving the past.

Flores del volcán/Flowers from the Volcano

The first translation of one of Alegría's works into English was *Flores del volcán/Flowers from the Volcano*, a bilingual edition. It is through the efforts of the translator, prizewinning poet Carolyn Forché, that Alegría first came to the attention of readers in the United States. Many of the poems chosen for this collection come from the 1978 collection *Sobrevivo*. The title of the work is an indication of its contents: The volcano represents Central America as a region and El Salvador as a country, as part of the Pacific Ring of Fire, but the volcano also represents the eruption, violence, and death caused by the civil wars of the 1970's and 1980's in Nicaragua, Guatemala, and El Salvador, while flowers suggest beauty, hope, and life.

In the title poem, "Flowers from the Volcano," Alegría critiques the class structure in El Salvador, in which "the volcano's children/ flow down like lava/ with their bouquets of flowers," threatening the status quo of the well-to-do, "the owners of two-story houses/ protected from thieves by walls," who "drown their fears in whiskey." She remembers the dead in "Sorrow," with its "rosary of names," including Roque Dalton, the Salvadoran poet killed by government forces in 1975, and the Chilean folksinger Victor Jara, killed by security forces in the stadium of Santiago in 1973, along with many other Chileans.

Flowers from the Volcano contains some poems of nostalgic recollection of life in Santa Ana in simpler times, but the collection principally engages notions of class struggle and the brutal repression of liberty and life. As Forché notes in the volume's preface, five years passed between the summer that she and Alegría worked on the book and its publication, and in those five years "more than 40,000 people . . . died in El Salvador at the hands of security forces."

LUISA IN REALITYLAND

Sometimes called a novel, or a mixed-genre work, *Luisa in Realityland* combines brief autobiographical anecdotes and vignettes with poetry to tell the story of the childhood and adolescence of Luisa (who resembles Alegría) in a country much like El Salvador. (The poems from this volume also form one section of the collection *Y este poema-río*.)

For Luisa, like Alegría, the ceiba tree of her homeland (in "The Ceiba") is nearly mystical with meaning, ". . . the sentinel/ of [her] childhood." In this poem, as in most of the poems in this work, are the themes of exile and loss: "My absences/ have been lengthy/ innumerable," she says; "They won't let me return." Alegría's politics are clear in these poems. In "Personal Creed" she states:

> I believe in my people
> who have been exploited
> for five hundred years

In "From the Bridge," the adult Luisa/Alegría looks back in time at the little girl and adolescent she once was, but now through the eyes of experience:

> Do you remember the massacre
> that left Izalco without menfolk?
> You were seven years old.
> How can I explain it to you
> nothing has changed
> and they keep killing people daily.

Despite the violence and pessimism of many of the poems, however, the book ends with an invitation to a "rebellious/ contagious peace," a "return to the future."

WOMAN OF THE RIVER

Many of the poems in *Woman of the River* directly confront the political situation in Central America and condemn the United States' influence and its presence there. In "The American Way of Death," Alegría criticizes America's response to people's desire for a better life:

> if you choose the guerrilla path,
> be careful,
> they'll kill you.

> If you combat your chaos
> through peace,
> . . . . . .
> they'll kill you.
>
> If your skin is dark
> . . . .
> slowly they'll kill you.

"The American Way of Life" contrasts skyscrapers with undocumented workers, wealth with wanton destruction, and finds one dependent on the other. America, says Alegría, is a selfish "bitch" who "chews Salvadorans/ as if they were Chiclets/ chews up Nicaraguans." Perhaps here she refers to the massive U.S. funding of the war in El Salvador or the training of Salvadoran and Nicaraguan soldiers by the U.S. military.

The title poem, "Woman of the River," testifies to the results of U.S. support of the war, telling the tale of a woman who survives the 1980 Sumpul River massacre with her baby and youngest son by hiding in the river for hours after the security troops have killed everyone in their path, including her other three children.

FUGUES

With the wars over in Central America, Alegría's later work became less political. In *Fugues*, the main themes are love, death, and aging. In "Mirror Image," for example, the poet considers the aging process, speaking to an alien, skull-like image superimposed on her own as it stares at her from the mirror:

> Why do you insist
> on showing me day after day
> these sockets
> that used to be my eyes?
> . . . .
> I traverse your skin
> to embrace the little girl
> who still resides in me

Fugues also contains a fascinating series of poems relating female mythological or historical figures to contemporary psychology. In "Letter to an Exile," the legendary Penelope (from Homer's epic poem the *Odyssey*, c. 725 B.C.E.; English translation, 1614) writes to her husband Odysseus, asking him please not to return home. Each of the Greek mythical figures—Persephone, Demeter, Pandora, and Hecate—has her own poem, as does Malinche, an Aztec interpreter and lover of the Spanish conqueror Hernán Cortés and the mother of the first Mexican. Each of the poems presents an interpretation from the woman's perspective rather than the usual interpretation of a woman by a man.

Sorrow

Saudade = Sorrow was written as a series of love poems to Alegría's dead husband. As her translator Forché comments, *saudade* is "a Portuguese word for a vague and persistent desire for something that cannot be, a time other than the present time, a turning toward the past or future, a sadness and yearning beyond sorrow." *Saudade* means much more than the English title *Sorrow*. The "Nostalgia" of *Fugues*, in which she stops being herself and begins forever "being us," becomes "Nostalgia II" in *Sorrow*, in which she ceases "being us" and again becomes "this I/ with its burden of winter/ and emptiness."

However, the collection ends optimistically when the poet states that "sadness can't cope" with her. Although *Sorrow* does not have the political tone or content common to her earlier works, Alegría has not forgotten her rosary of names to remember the dead. As she says in "Every Time," the dead are resurrected when she names them. Just as she used her art as a weapon for the cause of justice and named the dead to keep them alive to memory, she now uses her art to keep her "deceased beloved" present.

Casting Off

Soltando Amarras = Casting Off continues Alegría's theme of bereavement. The poet, a widow approaching eighty years of age, has shifted from a focus on the political to a focus on the personal. She writes with delicacy and restraint about her life winding down. Alegría clearly is still mourning her husband as well as her other departed friends. The poems occupy a stark, grief-filled landscape that is both intimate and universal.

"Casting Off" refers to the difficulties of growing old and accepting death. Although reluctant to let go, Alegría does see death as a reunion with loved ones who have gone before her, leaving her entangled in memories and unable to sleep. "You Made the Great Leap" expresses the loneliness of being left behind as well as Alegría's readiness to meet death:

> You made the great leap
> and were reborn
> I am left on this shore
> crouched to spring

Alegría seems to rehearse her departure from this world by taking on the personae of mythological women such as Arachne, Antigone, Medea, Cassandra, and the Furies. Through them, she approaches death and accepts it, refusing to shy away from risk and expressing a willingness to accept change. As she writes in "Limbo," she feels good because she is "all alone/ with my dead," and soon she will join them. Alegría is content to conclude a well-lived life.

OTHER MAJOR WORKS

LONG FICTION: *Cenizas de Izalco*, 1966 (with Darwin J. Flakoll; *Ashes of Izalco*, 1989); *El detén*, 1977; *Pueblo de Dios y de mandinga*, 1985; *Despierta mi bein, despierta*, 1986.

SHORT FICTION: *Album familiar*, 1982, 1986 (*Family Album: Three Novellas*, 1991).

NONFICTION: *Nicaragua: La revolución sandinista, una crónica política, 1855-1979*, 1982 (with Flakoll); *No me agarran viva: La mujer salvadoreña en lucha*, 1983 (with Flakoll; *They Won't Take Me Alive: Salvadoran Women in Struggle for National Liberation*, 1987); *Para romper el silencio: Resistencia y lucha en las cárceles salvadoreñas*, 1984 (with Flakoll); *Fuga de Canto Grande*, 1992 (with Flakoll; *Tunnel to Canto Grande*, 1996); *Somoza: Expediente cerrado, la historia de un ajusticiamiento*, 1993 (with Flakoll; *Death of Somoza: The First Person Story of the Guerrillas Who Assassinated the Nicaraguan Dictator*, 1996).

TRANSLATION: *Cien poemas de Robert Graves*, 1981 (with Flakoll).

CHILDREN'S LITERATURE: *Tres cuentos*, 1958.

EDITED TEXTS: *New Voices of Hispanic America*, 1962 (with Flakoll); *Homenaje a El Salvador*, 1981; *On the Front Line: Guerrilla Poetry of El Salvador*, 1988 (translated with Flakoll).

BIBLIOGRAPHY

Aparicio, Yvette. "Reading Social Consciousness in Claribel Alegría's Early Poetry." *Cincinnati Romance Review* 18 (1999): 1-6. Contends that Alegría's earlier, more metaphorical and less overtly "resistant" poetry contains implicit social criticism and deals with issues of injustice and power relations in a more allegorical manner than her later overtly politicized poetry.

Beverly, John, and Marc Zimmerman. *Literature and Politics in the Central American Revolutions*. Austin: University of Texas Press, 1990. Traces the development of popular revolutionary poetry and testimonial narrative as reactions to historical events in Nicaragua and El Salvador, and stresses the importance of revolutionary Salvadoran women poets such as Alegría.

Boschetto-Sandoval, Sandra M., and Marcia Phillips McGowan. *Claribel Alegría and Central American Literature: Critical Essays*. Athens: Ohio University Center for European Studies, 1994. An excellent collection of essays on Alegría's major works and themes. One essay specifically treats her poetry. Includes an interview with the poet and a chronology of her life and works, along with a bibliography of publications by and about her.

Craft, Linda J. *Novels of Testimony and Resistance from Central America*. Gainesville: University Press of Florida, 1997. The chapter on Alegría examines two works written in collaboration with her husband, Flakoll, *Ashes of Izalco* and *They Won't Take Me Alive*, and the multigenre *Luisa in Realityland*.

Harrison, Brady. "'The Gringos Perfected It in Vietnam': Torture and the American Adviser in Claribel Alegría's *Family Album* and Carlos Martinez Moreno's *El Infierno*." *Atenea* 26, no. 2 (2006): 9-19. Examines the theme of the psychological trauma of torture while showing how Alegría's work exemplifies how torture can discipline dissidents and regime alike.

McGowan, Marcia P. "Mapping a New Territory: *Luisa in Realityland*." *Letras Femeninas* 19, nos. 1/2 (Spring/Fall, 1993): 84-99. Considers *Luisa in Realityland* a "new form of autobiographical discourse" that incorporates poetry, testimony, and elements of fiction.

Sternbach, Nancy Saporta. "Remembering the Dead: Latin American Women's 'Testimonial' Discourse." *Latin American Perspectives* 18, no. 3 (Summer, 1991): 91-102. Examines the testimonial voice of prose and poetry in *They Won't Take Me Alive* and *Flores del Volcán/Flowers from the Volcano*.

Treacy, Mary Jane. "A Politics of the Word: Claribel Alegría's *Album familiar* and *Despierta mi bien, despierta*." *Intertexts* 1, no. 1 (Spring, 1997): 62-77. Discusses the "elite" or "bourgeois" woman as a marginalized "woman of porcelain," aware of her privileged status but not its political and economic underpinnings. In contrast to the passive bourgeois woman depicted in many of the female characters in novels by Isabel Allende, Rosario Ferré, and Teresa de la Parra, the two works by Alegría examined here portray "the struggles of the bourgeois woman to extricate herself from domesticity and to forge an independence through a 'progressive' political identity."

Van Delden, Maarten. "Claribel Alegría, the Neustadt Prize, and the World Republic of Letters." *World Literature Today* (May/June, 2007): 45-48. Discusses the significance of the Neustadt Prize and Alegría's critical reception in the world of letters.

Van Delden, Maarten, and Yvon Grenier. *Gunshots at the Fiesta: Literature and Politics in Latin America*. Nashville, Tenn.: Vanderbilt University Press, 2009. Discusses the political thought of Latin American writers. The chapter on Alegría focuses on *Ashes of Izalco* to argue that a writer does not have to abandon cultural nationalism to achieve literary excellence.

Linda Ledford-Miller
Updated by Caryn E. Neumann

JORGE LUIS BORGES

Born: Buenos Aires, Argentina; August 24, 1899
Died: Geneva, Switzerland; June 14, 1986
Also known as: F. Bustos; H. Bustos Domecq; B. Suárez Lynch

PRINCIPAL POETRY
Fervor de Buenos Aires, 1923, 1969
Luna de enfrente, 1925
Cuaderno San Martín, 1929
Poemas, 1923-1943, 1943
Poemas, 1923-1953, 1954
Obra poética, 1923-1958, 1958
El hacedor, 1960 (*Dreamtigers*, 1964)
Obra poética, 1923-1964, 1964
Seis poemas escandinavos, 1966
Siete poemas, 1967
Elogio de la sombra, 1969 (*In Praise of Darkness*, 1974)
El otro, el mismo, 1969
Para las seis cuerdas: milongas, 1970 (illustrated by Héctor Basaldua)
El oro de los tigres, 1972 (translated in *The Gold of Tigers: Selected Later Poems*, 1977)
La rosa profunda, 1975 (translated in *The Gold of Tigers*)
La moneda de hierro, 1976
Historia de la noche, 1977
Sonetos a Buenos Aires, 1979
Antologia poética, 1923-1977, 1981
La cifra, 1981
Los conjurados, 1985
Obra poética, 1923-1985, 1989
Selected Poems, 1999

OTHER LITERARY FORMS

Jorge Luis Borges (BAWR-hays) is best known for his short stories, especially those written during the period when he made each the exploration of a metaphysical paradox, often with the pretense that he was summarizing some larger work. These metaphysical themes pervade most of his poems, which give them even more condensed treatment.

Achievements

The best measure of the achievement of Jorge Luis Borges is his enormous influence on world literature and literary criticism, especially on Latin American Magical Realism and North American fantasy. Borges, along with Samuel Beckett, received the International Publishers' Prize (Prix Formentor) in 1961. Other recognitions include the Ingram Merrill Foundation's Annual Literary Award (1966), various honorary degrees (beginning in 1971 with Columbia University), Israel's Jerusalem Prize (1971), Mexico's Alfonso Reyes Prize (1973), the Nebula Award for Best Short Story (1975), a Special Edgar Allan Poe Award from the Mystery Writers of America (1976), the World Fantasy Award (1979), Spain's Miguel de Cervantes Prize (1979, shared with Gerardo Diego), the International Balzan Prize (1980), France's Cino Del Duca World Prize (1980), the Ingersoll Foundation's T. S. Eliot Award for Creative Writing (1983), and the National Book Critics Circle Award in criticism (1999). Argentina honored him with the directorship of its National Library from 1955 to 1973. He became a member of the French Legion of Honor in 1983.

Biography

Jorge Luis Borges was born in Buenos Aires, Argentina, in 1899. Borges grew up bilingual in Spanish and English, largely because he had a British grandmother, and later learned some French, German, and Latin during the family's four years in Switzerland (1914-1919). The major conflict during his early years was between forcefulness and literary refinement. Before leaving for Switzerland (to seek treatment for his father's growing blindness), his family lived in a suburb plagued with knife-fighting gauchos and other criminals, a fascination with which often surfaced in Borges's writings. In partial contrast, his father was a lawyer, psychology teacher, and amateur novelist. Once, however, when Borges was being bullied by Argentine classmates, his father handed him a knife. Another incentive toward assertiveness may have come from his mother (a dominant figure until she died at the age of ninety-nine), who prided herself on being descended from famous warriors. Edwin Wilson's biography of Borges argues that he was made to feel that a literary life was less valid than a military one.

After a period in Spain, where he fell under the influence of Ultraists (who reduced poems to a series of metaphors), Borges and his family returned to Argentina in 1921. He cofounded the Ultraist journal *Prisma*, and in 1923, he published his first collection of poetry, *Fervor de Buenos Aires* (fervor of Buenos Aires), paid for by his father and with a cover by his sister. After the family returned to Europe later that year for his father's eye treatments, he received a positive review of the book in the Spanish journal *Revista de Occidente*; thus his literary reputation was founded.

Borges was seen as a Europeanized intellectual, whom critics contrasted with the populists. In protest at being classified as a member of the elite, he spent years exploring and writing about the Argentine lower class (for example, the kind of criminal nightclubs where the tango was then danced). From this time forward, he suffered from various unrequited loves, particularly of Norah Lange, whose house figures nostalgically in many of his poems.

By 1937, his father could no longer provide for the family, so Borges took a menial position in a library, where he would finish his duties quickly each day and spend the rest of the time reading, translating, and composing articles, including antifascist essays. In 1946, this political activity had caused him to be forced out of his job by the profascist government of the populist president Juan Perón, who had been elected that year. Borges's resistance to the Perónists continued throughout his life, sometimes placing him on the liberal (antifascist side) and sometimes on the conservative (antipopulist) side. His reputation had grown to the extent that he could earn a living by writing and giving lectures, which he continued to do, even after his hereditary eye disease brought eight operations for cataracts and then blindness. He served as professor of English and American literature at the University of Buenos Aires from 1956 to 1968. He married Elsa Astete Millán in 1967, but she was rejected by his intellectual friends, and the marriage ended in divorce in 1970. He left Argentina, disappointed by its 1982 invasion of the Falkland Islands, for Geneva. There, in 1986, the last year of his life, he was married to the photographer María Kodama. He died of liver cancer in Geneva.

Analysis

Even more obviously than his other writings, the poetry of Jorge Luis Borges focuses on psychological orientation, reconciling the cultural contradictions associated with the poet's place in the world. In the early poetry, this issue of place tends to be quite literal, especially in his first volume, *Fervor de Buenos Aires*, about various locations in that city. Inspired partly by the French Symbolist poets he had read during his high school years in Switzerland, he made urban landscapes into representations of modern angst—consonant with the cynicism he was gleaning at that period from his literary mentor Macedonio Fernándéz but juxtaposed with his mother's patriotism.

In his preface to a 1969 reprint of *Luna de enfrente* (moon across the way), he contrasts the introverted way he mapped the city in *Fervor de Buenos Aires* with the ostentation of the later volume. It ushers in a splattering of the lines with local slang, typical of those periods when he acted as if he had to prove his virility that way. This, however, never led him to abandon the allusive or metaphysical, since the goal was always to make the physical locations metaphors for states of mind. That situation becomes more explicit in his third volume, *Cuaderno San Martín* (San Martin copybook), with "Fundación mítica de Buenos Aires" ("The Mythical Founding of Buenos Aires"), in which, after speculating about the actual origins of Buenos Aires, he recognizes the place is for him an eternal mental state.

This marks a transition from his poetic apprenticeship toward his long second period of mastery. Beginning with his 1960 collection *Dreamtigers*, he tended to set poems in the mind itself (often in some version of a dream). After his mother's death in 1975, he gradually shifted into a third period, old age. Particularly in the 1980's during his relationship with Kodama, he achieved greater independence from his mother's influence (for example, a growing pacifism and a lessening of embarrassment over not being a warrior). During this time, his poems incorporated more short sentences as if sometimes gasping for breath and were prone to complain of ill health, but they also celebrated his new love. It was a time of dreams coming true (albeit awkwardly and belatedly), as with the prose poem "Mi última tigre" ("My Last Tiger"), about the time when, blind and frightened, he nonetheless managed the courage to pet a real tiger.

Fervor de Buenos Aires

Although less directly than during his middle period, self-division characterizes *Fervor de Buenos Aires*. In "Las calles" ("The Streets"), for example, the speaker of the poem situates his soul as being on those streets—yet not on the avaricious, crowded ones (the core of the city) but on nearly empty, suburban ones, diminishing into eternal expanses. Despite this antiurban sentiment, the poem ends with an injunction to literal flag waving in praise of his country. Since the center of Buenos Aires was expensive property and its suburbs much less so, his rejecting the former for the latter has perhaps a liberal slant but not a populist one, because of his denouncing crowds. The poet longs for the timeless peripheries, where the streets (and presumably the speaker's soul) end. Throughout Borges's entire poetic opus, this is a common metaphor—a longing to move outside time, even at the cost of extinction, but in interviews, he said repeatedly that he kept remarking this precisely because he feared loss of himself. Indeed, in "The Streets," the poet counters this drift toward the timeless void with the image of separate souls recognized as such by God and also by the poem's patriotic affirmation of his country at the end. The streets themselves thus become a metaphor for a place where the poet's soul connects difficult-to-join opposites. This poem establishes the ambivalent attitude of the volume.

Even as patriotic a poem as "Inscripción sepulchral" ("Sepulchral Inscription") ends with Isidoro Suárez turned not merely into glory but also into dust. Because he provides the fact that Suárez is his great-grandfather, Borges advertises himself as being the speaker. Conversely "Calle desconocida" ("Unknown Street") is about a longing for oblivion, imaged as night and a downward path, derived from the pessimism of his favorite philosopher Arthur Schopenhauer. The poem portrays life as a locus of pain, where every step one takes is on some site of agony, compared to the Golgotha of Christ's crucifixion. Despite all this, the poem's speaker feels tenderness toward the earthly locals. In "Unknown Street," his imaginative power is so intense that poetry seems real to him to the point that the most he can say of the silver evening's vividness is that it resembles that of verse. In contrast, "El sur" ("The South") merely lists pleasant but plain images, such as stars whose names he does not know, and it concludes lamely that the place, not his words, constitutes the true poem. The volume is thus even ambivalent about the poet's qualification as poet—a theme persistent enough in Borges's subsequent poetry to be presumably his own.

DREAMTIGERS

Even more than *Antología personal* (1961; *A Personal Anthology*, 1967), *Dreamtigers*, a collection of verse and prose poems, was one he considered a very personal selection of his works. The intense self-division of the volume is established with his most famous prose poem, "Borges y yo" ("Borges and I"). It describes the tension between his physical self and his literary one, who keeps robbing the former of its experiences, even though the two manage to live together in Buenos Aires fairly peacefully. Also impressive is his prose poem "Dreamtigers," its title in English, which for Borges was a literary language dissociated from his Argentine existence. The whole point of the poem is to contrast literary tigers he loves with real ones and lament the difficulty of fixing either in the dreaming imagination—a part of himself not entirely under his control.

THE GOLD OF TIGERS

The Gold of Tigers is a bilingual edition that contains Alastair Reid's translation of *El oro de los tigres* and *La rosa profunda*. It helped to establish Borges's American reputation as a poet and marked the close of his middle period. Like all the poetry of that middle period, it is pervaded by the theme of life as a dream; nonetheless, it foreshadows his final period. It already laments that time is running out; thus some desires (such as to master the German language) will never be fulfilled. Two of its major themes are that his blindness stripped his sight of all colors but gold and that certain objects (such as the rose and coins) have resonances of events once connected to them. They may thus perhaps unite one to the whole universe.

OTHER MAJOR WORKS

LONG FICTION: *Un modelo para la muerte*, 1946 (with Adolfo Bioy Casares, under joint pseudonym B. Suárez Lynch).

SHORT FICTION: *Historia universal de la infamia*, 1935 (*A Universal History of Infamy*, 1972); *El jardín de senderos que se bifurcan*, 1941; *Seis problemas para don Isidro Parodi*, 1942 (with Bioy Casares, under joint pseudonym H. Bustos Domecq; *Six Problems for Don Isidro Parodi*, 1981); *Ficciones, 1935-1944*, 1944 (English translation, 1962); "Tres versiones de Judas," 1944 ("Three Versions of Judas," 1962); *Dos fantasías memorables*, 1946 (with Bioy Casares, under joint pseudonym Domecq); *El Aleph*, 1949, 1952 (translated in *The Aleph, and Other Stories, 1933-1969*, 1970); *La muerte y la brújula*, 1951; *La hermana de Eloísa*, 1955 (with Luisa Mercedes Levinson); *Cuentos*, 1958; *Crónicas de Bustos Domecq*, 1967 (with Bioy Casares; *Chroni-*

cles of Bustos Domecq, 1976); *El informe de Brodie*, 1970 (*Doctor Brodie's Report*, 1972); *El matrero*, 1970; *El congreso*, 1971 (*The Congress*, 1974); *El libro de arena*, 1975 (*The Book of Sand*, 1977); *Narraciones*, 1980.

SCREENPLAYS: *"Los orilleros" y "El paraíso de los creyentes,"* 1955 (with Bioy Casares); *Les Autres*, 1974 (with Bioy Casares and Hugo Santiago).

NONFICTION: *Inquisiciones*, 1925; *El tamaño de mi esperanza*, 1926; *El idioma de los argentinos*, 1928; *Evaristo Carriego*, 1930 (English translation, 1984); *Figari*, 1930; *Discusión*, 1932; *Las Kennigar*, 1933; *Historia de la eternidad*, 1936; *Nueva refutación del tiempo*, 1947; *Aspectos de la literatura gauchesca*, 1950; *Antiguas literaturas germánicas*, 1951 (with Delia Ingenieros; revised as *Literaturas germánicas medievales*, 1966, with Maria Esther Vásquez); *Otras Inquisiciones*, 1952 (*Other Inquisitions*, 1964); *El "Martin Fierro,"* 1953 (with Margarita Guerrero); *Leopoldo Lugones*, 1955 (with Betina Edelberg); *Manual de zoología fantástica*, 1957 (with Guerrero; *The Imaginary Zoo*, 1969; revised as *El libro de los seres imaginarios*, 1967, *The Book of Imaginary Beings*, 1969); *La poesía gauchesca*, 1960; *Introducción a la literatura norteamericana*, 1967 (with Esther Zemborain de Torres; *An Introduction to American Literature*, 1971); *Prólogos*, 1975; *Cosmogonías*, 1976; *Libro de sueños*, 1976; *¿Qué es el budismo?*, 1976 (with Alicia Jurado); *Siete noches*, 1980 (*Seven Nights*, 1984); *Nueve ensayos dantescos*, 1982; *This Craft of Verse*, 2000; *The Total Library: Non-fiction, 1922-1986*, 2001 (Eliot Weinberger, editor).

TRANSLATIONS: *Orlando*, 1937 (of Virginia Woolf's novel); *La metamórfosis*, 1938 (of Franz Kafka's novel *Die Verwandlung*); *Un bárbaro en Asia*, 1941 (of Henri Michaux's travel notes); *Bartleby, el escribiente*, 1943 (of Herman Melville's novella *Bartleby the Scrivener*); *Los mejores cuentos policiales*, 1943 (with Bioy Casares; of detective stories by various authors); *Los mejores cuentos policiales, segunda serie*, 1951 (with Bioy Casares; of detective stories by various authors); *Cuentos breves y extraordinarios*, 1955, 1973 (with Bioy Casares; of short stories by various authors; *Extraordinary Tales*, 1973); *Las palmeras salvajes*, 1956 (of William Faulkner's novel *The Wild Palms*); *Hojas de hierba*, 1969 (of Walt Whitman's *Leaves of Grass*).

EDITED TEXTS: *Antología clásica de la literatura argentina*, 1937; *Antología de la literatura fantástica*, 1940 (with Bioy Casares and Silvia Ocampo); *Antología poética argentina*, 1941 (with Bioy Casares and Ocampo); *El compadrito: Su destino, sus barrios, su musica*, 1945, 1968 (with Silvina Bullrich); *Poesía gauchesca*, 1955 (with Bioy Casares; 2 volumes); *Libro del cielo y del infierno*, 1960, 1975 (with Bioy Casares); *Versos*, 1972 (by Evaristo Carriego); *Antología poética*, 1982 (by Leopoldo Lugones); *Antología poética*, 1982 (by Franciso de Quevedo); *El amigo de la muerte*, 1984 (by Pedro Antonio de Alarcón).

MISCELLANEOUS: *Obras completas*, 1953-1967 (10 volumes); *Antología personal*, 1961 (*A Personal Anthology*, 1967); *Labyrinths: Selected Stories, and Other Writings*, 1962, 1964; *Nueva antología personal*, 1968; *Selected Poems, 1923-1967*, 1972 (also includes prose); *Adrogue*, 1977; *Obras completas en colaboración*, 1979 (with others); *Borges: A Reader*, 1981; *Atlas*, 1984 (with María Kodama; English translation, 1985).

BIBLIOGRAPHY

Boldy, Steven. *A Companion to Jorge Luis Borges*. Rochester, N.Y.: Tamesis, 2010. Provides biographical information and a general appreciation of Borges's themes.

Cortinez, Carlos. *Borges the Poet*. Fayetteville: University of Arkansas Press, 1986. Three interviews with Borges about poetry, followed by articles on his poetry, including an essay by María Kodama about his haiku.

Egginton, William, and David E. Johnson, eds. *Thinking with Borges*. Aurora, Colo.: Davies Group, 2009. Contains essays on Borges, including one on his poetry.

Jenckes, Kate. *Reading Borges After Benjamin: Allegory, Afterlife, and the Writing of History*. SUNY Series in Latin American and Iberian Thought and Cure. New York: State University of New York, 2007. Interprets his works, particularly his early poetry, as metaphors for a nonlinear approach to the history of Buenos Aires.

McNeese, Tim. *Jorge Luis Borges*. New York: Chelsea House, 2008. This biography, part of the Great Hispanic Heritage series, examines Borges's life and works. Contains a chapter on his poetry.

Milne, Ira Mark, ed. *Poetry for Students*. Vol. 27. Detroit: Thomson/Gale Group, 2008. Contains an analysis of Borges's "Borges and I."

Waisman, Sergio. *Borges and Translation: The Irreverence of the Periphery*. Lewisburg, Pa.: Bucknell University Press, 2005. Because Borges's writings have multilingual sources related to translations he made and because he sometimes took a very active part in the translation of his works into English, this is an important source.

Williamson, Edwin. *Borges: A Life*. New York: Viking, 2004. A generally convincing interpretation of his literary themes as disguised autobiography.

Wilson, Jason. *Jorge Luis Borges*. London: Reaktion, 2006. Part of the Critical Lives series, this biography looks at the life and works of Borges.

Woodall, James. *Borges: A Life*. New York: BasicBooks, 1996. Provides a wealth of photographs and anecdotal material derived from Borges's friends.

James Whitlark

ERNESTO CARDENAL

Born: Granada, Nicaragua; January 20, 1925

PRINCIPAL POETRY
Gethsemani, Ky., 1960
La hora cero, 1960
Epigramas: Poemas, 1961 (*Epigramas*, 1978)
Oración por Marilyn Monroe, y otros poemas, 1965 (*Marilyn Monroe, and Other Poems*, 1975)
El estrecho dudoso, 1966 (*The Doubtful Strait*, 1995)
Antología de Ernesto Cardenal, 1967
Salmos, 1967 (*The Psalms of Struggle and Liberation*, 1971)
Mayapán, 1968
Homenaje a los indios americanos, 1969 (*Homage to the American Indians*, 1973)
Poemas reunidos, 1949-1969, 1969
Antología, 1971
La hora cero, y otros poemas, 1971 (*Zero Hour, and Other Documentary Poems*, 1980)
Poemas, 1971
Canto nacional, 1973
Oráculo sobre Managua, 1973
El Evangelio en Solentiname, 1975 (*The Gospel in Solentiname*, 1976)
Poesía escogida, 1975
Apocalypse: And Other Poems, 1977
Antología, 1978
Canto a un país que nace, 1978
Nueva antología poética, 1979
Poesía, 1979
Poesía de uso: Antología, 1949-1978, 1979
Tocar el cielo, 1981
Antología: Ernesto Cardenal, 1983
Poesía de la nueva Nicaragua, 1983
Wasala: Poems, 1983
Vuelos de Victoria, 1984 (*Flights of Victory*, 1985)
Quetzalcóatal, 1985
With Walker in Nicaragua, and Other Early Poems, 1949-1954, 1985
From Nicaragua with Love: Poems, 1976-1986, 1986

Cántico cósmico, 1989 (*The Music of the Spheres*, 1990; also known as *Cosmic Canticle*, 1993)
Los ornis de oro, 1991
Golden UFOs: The Indian Poems, 1992
El Río San Juan: Estrecho dudoso en el centro de América, 1993
Telescopio en la noche oscura, 1993
Antología nueva, 1996
Versos del pluriverso, 2005
Pluriverse: New and Selected Poems, 2009 (Jonathan Cohen, editor)

Other literary forms

Part 1 of the autobiography of Ernesto Cardenal (kahr-day-NAHL), *Vida perdida* (lost life), was published in 1999 by Seix Barral in Barcelona. It is an excellent biographical resource and starting place for exploring the poet's fascinating life and thought. The chapters devoted to his years as a Trappist monk in Gethsemani, Kentucky, and his correspondence with the Catholic mystic, theologian, and writer Thomas Merton enlighten the reader attempting to comprehend the corpus of Cardenal's poetry.

Cardenal wrote essays and other prose works as he served as minister of culture in Nicaragua and as a director of Casa de los Tres Mundos, a literary and cultural organization in Granada, Nicaragua. *Vida en el amor* (1970; *To Live Is to Love*, 1972; *Abide in Love*, 1995) is a collection of meditations written after his novitiate years at Gethsemani.

Achievements

Ernesto Cardenal was instrumental in the rebirth of Nicaragua's identity as "a nation of poets," as it became known after Rubén Darío immortalized the poet-nation at the beginning of the twentieth century. Cardenal's life is as fascinating as his poetry. Controversy over the literary and political value of his work resulted from his attempts to reconcile the many roles he had played, from monk to priest to governmental official to promoter of literacy and the arts. His political ideology seemed inconsistent as he switched public roles. From a bourgeois family background, he espoused Marxism and militancy, then Christianity and nonviolent resistance. This dichotomy is evident in his work, but these ideological conflicts enhance rather than detract from his poetic corpus.

Consistent in his belief that art is linked to politics, his poetry actively supported the revolution that in 1979 overthrew the regime begun by dictator Anastasio Somoza García. After a functional social democracy was established in Cardenal's homeland, he served as an unofficial yet visible cultural ambassador. He was instrumental in the organization of community-based literacy and poetry workshops that have earned national as well as international success.

The poet has also been praised as an artist. His sculpture won recognition in the

United States as well as in Central America and Mexico. A stone sculpture of Christ dominates the courtyard of the Trappist monastery in Gethsemani, Kentucky, where he served as a novitiate from 1957 to 1959.

Cardenal has been honored with several awards for his literary achievements as well as for his public service. In 1972, he received the Christopher Book Award for *The Psalms of Struggle and Liberation*. In 1980, he received the Premio de La Paz grant, sponsored by Libreros de la República Federal de Alemania. He has received state-sponsored honors and honorary doctorates from several European nations. Cardenal was nominated for the 2005 Nobel Prize in Literature and received the Pablo Neruda Ibero-American Poetry Prize in 2009.

Biography

Ernesto Cardenal Martínez was born in 1925 in Granada, Nicaragua. He studied at the Universidad Nacional Autónoma de México. After graduating in 1947, he moved to the United States to study North American literature at Columbia University in New York from 1948 to 1949.

After traveling for a year throughout Europe, Cardenal returned to Nicaragua. He translated and published North American poetry and anonymously wrote political poems against the dictatorship of Somoza. The Chilean poet Pablo Neruda published works by the then-unknown Cardenal in *La Gaceta de Chile*. While in Nicaragua, Cardenal managed a bookstore that promoted national writers and published *El hilo azul*, a poetry journal.

In 1954, Cardenal participated in an armed assault against the Somoza regime known as the April Rebellion and continued to write anonymous political poems. Three years later, he drastically changed directions by entering the monastery of Our Lady of Gethsemani in Kentucky, where he met Thomas Merton, his spiritual mentor and lifelong friend. Poor health forced Cardenal to transfer to the Benedictine monastery in Cuernavaca, Mexico. There, he wrote his poetry collection *Gethsemani, Ky.* and the meditations *Abide in Love*. He continued his theological studies at the seminary of La Ceja in Colombia. While at the seminary, he wrote poems later collected and translated as *Homage to the American Indians*. He was ordained a Roman Catholic priest in 1965.

With the guidance of Merton, Cardenal planned to establish the spiritual community of Solentiname on Lake Nicaragua. He created a school for the native folk arts, poetry workshops, and the political movement of liberation theology. He visited Cuba to study its revolutionary process. In 1976, he represented Solentiname in the Russell tribunal for human rights violations in Latin America. In 1977, after Sandinista leaders had ordered Cardenal on a diplomatic mission, Somoza's army destroyed Solentiname. Cardenal was exiled from Nicaragua until the government of reconstruction appointed him minister of culture in 1979. He served internationally in the cause of peace and disarmament. After earning the Rubén Darío Prize, the highest Nicaraguan honor, he was honored by the governments of France and Germany, among those of other nations. Several international universities bestowed honorary doctorates upon Cardenal.

Cardenal's autobiography, *Vida perdida*, is an excellent source for biographical information, though not necessarily more accurate than objective sources. References to literary influences and Cardenal's creative contemporaries permeate the text. His complex values and belief system shine through his personal history as he reminisces about his literary production as spiritual experiences, with an unaffected style laced with self-effacing humor.

In *Vida perdida*, Cardenal defines himself as a Christian Marxist whose first calling is to serve God. His service is politically committed, focusing on the Central American peasants. His poems not only spoke for the voiceless; they enabled Cardenal to promote and publish poetry collections by "ordinary people," allowing them a personal as well as collective poetic voice.

Analysis

Revolutionary political ideology is blended with Roman Catholic theology in Ernesto Cardenal's poetry. Like Pablo Neruda, he hopes to motivate readers to change social injustices. His overt messages do not overshadow their poetic forms, and technical mastery is not compromised by theme. Cardenal's poetry is not just his second calling. Rather, it serves as an integral part of his first calling, operating as a tool of his spiritual mission to convert and enlighten. His poems reveal hard and ugly truths about Nicaragua and contemporary societies as they evangelize.

He developed the concept of *exteriorismo* with his poet friend José Coronel Utrecho. Through this technique, words present the world directly through its object rather than by abstraction. Cardenal referred to impure poetry as that seeming closer to prose for its prosaic references. *Interiorista* poetry is composed of abstract or symbolic words that have traditionally poetic connotations. Utrecho and Cardenal believed that the only poetry that could express the Latin American reality and reach the people in a revolutionary way was *exteriorista*. Cardenal's presentation of prosaic elements is innovative, and he connects images through techniques of montage, interpolation, and intertextuality.

"Zero Hour"

Among the most militant political poems that serve as a call to action, "La hora cero" ("Zero Hour") epitomizes Cardenal's *exteriorista* mission of words: "I did it," dijo después Somoza./ "I did it for the good of Nicaragua./ . . . de armas;/ todos marcados U.S.A., MADE IN U.S.A. . . ." The vivid reality of the United States supplying arms to the Nicaraguan dictatorship is juxtaposed with William Walker's invasion and scenes of exploitation, oppression, and glimpses of truth filtered through sound bites, news clips, and elements from the mass media.

"Marilyn Monroe"

"Oración por Marilyn Monroe" ("Marilyn Monroe") exemplifies *exteriorismo* as it is applied to themes beyond the Nicaraguan experience. This prayer reveals how a woman was destroyed by Hollywood. Cardenal relates the cultural icon to the degradation and exploitation of women. This poem connects Monroe to the Virgin Mary and demonstrates how both images of the ideal woman have been desecrated and violated by a godless, hedonistic society. He begins his prayer:

> Father
> Receive this girl known throughout the world as
>   Marilyn Monroe
> though that was not her real name
> (but You know her real name, that of the orphan raped
>   at nine
> and the shopgirl who had tried to kill herself at just 16.)
> and who now appears before You without makeup
> without her Press Agent
> without photographs or signing autographs
> lonely as an astronaut facing the darkness of outer
>   space . . .

The Music of the Spheres

Cardenal developed the genre of the canto in the way that Ezra Pound and Neruda created their own cantos. Cardenal credited Pound as a major influence on his poetic style. Disparate images are juxtaposed, lyrical and prosaic lines are mingled, and spiritual elements are combined with images of materialism and consumerism, in which commercialization replaces emotional and spiritual spontaneity. Technical skill is balanced by immediate and relevant messages.

The Music of the Spheres encapsulates the canto form. More than forty cantos create a vision of cosmic development that refers to astronomy, biology, physics, history, mythology, philosophy, politics, and theology. Science blends with spirituality to form a harmonic whole.

The organization of interconnected canticles resembles Pound's subdivisions of a long poem into thematic units. As a whole, the canticles' lyric quality predominates. They sing their praises to creation as they reach out to the cosmos to grasp its elemental clues to origins. These cantos chronicle political and economic realities, harmoniously combined with spiritual transcendence.

Cardenal's original masterwork follows the tradition of epic poems from Homer to Dante to Pound.

OTHER MAJOR WORKS

NONFICTION: *Vida en el amor*, 1970 (*To Live Is to Love*, 1972; also known as *Abide in Love*, 1995); *En Cuba*, 1972 (*In Cuba*, 1974); *Cardenal en Valencia*, 1974; *La santidad de la revolución*, 1976; *La paz mundial y la revolución de Nicaragua*, 1981; *Vida perdida*, 1999; *Los años de Granada*, 2001; *Las ínsulas extrañas*, 2002; *Memorias*, 2003; *La revolución perdida*, 2004; *Thomas Merton—Ernesto Cardenal: Correspondencia (1959-1968)*, 2004.

TRANSLATIONS: *Catulo-Marcial en versión de Ernesto Cardenal*, 1978 (of Gaius Valerius Catullus); *Tu paz es mi paz*, 1982 (of Ursula Schulz's *Dein Friede sei mein Friede*).

EDITED TEXTS: *Antología de la poesía norteamericana*, 1963 (with Coronel Urtecho); *Literatura indígena americana: Antología*, 1966 (with Jorge Montoya Toro); *Poesía nicaragüense*, 1973; *Poesía nueva de Nicaragua*, 1974; *Poesía cubana de la revolucíon*, 1976; *Antología de poesía primitiva*, 1979; *Poemas de un joven*, 1983 (by Joaquín Pasos); *Antología: Azarias H. Pallais*, 1986.

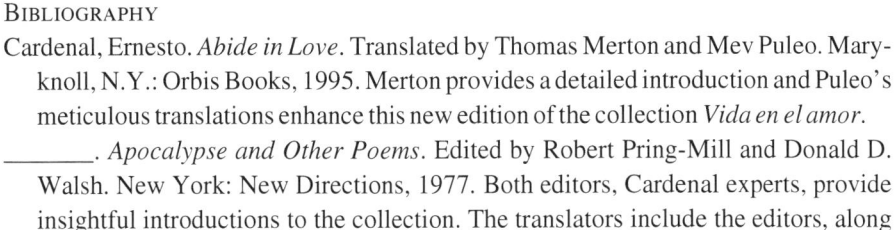

BIBLIOGRAPHY

Cardenal, Ernesto. *Abide in Love*. Translated by Thomas Merton and Mev Puleo. Maryknoll, N.Y.: Orbis Books, 1995. Merton provides a detailed introduction and Puleo's meticulous translations enhance this new edition of the collection *Vida en el amor*.

_____. *Apocalypse and Other Poems*. Edited by Robert Pring-Mill and Donald D. Walsh. New York: New Directions, 1977. Both editors, Cardenal experts, provide insightful introductions to the collection. The translators include the editors, along with Thomas Merton, Kenneth Rexroth, and Mireya Jaimes-Freyre.

_____. *The Doubtful Strait = El estrecho dudoso*. Translated by John Lyons. Bloomington: University of Indiana Press, 1995. Tamara Williams provides a substantial introduction to this collection. It is a detailed critical study of its genesis, technical, thematic, and stylistic elements, and historical and literary influences. Demonstrates how an epic quality is developed through the continuous thread of the quest throughout this collection.

_____. "Ernesto Cardenal Describes Sandinista Split." Interview by Leslie Wirpsa. *National Catholic Reporter* 31, no. 30 (May 26, 1995): 9. Cardenal describes Nicaraguan politics and reflects on the efforts made during the years immediately following the establishment of the Sandinista government.

_____. *Flights of Victory*. Translated by Marc Zimmerman. Maryknoll, N.Y.: Orbis Books, 1985. Presents the collection with a critical study of the historical context as well as technical and thematic elements that distinguish it from other works. Zimmerman examines the elements of *exteriorismo*, which was influenced by the Central American vanguards of revolutionary poets. This study demonstrates how Cardenal utilized *exteriorismo*.

Dawes, Greg. *Aesthetics and Revolution: Nicaraguan Poetry, 1979-1990*. Minneapolis: University of Minnesota Press, 1993. The chapter "Poetry and Spiritual Materialism: Ernesto Cardenal" discusses how Cardenal's Marxism, seen through a Christian lens, affected his poetry. Dawes believes that Cardenal's work reinterprets theology itself. Through liberation theology, religious states such as faith and salvation are returned to the social sphere. Examines Cardenal's impact on Nicaraguan politics and literature.

Elias, Edward. "Prophecy of Liberation: The Poetry of Ernesto Cardenal." In *Poetic Prophecy in Western Literature*, edited by Jan Wojcik and Raymond-Jean Frontain. Cranbury, N.J.: Associated University Presses, 1984. The author considers Cardenal's poetry within the Old Testament context of prophecy. He notes the poet's continuous efforts to move others to action and makes comparisons to the Hebrew prophets of old.

Gibbons, Reginald. "Political Poetry and the Example of Ernesto Cardenal." *Critical Inquiry* 13, no. 3 (Spring, 1987): 648-671. The poet speaks against injustice and oppression and in favor of compassion and revolution. It is impossible to separate the political from the poetic in Cardenal's work, Gibbons suggests.

Lee, Jongsoo. "The Colonial Legacy in Ernesto Cardenal's Poetry: Images of Quetzalcoatl, Nezahualcoyotl, and the Aztecs." *Hispania* 87, no. 1 (March, 2004): 22-31. Argues that Cardenal, in his poetry, "presents the Aztecs as a symbol of evil due to their militarism and practice of human sacrifice, while the two pre-Hispanic Mexican heroes, Quetzalcoatl and Nezahualcoyotl, symbolize righteousness because of their peaceful religious and civilized practices." Offers further critical analyses of Cardenal's representations.

Rowe, William. *Poets of Contemporary Latin America: History and the Inner Life*. New York: Oxford University Press, 2000. In the chapter "Ernesto Cardenal: Eros and Belief Under Epic Necessity," Rowe explores the poems as differing proposals of attention for each collection. He avoids making critical artistic decisions from political, religious, or erotic perspectives. Rowe believes that these preconceptions make the poems' words a vehicle for a higher cause, rather than enable them to be appreciated for their intrinsic artistic value.

Sarabia, Rosa. *Poetas de la palabra hablada*. London: Tamesis, 1997. This study, in Spanish, examines the oral nature of several Latin American writers. The chapter "La historia como musa en la poesía de Ernesto Cardenal" focuses on historical influences, including Native American mythology. The contemporary reality also influences the politically conscious poet as spokesman for the voiceless who are suffering injustices. This study demonstrates how past and contemporary realities, along with an oral tradition, find their voices in Cardenal's poetry.

Carole A. Champagne

SOR JUANA INÉS DE LA CRUZ

Born: San Miguel Nepantla, New Spain (now in Mexico); November, 1648
   (baptized December 2, 1648)
Died: Mexico City, New Spain (now in Mexico); April 17, 1695
Also known as: Sor Juana

PRINCIPAL POETRY
Inundación castálida, 1689
Segundo volumen de las obras, 1692 (the long poem *Primero sueño* is translated as *First Dream*, 1983)
Fama y obras póstumas, 1700
The Sonnets of Sor Juana Ines de la Cruz in English Verse, 2001

OTHER LITERARY FORMS

The most readable prose work of Sor Juana Inés de la Cruz (WAH-nah ee-NAYS day lah krews), *Respuesta de la poetisa a la muy ilustre Sor Filotea de la Cruz* (1700; *The Answer*, 1994), is an appealing autobiographical defense of her precocious interest

Sor Juana Inés de la Cruz.
(Library of Congress)

in learning, an emotional plea for acceptance as a woman and a scholar, and an obsessive declaration of faith. Sor Juana tries to convince her superiors that, despite her lifelong curiosity about the material world, theological concerns are still the most important to her.

El divino Narciso, pr. c. 1680 (*The Divine Narcissus*, 1945), a religious one-act play, is a tasteful and imaginative treatment of divine love in which Narcissus, as a figure of Christ, falls in love with human nature as a reflection of himself. With this short play, the fantasy of desire that takes so many forms throughout Sor Juana's work finds its ultimate synthesis of eros and agape.

Achievements

Sor Juana Inés de la Cruz was a Mexican literary virtuoso who was called the tenth muse during her lifetime and who is generally considered the most important writer of colonial Spanish America. Although she wrote more than four hundred poems, twenty-three short plays, two full-length comedias, and various prose works, Sor Juana's reputation rests on a handful of poems (about two dozen in all), *The Divine Narcissus*, and *The Answer*. Although a reassessment of her works begun in the 1950's promises a more extensive list of her most important writings, it is likely that, with the exception of her extremely complex *First Dream*, the few pieces that earned her the admiration of Marcelino Menendez y Pelayo one hundred years ago will continue to be the ones that will ensure her a place of prominence in Spanish letters.

At her best, Sor Juana was able to manipulate the often unwieldy and intricate language of the Spanish Baroque, with its rich heritage from the Golden Age, into expressions of delicate, feminine vision and sensibility. Her aesthetic documentation of the search for knowledge, love, and God is the most complete personal and artistic record of any figure from the colonial period. Sor Juana's love poetry appears to reflect frustrating and painful experiences before her entry into the convent at about the age of seventeen. Few of the poems are concerned with fulfillment or the intimate communication of personal feelings; most are, instead, variations on the themes of ambivalence and disillusionment in love. Sor Juana's philosophical poems are linked to her amatory verse by a sense of disenchantment. An exception to her general pessimism is *First Dream*, in which the poet takes delight in depicting the joys and dangers of her intellectual explorations. More of Sor Juana's writings bear witness to her theological concerns. Although some of her religious lyrics express the same kind of anguish about God's love that she expressed about human love, she clearly attempted in her *villancicos* to use her poetic talent in the service of the Roman Catholic Church.

Biography

Juana Inés de Asbaje y Ramírez de Santillana was born in November, 1648, in San Miguel Nepantla, some sixty kilometers southeast of Mexico City. She was the illegitimate child of a Spanish captain and a Creole mother. In the charming *The Answer*, she tells how she learned to read at the age of three and tagged along with one of her sisters to La Amiga, an elementary school, where she took her first formal lessons. She says that, at the age of eight, she begged her mother to let her cut her hair and dress like a boy so she could attend the university. That being denied her, she continued her self-education by reading the classics she found in her grandmother's house. Around 1659, she was allowed to go to Mexico City and live with the family of one of her aunts. Although not enrolled in the university, Juana privately continued her studies, which included twenty lessons in Latin. Twenty was apparently sufficient, for subsequently she was able to write Latin poetry as well as anyone in the viceroyalty.

By 1664, Sor Juana was a member of the viceregal court and was the darling of the vicereine. She so impressed the viceroy, the marques de Mancera, with her knowledge, that he arranged for forty professors from the university to give her tests. Sor Juana passed them all, amazing the local elite. Her several years of court life must have been intense, emotional years. She was a beautiful woman and was doubtless wooed by gentlemen of some wealth and position. Nevertheless, by 1669, she had entered the convent and had taken religious vows, as much from aversion to marriage as from attraction to the celibate life. It was her desire to be free to learn, she states in *The Answer*, that was the primary motivation for her vocation.

For the next twenty-three years, Sor Juana was the major literary figure in colonial Spanish America, composing everything from love sonnets to a treatise on music, almost all her writing being done on request from high-ranking officials of the Roman Catholic Church or the state. She wrote elaborate pieces for performance at liturgical functions, occasional verse for political events, and scenarios and scripts for afternoons of royal entertainment. Not long after the brilliant defense of her studies in *The Answer*, and at the height of her career, when her collected works were beginning to be published and acclaimed in Spain, pressures by her religious superiors induced her to give away her library of more than four thousand volumes and all her scientific and musical instruments and to abandon writing altogether. Several years later, on April 17, 1695, she died in an epidemic that swept Mexico City.

Analysis

Although most of the compositions have merit, the lyric poems, in the order of their treatment here, are usually considered to be the best, and they may be used as a point of departure for delineating a canon of Sor Juana Inés de la Cruz's most significant writings.

Sor Juana was a deeply passionate and intelligent woman who dedicated her life to knowledge and spiritual perfection. On one hand, she seems to have renounced love for intellectual freedom, and from her amatory and philosophical writings, it appears that her renunciation of the world, along with her commitment to learning, paradoxically caused an obsession with intimacy and a profound disillusionment with any reality except that of spiritual intimacy. On the other hand, judging from her other prose and verse, Sor Juana was also a writer engaged with her society, closely involved with its institutions and its native culture. An anthology of Sor Juana's most popular compositions may slight this more social side of her personality, but it is important to remember as one reviews her major poems of love and disillusionment that the poetess wrote more concerning religion than about any real or imaginary love and that she was as adept at elaborate versification about current events and visitors to the viceroyalty as at revealing her most private feelings. It is not difficult to dwell on the more romantic side of the "tenth muse," to use certain of her poems to enhance the image of a jilted, precocious, disenchanted teenage intellectual sequestering herself in a convent and spending her life in extremely elaborate sublimation. Her most famous pieces contribute to such an image, but as the reader is exposed to a wider spectrum of her talents, a more balanced picture emerges; a trajectory of maturation becomes visible in which Catholicism and the Baroque are means to the self-fulfillment and self-expression originally thwarted in her youth by her lack of social position and her fascination with scholarship.

Progression of love

If one reads Sor Juana's writings to observe a progression from human to divine love, it is appropriate to begin with the sonnet "Esta tarde, mi bien" (this afternoon, my love). The poem is one of the few in which she relates a moving encounter with another person, and it contrasts the impotency of words with the efficacy of tears in the communication of love. Here, there is none of the love-hate dialectic that colors most of her amatory poems; instead, one finds the description of a delicately feminine, sensitive, and formidably talented personality in a moment of unguarded abandon. It is only a slight exaggeration to say that after "Esta tarde, mi bien," one sees in Sor Juana's verse the psychological effects of an unhappy affair rather than the experience of love itself. Even the tender *lira* "Amado dueño mio" (my beloved master), while documenting in a poetic sense the dimensions of intimacy, is a conventional lament of the lover separated from the beloved. The lover, like a Renaissance shepherdess, tells her misfortunes to the wind, which carries her complaints, her passion, and her sadness to the distant partner. Alfonso Méndez Plancarte states that the poem contains some of Sor Juana's finest lines and that it may surpass the eclogues of Garcilaso de la Vega. The comparison with Garcilaso is appropriate, and poetry in his likeness is fitting to express the absence of consummation rather than its presence; significantly, the *lira* keynotes a thematic transformation from completion to emptiness.

The sonnet "Detente, sombra de mi bien esquivo" (stay, shadow of my scornful love) can be considered an introduction to a series of poems that admit both the positive and negative effects of passion as well as the inconclusive status of unconsummated love. In "Detente, sombra de mi bien esquivo," the beloved himself eludes the poet, but his image cannot escape the prison of her fantasy. Important in this and the poems under discussion below is the counterpoint of conceits and emotions about the love "por quien alegre muero" (for whom I would happily die) but also "por quien penosa vivo" (for whom I live in agony), which develops to an extreme in the sonnet "Al que Ingrato me deja, busco amante" (I seek the one who spurns me) and "Que no me quiera Fabio, al verse amado" (that Fabio does not love me as I love him), and the *redondilla* "Este amoroso tormento" (this torment of love). In the latter piece, as in the other poems of this group, the poet never finds fulfillment, "porque, entre alivio y dolar, hallo culpa en el amor y disculpa en el olvido" (because between relief and pain, I find blame in love and exoneration in forgetfulness).

Beyond frustration and the love-hate duality that the poet attributes to romantic feeling lie disillusionment and bitterness. The sonnets "Silvio, yo te aborezco" (I hate you, Silvio), "Amor empieza por desasosiego" (love begins uneasily), and "Con el dolor de la mortal herida" (with the pain of a mortal wound) are among Sor Juana's strongest denunciations of the men she once might have loved, as well as of herself for having given in to loving them: "no solo a tí, corrida, te aborrezco,/ pero a mí por el tiempo que te quise" (not only do I abhor you/ but myself for the time that I loved you). Here the bittersweet of "Este amoroso tormento" turns to anger. The image of the lover purposely retained in "Detente, sombra de mi bien esquivo" is repeatedly banished, and it is a logical movement from such rejection to the *sátira filosófica*, "Hombres necios" ("Foolish Men"), one of Sor Juana's more popular denunciations of men as the source of all women's problems. In these feminist *redondillas*, the poet exposes the ways in which men "acusan lo que causan" (blame us for the things they cause). Why, she asks, do men want women to be good if they tempt them to be bad? Who, she questions, is the greater sinner, "la que peca por la paga o el que paga por pecar" (she who sins for pay or he who pays for sin)?

Because Sor Juana's poems are not usually dated, there is no way of knowing whether the progression from the delicate, loving "Esta tarde, mi bien" to the sarcastic "Hombres necios" reflects the sequential effects of an increasingly unhappy situation. In any case, these poems of erotic experience do fit a pattern that begins with brief reciprocal affection and degenerates into ambivalence, then finally into contempt. There are, at the same time, a great number of poems written to women which do not fit this generalization. Sor Juana apparently had very meaningful relationships with the wives of two of the Mexican viceroys, and her many verses to Lysi show a far more consistent emotional response than that depicted in poems of male-female interaction. Certainly the Lysi poems, perhaps especially the ornate "Lámina sirva el cielo al retrato" (the sky is lamina of your portrait), are a moving contrast to her more widely read poems' heterosexual canon.

Philosophic poems

Sor Juana's philosophic poems complement her negative attitude toward worldly love. "Verde embeleso de la vida humana" (green charm of human life) rejects illusions and hope as deceptive: "solamente lo que toco veo" ("I only see what I can touch"). It represents the repression of vain dreams, the acceptance of life without romance or even platonic fantasy. "Diuturna enfermedad de la Esperanza" (lasting infirmity of hope) reiterates this concept, and "Este que ves, engaño colorido" (this painted lie you see), a sonnet on her portrait, is an intense affirmation of the Roman Catholic view that the flesh is "polvo, es sombra, es nada" ("is dust, is a shadow, is nothing"). Her "Rosa divina" (divine rose) is a variation on the universal theme of the brevity of beauty and life. Perhaps her most powerful renunciation is "Finjamos que soy feliz" (pretend that I am happy), in which she denies the validity of knowledge and maintains that because humans can know nothing for certain, ignorance is preferable to imperfect knowing: "aprendamos a ignorar" ("let us learn to not know"). "Finjamos que soy feliz" is a moment of despair within the context of Sor Juana's self-confessed lifelong passion, the pursuit of knowledge. Her monumental *First Dream*, the only work that she admitted to writing for her own pleasure and not to please someone else, is far more balanced in presenting her attitude toward learning.

First Dream

First Dream, which is among the best philosophic poems in Spanish, is the height of Sor Juana's exploration of the Baroque. The poem begins with a description of nightfall, in which the entire physical world eventually succumbs to sleep. The human spirit, freed from the constraint of the body, soars upward to find a perspective from which it can comprehend the immensity of the universe. Once it glimpses the overpowering dimensions of creation, the soul retreats to the shadows. Finding a mental shore on the sea of knowledge, it decides to approach the challenge of learning by dividing things into categories and mastering each division separately. In spite of doubts that the mind can really know anything, echoes of the dark vision of "Finjamos que soy feliz," the soul continues its search for truth. Dawn arrives, however, and the dream ends inconclusively. Universal knowledge has eluded the soul, but the dreamer has not despaired.

Once considered to be on the fringe of literature because of its purposeful Gongorism, *First Dream* is enjoying the positive reconsideration accorded the entire Spanish Baroque, in the course of which Luis de Góngora y Argote himself has been reinstated into the canon of major Spanish poets. Accepting the style of this poem as not only valid but also essential to its meaning, one can better appreciate Sor Juana's most mature and complex statement about the human condition. It is the culmination of a lifetime of study and reflection.

Sacred ballads

Sor Juana's religious writings include several "sacred ballads," among which "Amante dulce del alma" (sweet love of my soul), "Mientras la Gracia me exita" (while Grace moves me), and "Traigo conmigo un cuidado" (I have a deep concern) are generally held in high regard. All three attempt to express the effects of divine love. "Amante dulce del alma" asks why Christ might have willed to visit the poet in Holy Communion: Has he decided to be present from love or from jealousy? She decides for the former, reflecting that since God knows all things, he can see into her heart and has no reason to be jealous. "Mientras la Gracia me exita" tries to clarify some of the feelings involved in the inner struggle between "la virtud y la costumbre" (virtue and habit). Like "Amante dulce del alma," this is a poem of scruples rather than a meditation of universal religious significance. "Traigo conmigo un cuidado" carries the analysis of spiritual love further and contrasts it with the poet's experience of human love. "La misma muerte que vivo, es la vida con que muero" ("the same death that I live is the life in which I die"), she writes at the end of the poem, attempting to sum up her contradictory mental state. Even though it is divine love that causes her to feel the way she does, there are parallels between the *contrarias penas* ("contradictory anxieties") of "Este amoroso tormento" and those expressed in "Traigo conmigo un cuidado."

It is more fruitful to look for a developed sense of religious experience in Sor Juana's *villancicos* and her play *The Divine Narcissus* than in her personal religious lyrics. Although these works have generally been neglected, scholar Méndez Plancarte and others have made convincing defenses of their genres as well as of the verse itself. *The Divine Narcissus* contains some of Sor Juana's best writing, and, with the *loa* (or one-act play) that precedes it, shows how she introduced local themes into her work. The most significant element of the play, however, is the successful depiction of divine love, sufficiently anthropomorphized to give it comprehensible human beauty. Here is also the full evolution of a spiritual maturity that finally quiets the older, worldly concerns.

OTHER MAJOR WORKS

PLAYS: *El divino Narciso*, pr. c. 1680 (*The Divine Narcissus*, 1945); *Los empeños de una casa*, pr. c. 1680 (adaptation of Lope de Vega Carpio's play *La discreta enamorada*; *A Household Plagued by Love*, 1942); *Amor es más laberinto*, pr. 1689 (wr. 1668; with Juan de Guevara); *El cetro de José*, pb. 1692; *El mártir del Sacramento, San Hermenegildo*, pr. c. 1692; *The Three Secular Plays of Sor Juana Inés de la Cruz*, 2000.

NONFICTION: *Neptuno alegórico*, 1680; *Carta atenagórica*, 1690; *Respuesta de la poetisa a la muy ilustre Sor Filotea de la Cruz*, 1700 (*The Answer*, 1994).

MISCELLANEOUS: *Obras completas de Sor Juana Inés de la Cruz*, 1951-1957 (4 volumes: I, *Lírica personal*, poetry; II, *Villancicos y letras sacras*, poetry; III, *Autos y loas*, drama; IV, *Comedias sainetes y prosa*, drama and prose; Alfonso Méndez Plancarte, editor); *A Sor Juana Anthology*, 1988.

BIBLIOGRAPHY

Bergmann, Emile L., and Stacey Shlau, eds. *Approaches to Teaching the Works of Sor Juana Inés de la Cruz*. New York: Modern Language Association of America, 2007.

Contains several essays about Sor Juana's poetry as well as a wealth of material on her life and other works.

Cruz, Sor Juana Inés de la. *A Woman of Genius: The Intellectual Autobiography of Sor Juana Inés de la Cruz*. Translated with an introduction by Margaret Sayers Pedén. Salisbury, Conn.: Lime Rock Press, 1982. Contains a translation of Sor Juana's defense of her life, *The Answer*. Also contains a list of basic sources at the end.

Flynn, Gerard. *Sor Juana Inés de la Cruz*. Boston: Twayne, 1971. Introduces the reader to Sor Juana and her work. The first chapter gives biographical information, and the others review her poetry and drama. A discussion of the criticism of several authors is included, as are a number of quotations from Sor Juana's work with English translations provided by Flynn.

Gonzalez, Michelle A. *Sor Juana: Beauty and Justice in the Americas*. Maryknoll, N.Y.: Orbis Books, 2003. A biography of Sor Juana that examines all aspects of her life, including her poetry.

Kirk, Pamela. *Sor Juana Inés de la Cruz: Religion, Art, and Feminism*. New York: Continuum, 1998. An examination of Sor Juana's role in the Roman Catholic Church as well as her literary efforts. Bibliography and index.

Lucianai, Frederick. *Literary Self-fashioning in Sor Juana Inés de la Cruz*. Lewisburg, Pa.: Bucknell University Presses, 2004. Four essays in a roughly chronological order that track how Sor Juana created a literary self in her writings.

Merrim, Stephanie. *Early Modern Women's Writing and Sor Juana Inés de la Cruz*. Nashville, Tenn.: Vanderbilt University Press, 1999. Situates the work of Sor Juana within the field of seventeenth century women's writing in Spanish, English, and French. The protofeminist writings of Sor Juana are used as a benchmark for the examination of the literary production of her female contemporaries. Includes bibliographical references and index.

_____, ed. *Feminist Perspectives on Sor Juana Inés de la Cruz*. Detroit: Wayne State University Press, 1991. A collection of essays by important literary critics and translators of Sor Juana. Discusses her life, time, and work in the context of feminist criticism.

Montross, Constance M. *Virtue or Vice? Sor Juana's Use of Thomistic Thought*. Washington, D.C.: University Press of America, 1981. Examines Sor Juana's use of Scholastic doctrine and methodology, specifically the ideas of Saint Thomas Aquinas. The author analyzes the combination of belief and questioning in the *Carta atenagórica*, *The Answer*, and *First Dream*. Extensive bibliography and the Spanish text of *First Dream* is included.

Paz, Octavio. *Sor Juana: Or, The Traps of Faith*. Translated by Margaret Sayers Pedén. Cambridge, Mass.: Harvard University Press, 1988. A biography of Sor Juana by a leading Mexican poet, essayist, and cultural critic. Paz emphasizes Sor Juana's uniqueness as a poet and focuses on her struggle for her intellectual and creative life.

Historical settings and traditions are detailed. Included are illustrations, among them portraits of Sor Juana, and a helpful listing of Spanish literary terms.

_____, ed. *Mexican Poetry: An Anthology*. Translated by Samuel Beckett. Reprint. New York: Grove Press, 1985. Contains a discussion of the place of Sor Juana in Mexican poetry as part of Paz's introduction to the history of Mexican poetry. Within the anthology itself are translations of twelve of Sor Juana's poems.

William L. Felker

RUBÉN DARÍO
Félix Rubén García Sarmiento

Born: Metapa (now Ciudad Darío), Nicaragua; January 18, 1867
Died: León, Nicaragua; February 6, 1916

PRINCIPAL POETRY
Abrojos, 1887
Rimas, 1887
Azul, 1888
Prosas profanas, 1896 (*Prosas Profanas, and Other Poems*, 1922)
Cantos de vida y esperanza, los cisnes, y otros poemas, 1905
Canto a la Argentina, oda a mitre, y otros poemas, 1914 (English translation, 1920)
Selected Poems of Rubén Darío, 1965 (Lysander Kemp, translator)

OTHER LITERARY FORMS

The fame of Rubén Darío (dah-REE-oh) rests primarily on his poetry, but he wrote serious prose as well. *Azul* (azure), his first major publication, contained poems and short stories alike. Both the poetry and the prose portions were widely acclaimed, but Darío's mature work includes almost no fiction. He published several volumes of essays based on his experience as a foreign correspondent, a traveler, and a diplomat, and two such collections have gained international attention: *La caravana pasa* (1903; the caravan passes) was among the earliest chronicles of the experience of American artists in Paris, while *Tierras solares* (1904; the sunny lands) is a collection of affectionate and melancholy essays celebrating the countryside of southern Spain, which Darío considered the common ground of Spanish and Latin American history. Darío also published literary criticism, political commentary, an autobiography, and exegeses of his own works.

The most famous of Darío's critical works is *Historias de mis libros* (1914; stories of my books), a compilation of three explanatory pieces he wrote about his greatest works of poetry, *Azul*, *Prosas Profanas, and Other Poems*, and *Cantos de vida y esperanza, los cisnes, y otros poemas*. In *Historias de mis libros*, he responded to the most frequent criticism of his work, that he had abandoned the traditional themes of Latin America in pursuit of a European art. He branded the criticism "myopic" and answered that the literature of the New World needed no more stylized odes to nature or patriotic battle hymns.

Achievements

Rubén Darío was a giant of Spanish-language literature and a pioneer of the literature of the American continents. One of the founders of the indigenous Latin American literary movement known as *Modernismo*, Darío introduced European influences—particularly from France—to the poetry of Latin America, but perhaps more important, he introduced the *Modernismo* of Latin America to Europe. His dramatic innovations in theme, language, meter, and rhyme influenced the poetry of both the New World and the Old.

The publication of *Azul* in 1888 was acclaimed by European as well as South American critics, and the book's title was adopted by the *Azure Review*, a Mexican journal that became a principal forum for South America's experimental *Modernista* poetry. When Darío was only twenty-one years old, the influential Madrid critic Juan Valera praised the Nicaraguan's "singular artistic and poetic talent" and the "pure Spanish form" of his writing. With the publication of later works, Darío's renown grew, and he was widely acknowledged as a spokesperson for Latin American culture.

Darío was a colorful public figure, equally at home in Paris, Madrid, and Latin America. He traveled constantly and was acquainted with literary figures throughout Europe and Latin America. He exerted a profound cultural influence through his poetry, his literary criticism, and his journalism. At the height of his fame, he was Nicaragua's minister to Spain; an internationally celebrated lecturer, poet, and journalist; and an éminence grise among artists of Europe and the Americas. In a 1934 tribute, Chile's Pablo Neruda and Spain's Federico García Lorca pronounced Darío "the poet of America and Spain."

Biography

Rubén Darío's life was adventurous and bohemian. He traveled constantly in Europe and the Americas, renowned for his literary achievements but dogged by debt, sickness, and alcoholism throughout his life.

Darío was born Félix Rubén García Sarmiento in 1867 to a poor, part-Indian family in rural Nicaragua. He published his first poem at the age of thirteen, and his early promise as a poet won for him scholarships that enabled him to gain an education.

In 1886, Darío left Nicaragua for Santiago, Chile. There, he suffered a life of severe poverty and wrote in obscurity until the publication of *Azul*. Through Darío's friend Pedro Balmaceda, the son of Chile's president, *Azul* came to the attention of Juan Valera, a Spanish critic attentive to South American literature. Valera published an encouraging review in Spain and Latin America in 1889, but although this brought Darío literary recognition, it did little to ease his poverty. In the same year, the poet returned to Central America, where his writing in literary journals and other periodicals won regional fame for him.

In 1892, Darío traveled to Europe as an assistant to a relative who was an official of the Nicaraguan government. He made his first visits to Madrid and to Paris, developing a lifelong love for the artistic communities of Europe. On his return to Central America, Darío called on Rafael Nuñez, a former president of Colombia, who was, like Darío, a writer. Nuñez arranged for a consular appointment for Darío in Buenos Aires, Argentina. Darío remained in Buenos Aires from 1893 to 1898, writing for many Latin American newspapers and other periodicals, including *La nación*, Argentina's most influential newspaper. In the course of his Argentine stay, Darío's literary reputation continued to grow. *Prosas Profanas, and Other Poems*, his second major volume, was published in 1896 and attracted critical attention in Spain and South America alike. Both the work's literary maturity and treatment of erotic themes ensured Darío's notoriety in the Spanish-speaking literary world.

In 1898, Darío returned to Europe as a foreign correspondent for *La nación*. In the course of the following ten years, he became a fixture of the literary life in Spain and France. He collaborated in establishing a number of fledgling literary journals, contributed to periodicals in Europe and Latin America, and produced important works of nonfiction as well as collections of poetry. Despite his commission from *La nación* and appointments to consular positions for Nicaragua in both Paris and Madrid, however, Darío's financial difficulties continued.

In 1907, Darío returned to Nicaragua to an enthusiastic public reception but stayed in his native country only briefly; he remained restless until his death, spending the last ten years of his life traveling throughout Central America and Europe, holding a variety of diplomatic and ceremonial posts, lecturing, and publishing poetry and essays in periodicals of both continents. In 1914, he published his last major work, *Canto a la Argentina, oda a mitre, y otros poemas*, commissioned by *La nación* on the occasion of Argentina's centenary of independence.

In 1915, Darío took his last trip home from Europe. His health was poor, and he died the following year in León, Nicaragua, at the age of forty-nine.

Analysis

Rubén Darío is remembered as one of the first poetic voices of postcolonial Latin America, enormously influential as a founder of *Modernismo*. His work, however, underwent constant change, and no single school can claim him. He was acclaimed a Prometheus who brought modern trends of European art to newly independent Latin America; at the same time, he was an innovator in poetic form who exercised a major influence on the poetry of twentieth century Spain. In his later years, Darío retreated from the exotic imagery of *Modernismo* and returned to more traditional Latin American themes, including patriotism and religion.

The birth of *Modernismo* in Latin America coincided with South America's transition from colonialism to independence. The declining influence of Spanish culture made way for new literary sources. Latin American intellectuals had long recognized

French culture as the navigational star for their society, which was throwing off the control of monarchies. Thus, in the late nineteenth century, with much of Latin America freed from the cultural sway of Spain, the influence of France was everywhere ascendant, particularly in the universities and in the world of the arts. Darío's work in particular and *Modernismo* in general derived primarily from the interplay between French and Spanish culture, with a rich diversity of other foreign influences.

At its heart, *Modernismo* was an assertion of artistic freedom—the manifesto of those whom Darío described as a "new generation of American writers [with] an immense thirst for progress and a lively enthusiasm." The *Modernistas* idealized art, seeking to range freely for symbolic images in the worlds of the fantastic, the mysterious, and the spiritual. Emphasizing the eclectic internationalism that characterized the movement, Darío spoke of a "close material and spiritual commerce with the different nations of the world."

Darío's work spanned thirty-five years. It consists of thousands of poems, most of them short and many of them in sonnet form. Darío's best-known works also include longer pieces, and his shorter works are sometimes grouped as suites of poems with common themes.

The most common subjects of Darío's poetry are the members of his international family of friends, his romantic loves, and the world of nature. In the tradition of French Parnassianism, he portrayed his subjects through dramatic ideals, using lavish symbolic imagery. Whatever the subject, Darío's portraits are rich in exotic imagery and symbolism. The world of his images is European as much as it is American. In places real and imagined, the reader finds unusual animals and woodland flora, and characters plucked from myth and history. Darío's poetry abounds in allusion, and he often arrays his poetic portraits of the most commonplace themes with the exotic trim of myth and history.

"A Víctor Hugo"

Early evidence of Darío's debt to French art and literature appears in the 1884 poem "A Víctor Hugo" (to Victor Hugo), a paean directed not only to the French master but also to an enumerated multitude of figures who inspired the seventeen-year-old Darío: authors, scientists, and philosophers from Europe and the United States as well as figures from mythology and the Bible. The poem describes the explosion that Hugo touched off in the heart of the self-proclaimed "sad troubadour from the New World." Throughout the work, Darío blends his pious attention to the noise and movement of nature with the voices of myth and history. The influential Spanish critic Juan Valera acknowledged the obvious: The poetry of the young Darío was marked by an immersion in the images and ideas of centuries of Western civilization. Throughout his literary life, Darío wore his new religion proudly.

"A Víctor Hugo" explodes with pithy tributes to Darío's Olympus of heroes. Venus smiles. Apollo discourses with Erato, the Muse of love poetry, and with her sister

Muses. Christ preaches and dies. Galileo utters his apocryphal words of defiance ("And still, I say, it moves"). Benjamin Franklin, Robert Fulton, and Ferdinand de Lesseps move Earth with their inspired plans.

International recognition did not immediately follow the publication of "A Víctor Hugo," but the work heralded Darío's fame. In it, he affirmed his proud association with the artist. His profusion of references to the geniuses of Western civilization, too, reflected his captivation by European art and writing. Finally, his portrait of the world was of an extraordinary setting, a site of spectacular animation, anticipating explicitly *Modernista* works. Although emotional and sincere, his descriptions were not so much true to life as true to an ideal.

At the close of "A Víctor Hugo," the New World's sad but well-read troubadour echoes a famous theme of Spain's first poet of the modern era, Gustavo Adolfo Bécquer: the yearning to give voice to the transcendent and the frustration at the limits of language. Darío unconvincingly gasps: "Oh, but I am left breathless at my lyre/ And unable to continue my song." The breathless recollection of Hugo, France's "immortal genius" and "prophet," however, provides a reviving breeze: "Thoughts of your just fame/ Echo in my mind/ And ardor inflames my heart. . . ."

AZUL

The publication of *Azul* in 1888 marked the beginning of Darío's international recognition. An unusual combination of short stories and poetry, the collection revealed not only Darío's ebullience but also his sympathy with Parnassianism, with its exotic symbolism, lavish portrayal of ideals through striking imagery, and departure from metric formalities.

The centerpiece of *Azul* is the suite of four poems that constitute "El año lírico" (the lyrical year), corresponding to the seasons and beginning with spring. The poems describe settings rich in exotic scenery and stirring with activity. "Primaveral" (spring) is by far the most dramatic. It portrays a vast forest alive with the awakening activity of nature. Darío's treatment of the arrival of spring, with suggestions of pagan and mythic ritual, reveals his fascination with a favorite theme of nineteenth and twentieth century European art and literature: the vision of untamed nature as the face of the savage world. The theme received its most celebrated treatment in Igor Stravinsky's ballet *Le Sacre du printemps* (*The Rite of Spring*), which premiered in Paris in 1913. Darío's "Primaveral" begins with an invitation to the same celebration. The poem is composed of six stanzas of nearly uniform length, five of which end with the antiphonal cry: "Oh, my beloved, It is the sweet springtime!" The grand forest hosts the bathing nymphs, a stalking Pan, and the stirring Muses. Throughout the poem, colors flicker in the light. The locusts chirp to the sun, and all of nature highlights the beauty of a woman's face. "Primaveral" is not simply a seasonal celebration of love; the forest is the beautiful face of the world.

Azul also introduced influential formal innovations. The traditional Spanish sonnet of the nineteenth century consisted of rhymed lines with an even distribution of metric feet within the lines. Darío's sonnets generally abide by those conventions, but he experimented with longer lines and innovative patterns of rhyme. His sonnet "Caupolicán" (added to editions of *Azul* after 1890) is an early example. Each of its lines far exceeds the conventional eleven metric feet; in addition, Darío's rhyme scheme is unorthodox, and instead of the usual rhyming device of assonance, he employs sharp, syllabic rhymes. The first quatrain of the sonnet is representative:

> Es algo formidable que vio la vieja raza;
> robusto tronco de árbol al hombro de un campeón
> salvaje y aguerrido, cuya fornida maza
> blandiera el brazo de Hércules, o el brazo de Sansón.

> They saw Something formidable, the now-gone ancient
>   race:
> A robust tree trunk on the shoulder of the champion
> Savage and war-wise with the mighty mace
> Fit for the arm of Hercules or the arm of a Samson.

Azul, if not the first *Modernista* work in Latin America, is a literary landmark and supremely representative of the movement. Its departure from formality and its thematic audacity reveal the literary freedom of what was then a new, and largely young, generation of artists in Latin America, apace of Europe's artistic evolution.

PROSAS PROFANAS, AND OTHER POEMS

With his next major collection, Darío established his reputation as a mature poet and aroused controversy as well. Published in 1896, while Darío was living in Argentina, the work received considerable attention in Spain. Although it developed themes familiar to readers of *Azul*, it also included many poems exalting erotic love. The Spanish poet Pedro Salinas, a Darío partisan, describes the work as the "daydream of a cultured and erotic man."

In exploring sexual themes, Darío was both playful and frank, enhancing his reputation as a libertine and a rascal, and he provoked predictable outrage from some conservative critics. Others saw uncommon beauty and innovation in the work, and *Prosas Profanas, and Other Poems* won acclaim, particularly among young readers in Europe.

One of the best-known poems in the collection *Prosas Profanas, and Other Poems*, "Blasón" ("Blazon") is a panegyric to the swan (*Modernista* doctrine and French Parnassians). The work contributed to one of literary history's most colorful exchanges, a contest between Darío and his contemporary, the Mexican poet Enrique González Martínez, fought by symbolic proxies.

In "Blazon," Darío proudly adopts the swan as his blazon—his emblem. He sings of the swan's haunting unreality and decorative beauty in numerous poems, extolling its mythic and regal qualities—"Olympic is the swan, . . . Wings, short and pure . . . as the sun they seek." In time, the swan became closely associated both with Darío and with *Modernismo*, symbolizing the depiction of the exquisite, for which the *Modernistas* strived.

Some Latin American artists believed that Darío was guilty of excessive fidelity to the symbols, themes, and forms of European art. The growing "New World" movement did not entirely reject *Modernismo* but rather scolded what it perceived as its symbolic excesses and favored development of truly Latin American themes. In his later works, Darío himself showed just such an inclination, but at the height of his swan worship, he was a target of the New World movement.

González Martínez chose to attack the symbol of the swan in his famous repudiation of the elegant excesses of *Modernismo*, "Tuércele el cuello al cisne" ("Wring the Swan's Neck"), something of a New World credo. The 1911 work began, "Wring the neck of the deceitfully-plumed swan/ Who sings his white note to the blue of the fountain." Ironically, by the time "Wring the Swan's Neck" was published, Darío had turned to themes more conspicuously South American, including traditional Christian subjects and songs to the awakening continent.

CANTOS DE VIDA Y ESPERANZA, LOS CISNES, Y OTROS POEMAS

This growing South Americanism is obvious in the last of Darío's three great collections, *Cantos de vida y esperanza, los cisnes, y otros poemas*. Published when Darío was thirty-eight and in the depths of ill health and despondency, the work was widely acclaimed in Europe and South America and recognized as a new departure for the poet. Although it carries on themes associated with Darío's early works, it also includes a number of poems featuring traditional Christian imagery as well as several political poems—both uncommon in his previous collections.

"A Roosevelt" ("To Roosevelt"), the best known of the *Cantos de vida y esperanza, los cisnes, y otros poemas*, is sharply political. It voices a stern warning to the United States to forswear colonial designs on Latin America. The poem is a confident address to President Theodore Roosevelt, a celebrated big-game hunter, whose personification of the United States is clear.

"To Roosevelt" followed close on the heels of Spanish defeat in the Spanish-American War. Voicing as it did a solemn warning to the United States and a disarming affinity with Spain, the poem did much to enhance the reputation of Darío, then living in Europe, as a spokesperson of Latin America. The poem boasts of the proud Spanish spirit and the strong literary traditions of Latin America—both ironic choices for Darío—as the sources of South America's potential resistance to the United States.

Darío enjoys a lasting place in Hispanic literature. His art reunited Spain and its former empire after the wars of independence. He infused Latin American literature with the cosmopolitanism of the European avant-garde, while his own achievement drew

European critical attention to the literary activity of Latin America. He was, to many, the quintessential American artist: an earnest student of tradition and an eager captive of the future.

OTHER MAJOR WORKS

SHORT FICTION: *Cuentos completos de Rubén Darío*, 1950 (Ernesto Mejía Sánchez, editor).

NONFICTION: *La caravana pasa*, 1903; *Tierras solares*, 1904; *Historias de mis libros*, 1914.

MISCELLANEOUS: *Obras desconocidas de Rubén Darío*, 1934 (Raúl Silva Castro, editor); *Escritos inéditos de Rubén Darío*, 1938 (Erwin K. Mapes, editor); *Rubén Darío, Obras completas*, 1950-1953 (5 volumes).

BIBLIOGRAPHY

Acereda, Alberto, and Rigoberto Guevara. *Modernism, Rubén Darío, and the Poetics of Despair*. Lanham, Md.: University Press of America, 2004. An examination of *Moderismo* and how it was expressed in the works of Darío.

LoDato, Rosemary C. *Beyond the Glitter: The Language of Gems in Modernista Writers Rubén Darío, Ramón del Valle-Inclán, and José Asunción Silva*. Lewisburg, Pa.: Bucknell University Press, 1999. A critical study of Latin American and Spanish modernist writers. Includes bibliographical references and index.

Morrow, John A. *Amerindian Elements in the Poetry of Rubén Darío: The Alter Ego as the Indigenous Other*. Lewiston, N.Y.: Edwin Mellen Press, 2008. An analysis of Darío's works that looks at the Indian influence on his work.

Mujica, Barbara. "Uncovering a Literary Treasury." *Americas* 44, no. 2 (1992): 53. A profile of the early modernist magazine *Revista de América* and its publishers, including Rubén Darío.

Solares-Larrave, Francisco. "A Harmony of Whims: Towards a Discourse of Identity in Darío's 'Palabras Liminasies.'" *Hispanic Review* 66, no. 4 (Autumn, 1998): 447-465. An examination of Rubén Darío's ability to manipulate words to evoke a "soul" and to create beauty.

Torres-Rioseco, Arturo. *The Epic of Latin American Literature*. Berkeley: University of California Press, 1964. History and criticism of Latin American literature. Includes commentary on Rubén Darío's poetry and an index.

Watland, Charles. *Poet Errant*. New York: Philosophical Library, 1965. A biography of Darío with bibliographic references.

David Nerkle

CARLOS DRUMMOND DE ANDRADE

Born: Itabira, Brazil; October 31, 1902
Died: Rio de Janeiro, Brazil; August 17, 1987

PRINCIPAL POETRY
Alguma poesia, 1930
Brejo das almas, 1934
Sentimento do mundo, 1940
Poesias, 1942
A rosa do povo, 1945
Poesia até agora, 1947
Claro enigma, 1951
Viola de bolso, 1952
Fazendeiro do ar, 1953
Cincoenta poemas escolhidos pelo autor, 1958
Poemas, 1959
Antologia poética, 1962
Lição de coisas, 1962
In the Middle of the Road, 1965
José e outros: Poesia, 1967
Boitempo, 1968
A falta que ama, 1968
Reunião: 10 livros de poesia, 1969
Seleta em prosa e verso, 1971
As impurezas do branco, 1973
Menino antigo, 1973
Esquecer para lembrar, 1979
The Minus Sign: Selected Poems, 1980
A paixão medida, 1980
Carmina Drummondiana, 1982 (with Silva Belkior)
Nova reunião: 19 livros de poesia, 1983
Corpo, 1984
Sessenta anos de poesia, 1985
Travelling in the Family, 1986
Amar se aprende amando: Poesia de convívio e de humor, 1987
Poesia errante: Derrames líricos (e outros nem tanto, ou nada), 1988
O amor natural, 1992
José: Novos Poemas, 1993

A paixão medida: Poesia, 1993
Carlos Drummond de Andrade: Poesia, 1994
Poesia completa: Conforme as disposições do autor, 2002

OTHER LITERARY FORMS

In addition to many books of poetry, Carlos Drummond de Andrade (druh-muhnd juhn-DRAH-juh) published three volumes of stories, nine collections of *crônicas* (journalistic "chronicles," or short prose pieces which may take the form of anecdotal narratives or commentary on current events or behavior), and numerous Portuguese translations of works of French literature. The language of many of his prose-narrative poems is closely related to that of his *crônicas*.

ACHIEVEMENTS

In a distinguished career spanning six decades, Carlos Drummond de Andrade produced a formidable body of poetry and prose. Appealing to connoisseurs of literature and the broader public alike, he became one of Brazil's most beloved modern writers. With a vast poetic repertory of considerable thematic and stylistic variety, Drummond is widely regarded as the leading Brazilian poet of the twentieth century; many consider him to be the most important lyrical voice in that nation's entire literary history. He rightly stands alongside the great Portuguese-language poets, the classic Luís de Camões and the modern Fernando Pessoa, as well as the major contemporary Latin American poets Pablo Neruda, César Vallejo, and Octavio Paz.

Brazilian *Modernismo* of the 1920's and 1930's sought to free poetry from the lingering constraints of Parnassian and Symbolist verse. Iconoclast writers combated conservative tradition, infusing poetry with New World awareness and revitalizing lyric through application of avant-garde techniques. Perhaps more than any other poet of *Modernismo*, Drummond was capable of crystallizing the aims of the movement to institute newness and give value to the national variety of the Portuguese language, while forging an intensely personal style with universal scope.

Drummond received numerous literary prizes in Brazil for individual works and overall contribution, including those of the PEN Club of Brazil and the Union of Brazilian Writers. He was twice nominated (in 1972 and 1978) for the Neustadt International Prize for Literature awarded by *World Literature Today*. His work has had a tremendous and continuing impact on successive generations of Brazilian artists, influencing emerging lyric poets since the 1930's. On another front, more than seventy musical settings of his poems have been made. Composers inspired by Drummond include the renowned Heitor Villa-Lobos (who set Drummond's poems to music as early as 1926) and the popular vocalist Milton Nascimento. Academic studies of Drummond's work abound; hundreds of articles and dozens of book-length analyses of his poetry have appeared in Brazil.

BIOGRAPHY

Carlos Drummond de Andrade was born in a small town in the interior of Brazil, the ninth son of a rancher with strict traditional values. His rural origins and family life were to be constant sources of inspiration for his poetry. As a rebellious youth, he studied in Belo Horizonte, the capital city of the state, where the family moved in 1920. The young Drummond had already published several items when, in 1922, he became aware of the Modern Art Week in São Paulo, an event that officially launched *Modernismo* as a program of artistic renovation and nationalist spirit.

In 1924, two leaders of the movement from São Paulo, Oswald de Andrade and Mário de Andrade (no relation), took Swiss-French poet Blaise Cendrars on a tour of Brazil; Drummond met them in Belo Horizonte. The young poet from Minas corresponded with Mário de Andrade, one of Brazil's most influential men of culture, until the death of the latter. Still in his home state, Drummond was a cofounder, in 1925, of *A revista* (the review), a modernist organ which lasted through three issues. In the same year, Drummond received a degree in pharmacy, a profession which he never practiced. Instead, he began to earn his living in journalism. In 1928, Oswald de Andrade's radical literary journal *Revista de antropofagia* (review of anthropophagy) published a neoteric poem by Drummond which generated much controversy and some early notoriety for the author. His first two books of verse were published in 1930 and in 1934, the year Drummond moved to Rio de Janeiro, the political and cultural capital of the nation.

In Rio, the writer from Minas served as chief of staff for the minister of health and education and collaborated on magazines and literary reviews. By 1942, he had been contracted by a major publishing house that would regularly publish cumulative editions of the poet's work, affording renewed exposure to poetry that had originally appeared in limited first editions of narrow circulation. Drummond lost his position in the ministry when the government fell in 1945. For a brief period, he was part of the editorial board of the tribune of the Communist Party. Later in that same year, he found work with the directorship of the National Artistic and Historical Patrimony, a bureaucratic position he held until his retirement in 1962.

During his years of public service, Drummond kept up a prolific pace as a journalist, narrator, and poet of diverse talents. In 1954, he obtained a permanent column in a major Rio daily to publish his *crônicas*; he maintained this activity until the early 1980's. Throughout these four decades, the author periodically joined the best of his journalistic prose pieces with other original writings for publication in volumes. A significant part of his wide-ranging recognition and popularity can be attributed to these endeavors. During this time, Drummond's reputation as a poet steadily grew. His work has been translated into Spanish, German, French, Swedish, Bulgarian, Czech, Russian, and English.

ANALYSIS

In 1962, Carlos Drummond de Andrade edited an anthology of his own poetry. Rather than follow a standard chronological sequence or order selections according to the book in which they originally appeared, the author chose poems from each of his collections and organized them into nine representative thematic divisions. This self-characterization reflects, in very general terms, the main preoccupations of Drummond's poetry before and after the publication of the anthology. Each of what the poet calls his "points of departure" or "materials" corresponds to a titled subdivision: the individual ("Um eu todo retorcido," a totally twisted self), the homeland ("Uma província: Esta," a province: this one), the family ("A família que medei," the family I gave myself), friends ("Cantar de amigos," singing of friends), social impact ("Amar-amaro," better-bitter love), knowledge of love ("Uma, duas argolinhas," one, two jousts), lyric itself ("Poesia contemplada," contemplated poetry), playful exercises ("Na praça de conuites," in the square of invitations), and a vision, or attempt, of existence ("Tentativa de exploração e de interpretação do estar-no-mundo," efforts at exploration and interpretation of being-in-the-world).

These are, as the author himself noted, imprecise and overlapping sections. Indeed, any effort at classificatory or chronological categorization of Drummond's poetry, like that of any complex and prolific verse maker, is subject to inconsistencies and inaccuracies. In addition to the wide thematic concerns enumerated above, several stylistic constants run through the whole of Drummond's work. Certain traits of form and content fade and reappear; other aspects merit consideration from a cumulative point of view. There is much transitional overlap between the broadly defined phases of his production. With these caveats in mind, the general lines of Drummond's poetic trajectory can be traced.

His earliest production, in the 1930's, following the antinormative paths of *Modernismo*, is direct, colloquial, and circumstantial. Sarcastic tones abound within a somewhat individualistic focus. Broader perspective is evident in the next stage, in the 1940's, as the poet explores the physical and human world around him. Existential questions are raised within the context of community; social and historical events move the poet, whose own anguish is a reflection of a generalized crisis of consciousness. A third phase, in the 1950's, incorporates personal and social concerns into an all-encompassing consideration of humanity and the environment from a philosophical standpoint. A certain formal rigidity accompanies this more contemplative and speculative poetry.

The development of Drummond's verse from the 1930's to the 1950's reveals, in broad strokes, a process of opening and expansion. This unfolding can be described with a tripartite metaphor of sight and attitude. The dominant voice of the early poetry is ironic yet timid; the poet observes but the lyric vision is uninvolved, hardly surpassing the limits of self. As the poet begins to confront the surrounding world, he looks more intently at the faces of reality. Existential meditations lead to a project of encounter; the struggles of others are seen and internalized. In his most mature stage, the poet not only observes and looks but also contemplates objects and subjects in an effort to see essences or the roots of contradictions. Having developed this broader vision, Drummond returns, in a cycle of books beginning in 1968, to examine his provincial origins. These latest works—in a reflection of the predominance of paradigms over temporal progression in Drummond's work—are permeated with the vigorous irony that characterized his earliest verse.

A thoroughly modern poet, Drummond can be inspired by and effectively use almost any source for his poetry. Much of his raw material is quotidian; the molding of everyday reality into poetic frameworks may be anecdotal or manifest utopian aspirations. One of his notable strengths is the ability to strike a balance between the light, vulgar, direct, or colloquial and the heavy, elevated, evocative, or contemplative. He is at home with the concrete and the abstract, finding the structures of language most adequate for a particular situation. His is a poetry of discovery, whether of a provincial past in its psychic and mythical dimensions or of the relationships and values that form modern society. Drummond's literary discoveries are not presented as truths or absolutes. His poetry is informed by a fundamental skepticism; however, bouts with relativism and anguish do not result in nihilism or cynicism. His lyric universe is fundamentally secular, and his speculative and metaphysical considerations of essences and human experience rarely involve concepts of gods or divinity.

Throughout, there operates a dialectic of inner examination and outward projection, of introspection and denunciation of social problems. Expressions of anguish and impotence unveil emblematic poetic selves threatened by technology and a hostile world. The poet seeks to apprehend the profound sense of unresolved differences and change for the individual, the family and affective relationships, society at large, his nation, and the community of humankind. When he bares himself and his personal psychic states, well-tuned devices filter or block the potential for self-indulgence or confession. The revelation of oppressive senses of reality is related to a view of the human condition, to the crises of modern humanity and civilization. T. S. Eliot said that great poets writing about themselves are writing about their times. A clear sign of Drummond's greatness is his linkage of substances of private, public, and transcendent planes.

Words and meaning

A particularly important aspect of Drummond's poetry is the explicit preoccupation with words and expressive means. At the outset, the poet expressed his disquiet through attacks on worn values and stale traditions. As his impulsive impressionism evolved, he undertook an ever-expanding search for nuances, keywords, the secrets of language and its virtualities. Words themselves and the making of poetry are the themes of some of Drummond's most important poems. In such works, the necessity of expression may be played against incommunicability or the imperfections of language. There is no tendency or approach in his poetry without a corresponding questioning of linguistic instruments or the sense of poetry. The modernist period in Western culture has been characterized as the age of criticism. Drummond's poetry is marked by self-consciousness; he is a constant critic of his own art. After *Modernismo* had effectively dissolved as a movement in Brazil, only its most complete poet would be able to write: "And how boring it's become to be modern/ Now I will be eternal."

Drummond's prime linguistic concern is with meaning. In his poetry, conceptual dimensions are generally more important than visuality or sonorousness. Occurrence, idea, and conceit dominate over imagery or symbolism. He seeks to use words in unusual and provocative combinations. Drummond's verse, moreover, is not very musical, in the sense of melodious and harmonious formation of words. There is notable formal variety in the poet's repertory, which incorporates everything from minimalist epigrams to long prose poems, both lyrical and narrative. Much of the poetry seems direct or simple. In the fashion of an Ernest Hemingway character who can "know that it's complicated and write it simple," Drummond, in the realm of poetry, has an uncanny ability to sculpt seemingly spontaneous airs. The simplicity of the poet is deceptive or even duplicitous. While Drummond's customary approach is free verse, he has written in consecrated forms such as the sonnet. He has cultivated the ode, the ballad, and the elegy as well.

Modernismo

Drummond's earliest work is written under the sign of *Modernismo* and demonstrates a combative frame of mind with respect to conservative notions of belles lettres associated with Parnassian and Symbolist traditions, long surpassed in Europe but slow to die in South America. Following the Brazilian modernists who preceded him in the 1920's, Drummond sought, once and for all, to pierce the "sacred air" of poetry by abandoning the idea of "noble" thematics and insisting on a more colloquial approach. In 1930, *Modernismo* had already conquered some ground. Thus, Drummond's poetry could not constitute rebellion alone. He was presented with the challenges that liberation presents and had to forge an iconoclasm of the second degree. Drummond succeeded in delivering the coup de grace on propriety, academic language, and mandatory stylization of diction. Humor and irony, never perverse, permeate the early poems, several of which can be called, in the Brazilian fashion, "joke-poems."

"In the Middle of the Road"

Two memorable selections from Drummond's first book, modestly titled *Alguma poesia*, illustrate the poet's characteristically daring and provocative attitudes. In the ten lines of the poem "No meio do caminho" ("In the Middle of the Road"), the speaker simply announces, in a starkly unadorned and repetitive fashion, that he, with "fatigued retinas," will never forget that "there was a stone in the middle of the road." Readers wondered whether the poem was sheer mockery or designed to baffle. Conservative critics laughed at the author, some even suggesting that the poem demonstrated a state of schizophrenia or psychosis. The extent of the controversy enabled Drummond, many years later, to edit a book consisting solely of commentaries and critiques of the neoteric set of verses. On the positive side, the poem can be read as a drama of obsession with ideas or as an expression of a monotonous human condition. It can also represent confrontation with impediments of any kind, be they personal, related to self-fulfillment, or literary (that is, ingrained norms). "In the Middle of the Road" can further be considered as a premonition of the hermetic mode in which Drummond would operate in subsequent poetry.

"Poem of Seven Faces"

Another symptomatic modernist work is the seemingly disjunct "Poema de sete faces" ("Poem of Seven Faces"). The opening lines—"When I was born, a crooked angel/ one of those who live in shadows/ said: Go on, Carlos! be *gauche* in life."—embody senses of repudiation, marginality, and awkwardness that inform the poet's early work and never completely disappear. This is the first presentation of the "twisted self" that inhabits Drummond's poetic world. The penultimate group of verses of the heptagonal poem alludes to a neoclassical poem, well known by Brazilian readers, to present aspects of a new poetics: "World world oh vast world/ If I were called Earl'd/ it would be a rhyme, it wouldn't be a solution." Here Drummond attacks the canons of rhyme and meter as external formalities that restrict expressive plenitude. This aggressive insistence on artistic freedom is again formulated with reference to rhyme in "Considera ção do poema" (consideration of the poem), in which the poet writes that he will not rhyme *sono* (slumber) with "the uncorresponding word" *outono* (autumn) but rather with "the word flesh/ or any other for all are good for me." Such statements should not be misconstrued, for Drummond has utilized delicately all manners of rhyme (verse-initial, verse-final, horizontal, vertical, diagonal, and internal), especially in his middle years. The question is not rhyme per se but the adaptation of form to the exigencies of particular poetic situations. In the early years of modernist enthusiasm, free verse indeed dominates Drummond's output.

Nationalism

As for the nationalistic concerns of *Modernismo*, the young Drummond did present a series of poetic snapshots of Brazil, focused on his home state of Minas Gerais, but these poems were not strictly regionalist. Even the validation of national reality did not escape the ironic provocations of the young poet. In a poem titled "Também já fui brasileiro" (I have been Brazilian too), he writes: ". . . I learned that nationalism is a virtue/ But there comes a time when bars close/ and all virtues are denied." Unwillingness to be restricted by the imposition of new values can also be read between lines such as "A garden, hardly Brazilian . . . but so lovely." Drummond's all-encompassing irony is crystalline in a poem called "Hino naçional" (national anthem), which begins, in typical Brazilian modernist fashion "We must discover Brazil!" only to declare, toward the conclusion of this exercise in skepticism, "We must, we must forget Brazil!" This distancing effect is a good measure of the poet's independence and unyielding search for revelations beyond given and constituted frames of reference, above and below evident surfaces.

SOCIAL-HISTORICAL PHASE

The social phase of Drummond's poetry is identifiable not so much by formal development but rather by attitudinal and ideological shifts. The titles of two of his early collections, *Sentimento do mundo* (feeling of the world) and *A rosa do povo* (the people's rose), clearly indicate in what directions the poet moved. Personal and family preoccupations are linked to the surrounding world, as the poet explores the consequences of pragmatism, mechanization, and the reification of humanity. The disquiet of the ironic self gives way to concerns with the other and with more far-reaching societal problems. Within this orientation, one of Drummond's masterpieces is "Canto ao homem do povo Charlie Chaplin" ("Song to the Man of the People C. C."). Harry Levin has written that Chaplin was one of the greatest modernists for his brilliant renderings of the frustrations and incongruities of modern urban life. Drummond, master of Brazilian *Modernismo*, pays homage to that cinematographic genius and incorporates reverberations of his work into a long (226-line) Whitmanesque piece that speaks for the "abandoned, pariahs, failures, downtrodden." In general, Drummond's poetry of this period gives rise to an existential raison d'être that is determined via interaction and giving. Individuality is encompassed by new perspectives: ethics, solidarity with the oppressed and the international community. The symptomatic poem "Os ombros suportam o mundo" ("Shoulders Bear the World") establishes a vital perspective—"Just life without mystifications"—alongside "Mãos dadas" ("Hand in Hand"), which presents the poetic voice of commitment: "I am shackled to life and I see my companions/ They may be taciturn but they nourish great hopes/ It is among them that I consider the enormity of reality." The 1940's were marked by the ravages of world war, and events touched Drummond the poet. The effects of the war in Europe are reflected, for example, in his "Congresso internacional do medo" (international congress of fear). Antifascist positions and socialist sympathies are evident in such representative poems as "Carta a Stalingrado" (letter to Stalingrad) and "Con o russo em Berlin" (with the Russians in Berlin).

"RESIDUE" AND "SEARCH FOR POETRY"

In the midst of this social and historical commotion, Drummond wrote two of his most enduring poems, "Resíduo" ("Residue"), an instigating inventory of emotive and objective presences, and "Procura da poesia" ("Search for Poetry"), which voices an ideal poetics. Here the persona speaks against making poetry of events, feelings, memories, or thoughts. Instead, he advises one to "penetrate quietly the kingdom of words" and contemplate the "thousands of secret faces under the neutral face" of each word. This advice might seem to point out inner contradictions, for much of Drummond's poetry itself derives from the sources he seems to reject. Without discounting a touch of ironic self-commentary, a less literal reading would not hold occurrences, sentiment, recollection, and ideas to be, in themselves, ill-advised for poets. Indeed, unmediated experience will not yield poetry; the true search is for a linguistic craft capable of reformulating experience into viable art.

Neoclassical phase

Formal and thematic properties alike permit establishing a third phase in Drummond's poetic career, beginning in the 1950's and continuing into the next decade. The free-verse and colloquial emphases of his eminently modernist and *engagé* poetry give way to somewhat neoclassical methods. The poet rediscovers the sonnet (and other measured forms) and withdraws from events into a philosophical mode. Reflection on the self, the world, and words takes place at the level of abstract expression. Drummond's confrontation with issues of metaphysics and transcendence signifies an interpretative poetry, which becomes somewhat hermetic. The book titles *Claro enigma* (clear enigma) and *Fazendeiro do ar* (farmer of the air) are suggestive of the evolution of the poet's endeavors, as are the names of specific poems such as "Ser" ("Being"), "Entre o ser e as coisas" ("Between Being and Things"), "Aspiração" ("Aspiration"), "Dissolução" ("Dissolution"), and "Contemplação no banco" ("Contemplation on a Bench"). In this more "pure" poetry, love (carnal and psychic) may constitute a means of sublimation. Consideration of family and of the past may evoke wonder about immortality or heredity as a cognitive category. What Drummond calls the most representative poem of this period, "A máquina do mundo" ("The Machine of the World"), is not to be understood in terms of personal accommodation or social structure but as phenomenological totality with mythical and archetypal dimensions. The poet reports an awakening:

> the machine of the world half-opened
> for whom its breaking was avoiding
> and at the very thought of it moaning . . .
> the whole of a reality that transcends
> the outline of its own image drawn
> in the face of mystery, in abysms . . .

Such poetry of paradox and enigma is also present in *Poemas*, but narrative procedures and concrete referents are reminiscent at times of the more "realistic" poetry of earlier years. The title of the poem "Especulações emtornoda palavra homem" ("Speculations Around the Word Man") suggests its philosophical stance, but rather than affirmations, the poem is made up entirely of questions. In this way, one is reminded of the celebrated poem "José," which portrayed disillusionment and the potential for resignation through a series of questions. "A um hotel em demolição" ("To a Hotel Under Demolition") is a long, digressive work which was inspired by an actual event and has prosaic moments. The wandering poem is anchored at the end of the metaphor of the hotel, as the speaker, who has "lived and unlived" in the "Great Hotel of the World without management," finds himself to be "a secret guest of himself." Here Drummond balances narrative and lyrical impulses, private and social dimensions, as well as observation and contemplation.

Lição de coisas

The two most important selections of *Lição de coisas* (lesson of things), which represents fully the author's mixed style, operate within strict binomial structures. Philosophical speculation is tempered in (by) "A bomba" (the bomb), an extended series of reactions to and statements about atomic explosive devices, the most humbling and frightening invention of modern technology. Each line begins with "the bomb," except the last, in which "man" appears with the hope that he "will destroy the bomb." The realism of this lyric contrasts, but ultimately links, with the experimental "Isso é aquilo ("this is that). This second work is measured and balanced, consisting of ten numbered sets of ten, two-item lines. The pairs of words or neologisms in each line are determined by free lexical, morphological, or semantic associations, for example, "The facile the fossil/ the missile the fissile. . . . the atom the atone . . . the chastity the castigate . . ." The final two lines have but one item—"the bombix/ the pytx"—and connect the playful linguistic exercise to the thematic of destruction. These two poems reflect how philosophical, humanitarian, and poetically inventive concerns can interpenetrate and synthesize in Drummond's poetry.

Boitempo

The publication of *Boitempo* (oxtime) begins a homonymous trilogy that incorporates hundreds of poems. This production constitutes a detailed return to historical roots and rural origins. The poet sets out to explore memories, incidents, and personages of his childhood and adolescence in Minas Gerais, much as he did in the 1930's. Inherent in this project is the potential for self-indulgence, cathartic sentimentalism, or autobiographical nostalgia. However, Drummond undertakes this effort with all the perspective of his varied poetic activities—modernist struggles, committed verse, metaphysical divagations, and metapoetics—and makes poetic distance of the chronological distance that separates him from his material. His moods are serene, and a generalized irony tempers the tenderness of memory. The poet is sufficiently detached to employ light, humorous tones in his review of a parochial (and paternalistic) past. There are certainly literarily self-conscious moments in the flow of Drummond's *Boitempo*. Passages that might appear to be dialogues with what was lived long ago are actually evocations of a literary oeuvre. There are returns to the birth of the "totally twisted self" as well as dramatizations of the genesis of nonconformity and rebelliousness. The poetry's comic character signifies a turning away from problematic relations as the center of poetic concern. Only about a tenth of the first set of the *Boitempo* poems are suggestive of Drummond's philosophical muses. The continuation of that mode is to be found in *A falta que ama* (loving lack) and in parts of the brief *A paixão medida* (measured passion).

Legacy

The contributions of Drummond to the modern art of poetry can be measured in regional, national, continental, and international terms. His regional role in *Modernismo* developed into Brazil's most powerful body of poetry. His reformulation of academic verse as idiomatic lyricism was unique in the diversity of tones, depth of psychological probing, and complexity of thought. With its linguistic flexibility, Drummond's poetry has the eminent capacity to represent metamorphoses, the mobility of sentiment, and the multiplicity of being. In his craft, he achieves a balance of emotion, intelligence, ethical senses, and irony. While Drummond's poetry has been a vehicle for expressions of social awareness, self-discovery, and transcendent inquiry, none of these is more fundamental than the poet's disquiet with the instrument of language itself. Drummond's truest vocation is not the profession of a literary creed or promulgation of any set of ideas but the very uncovering and shaping of words and verbal structures to reflect and explore multiple moods and attitudes.

Other major works

SHORT FICTION: *Contos de aprendiz*, 1951; *70 historinhas*, 1978; *Contos plausíveis*, 1981; *O sorvete e outras histórias*, 1993; *Histórias para o rei: Conto*, 1997; *As palavras que ninguém diz: Crônica*, 1997.

NONFICTION: *Confissões de Minas*, 1944; *Passeios na ilha: Divagaçoes sôbre a vida literária e outras matérias*, 1952; *Fala, amendoeira*, 1957; *Cadeira de balanço*, 1966; *Versiprosa: Crônica da vida cotidiana e de algumas miragens*, 1967; *Caminhos de João Brandão*, 1970; *A bôlsa e a vida*, 1971; *O poder ultrajovem*, 1972; *Os dias lindos*, 1977; *Discurso de primavera e algumas sombras*, 1977; *Setenta historinhas: Antologia*, 1978; *Boca de luar*, 1984; *O observador no escritório*, 1985; *Tempo, vida, poesia: Confissões no rádio*, 1986; *Moça deitada na grama*, 1987; *Conversa de livraria 1941 e 1948*, 2000; *Carlos e Mário: Correspondência completa entre Carlos Drummond de Andrade (inédita) e Mário de Andrade*, 2002 (Lélia Coelho Frota, editor); *Quando é dia de futebol*, 2002.

TRANSLATION: *Fome*, 1963 (of Knut Hamsun).

CHILDREN'S LITERATURE: *Historia de dois amores*, 1985.

EDITED TEXTS: *Rio de Janeiro em prosa e verso*, 1965 (with Manuel Bandeira); *Minas Gerais*, 1967; *Uma pedra no meio do caminho: Biographia de um poema*, 1967.

BIBLIOGRAPHY

Armstrong, Piers. *Third World Literary Fortunes: Brazilian Culture and Its International Reception.* Lewisburg, Pa.: Bucknell University Press, 1999. Contrasts Brazilian writers with their Spanish American counterparts and compares Drummond's poetic persona to such "paradigmatic antiheroes" as T. S. Eliot and Franz Kafka.

Di Antonio, Robert Edward. "The Confessional Mode as a Liberating Force in the Poetics of Carlos Drummond de Andrade." *Quaderni Ibero-Americani* 8, nos. 61/62 (December/January, 1986/1987): 201-207. Considers Drummond an existentialist with a personal, often humorous vision of the absurdity of existence.

Lima, Luiz Costa. "Carlos Drummond de Andrade." In *Latin American Writers*. Vol. 2. New York: Charles Scribner's Sons, 1989. This lengthy essay discusses Drummond's early work in the context of conflicting aspects of Brazilian *Modernismo*, his later work as evidence of "the corrosion principle," and his even later work as the "postcorrosion phase," in which memory is privileged over history.

Roncador, Sonia. "Precocious Boys: Race and Sexual Desire in the Autobiographical Poems of Carlos Drummond de Andrade." *Afro-Hispanic Review* 27, no. 2 (Fall, 2008): 91-115. Roncador discusses the relationships between boys in privileged households and the black maids and other servants, using numerous poems by Drummond.

Sternberg, Ricardo da Silveira Lobo. *The Unquiet Self: Self and Society in the Poetry of Carlos Drummond de Andrade.* Valencia, Spain: Albatros/Hispanófila, 1986. Analyzes Drummond's work as representing the inherent conflict in the relationship between self and others, and the tendency toward both withdrawal from and engagement with the world.

_____. "The World Within: Carlos Drummond de Andrade's *Alguma poesia*." *Luso-Brazilian Review* 21, no. 2 (Winter, 1984): 57-69. Focusing on Drummond's "first phase," from 1930 to 1945, Sternberg examines *o choque social*, or social shock inherent in the conflicts between individual and society, self and others, in Drummond's poetry.

Vargas, Claret M. "A Poetics of Bafflement: Ethics and the Representation of the Other in Carlos Drummond de Andrade's Poetry." *Neophilologus* 92, no. 8 (July, 2008): 457-470. Explores the self and the Other in three poems by Drummond: "Menino Chorando na Noite," "O Operário no Mar," and "Jose."

Charles A. Perrone

ENRIQUE GONZÁLEZ MARTÍNEZ

Born: Guadalajara, Jalisco, Mexico; April 13, 1871
Died: Mexico City, Mexico; February 19, 1952

PRINCIPAL POETRY
Preludios, 1903
Lirismos, 1907
Silénter, 1909
Los senderos ocultos, 1911
La muerte del cisne, 1915
El libro de la fuerza, de la bondad y del ensueño, 1917
Parábolas, y otras poemas, 1918
Jardins de Francia, 1919 (translation)
La palabra del viento, 1921
El romero alucinado, 1923
Las señales furtivas, 1925
Poemas truncas, 1935
Ausencia y canto, 1937
El diluvio del fuego, 1938
Tres rosas en el ánfora, 1939
Poesía, 1898-1938, 1939-1940
Bajo el signo mortal, 1942
Segundo despertar, y otras poemas, 1945
Vilano al viento, 1948
Babel, poema al margen del tiempo, 1949
El nuevo narciso, y otras poemas, 1952

OTHER LITERARY FORMS

The reputation of Enrique González Martínez (gohn-SOL-ays mor-TEE-nays) rests entirely on his poetry. He was active as a journalist, and his only published fiction—three short stories—appeared in a provincial newspaper and in a magazine that he coedited early in his career. These stories show a marked influence from the naturalist movement. The first one, "Una hembra" (a female), which appeared in *El heraldo de Mexico* in 1895, narrates the transformation experienced by a girl of the humblest class when the illicit love affair into which she is forced by the terrible circumstances of her life results in the birth of a child. The second story, "La chiquilla" (the girl), which was published in *Arte* in 1907, relates the sensual awakening of a young girl being reared in the house of a priest. In the third of the stories, "A vuelo" (ringing bells)—also published in *Arte*, in 1908—a sick boy dies when he is unable to suppress his desire to ring his favorite bell in the church on the day of the town fiesta.

González Martínez's acceptance speech on his admission to the Mexican Academy of Language, "Algunos aspectos de la lírica mexicana" (1932; some aspects of Mexican lyricism), examines the history of Mexican lyric poetry and draws the picture of its evolution, analyzing the best Mexican poets, pointing out weaknesses and virtues, and determining influences and trends. It has been considered one of his most refined prose pieces.

González Martínez wrote two autobiographical volumes *El hombre del búho* (1944; the man of the owl) and *La apacible locura* (1951; the peaceful madness). In these two books, written during the author's advanced years, he recalls the most important moments and events of his life in a plain and clear style, without literary pretentiousness. Sincerity and humility are perhaps the most impressive features of these two works, in which the poet talks about his contemporaries, describes his friends, and tells of his successes and his disappointments.

Achievements

Enrique González Martínez achieved his first literary success at an early age. When he was fourteen years old, he won first prize in a contest organized by the English-Spanish newspaper of Guadalajara, *The Sun*, for his translation of an English poem about John Milton. Later in his life, he was an effective member of the prestigious Mexican Academy of Language, president of the Athenaeum of the Youth of Mexico, member of the Seminary of Mexican Culture, founding member of the renowned National College of Mexico, president of the organizing committee of the American Continental Congress of Peace, and a professor of language and literature at various institutions of higher education. He received the Manuel Ávila Camacho Literary Award in 1944 and was a candidate for the Nobel Prize in Literature in 1949.

Biography

Enrique González Martínez was born in Guadalajara, the capital of the state of Jalisco, Mexico, on April 13, 1871. He was the son of a schoolteacher, José María González, and his wife, Feliciana Martínez. González Martínez attended the grade school directed by his father, and in 1881, he entered the preparatory school run by the Roman Catholic Church in the Conciliar Seminary of his native city. Five years later, when he was only fifteen, he entered the School of Medicine of Guadalajara.

González Martínez's fondness for poetry began at a very early age. As a child, he often amazed his parents and other adults with his achievements as a student as well as with his ability to write verse. Although he devoted himself with enthusiasm to the study of medicine during his student years, his interest in poetry grew. When he graduated as a medical doctor in 1893, he had already published a number of poems in newspapers and magazines, earning for himself a reputation as a provincial poet.

Despite his appointment upon graduation as an adjunct professor of physiology in the School of Medicine in Guadalajara, González Martínez did not have much success practicing medicine in his native city. At this time, González Martínez's father was offered the post of headmaster in a school that was going to be opened in Culiacán, the capital of the state of Sinaloa. It was an excellent opportunity to improve the family's economic situation, and since González Martínez had yet to establish himself as a physician, he decided to move to Culiacán with his parents and his younger sister, Josefina. They arrived there at the end of 1895, and for the next six months, González Martínez tried without success to establish his professional practice. After this time, he decided to move to the small town of Sinaloa, where he finally established himself and resided for the next fifteen years. In 1898, González Martínez married Luisa Rojo y Fonseca, a girl who had strongly impressed him when he had first seen her on his initial visit to Sinaloa. Their marriage produced four children—Enrique, María Luisa, Héctor, and Jorge—the youngest child, however, lived only sixteen months.

The fifteen years that González Martínez lived in Sinaloa were a period of intense professional activity as a doctor as well as of incessant literary production. For some time, the poet seemed to be content with publishing his poems in newspapers and magazines of the provinces as well as the capital, where he was beginning to be known. Nevertheless, in 1900, an event took place that prompted González Martínez to publish his first book of poetry. For reasons not yet fully understood, a newspaper in Guadalajara published a false report of his death. Several publications in different cities expressed their sorrow for the early death of such a promising poet and reprinted poems of his that had previously appeared in their pages. One of González Martínez's friends published a long article lamenting the death of the poet, recalling his life, listing his successes, and praising his virtues as a physician, a man of letters, and a citizen. When all this came to the attention of González Martínez in the small town where he lived, the poet rushed to deny the false information, and in a letter written in a joking tone he thanked his friend from Guadalajara for the informative and sorrowful article. After the uproar occasioned by this event had passed, the poet concluded that his poems must be good enough to be published in book form, and thus his first collection, titled *Preludios* (preludes), appeared in 1903.

Although González Martínez continued practicing medicine, his other activities seemed to multiply after the publication of his first book. In 1907, he published *Lirismos* (lyricisms), his second book of poetry, and between 1907 and 1909, he edited, along with his friend Sixto Osuna, the magazine *Arte*, which was published in Mocorito. Between 1907 and 1911, he occupied the position of political prefect in the districts of Mocorito, El Fuerte, and Mazatlán in the state of Sinaloa, and at the beginning of the Revolution of 1910, he was the secretary general of the government in Culiacán, the capital of the state of Sinaloa. In 1909, he published another book of poetry, *Silénter* (silently), and was appointed correspondent member of the Mexican Academy of Language.

In 1911, González Martínez published *Los senderos ocultos* (the concealed paths). That same year, he decided to abandon his medical career completely to devote the rest of his life to poetry, changing his residence and that of his family to Mexico City. There, he began to work as an editorial writer for the newspaper *El imparcial*. Finally, he was designated effective member of the Mexican Academy of Language and affiliated himself with the Athenaeum of the Youth of Mexico, becoming its president a year later. In 1912, he founded the magazine *Argos*, which appeared for only one year, and in 1913, he was appointed under secretary of public instruction and fine arts. After occupying this position for a year, he spent a year as secretary general of the government in Puebla. In 1915, he returned to Mexico City to devote himself to teaching and was appointed a professor of Spanish language and literature and of general literature in the National Preparatory School, as well as in the Normal School for Women. He was also appointed a professor of French literature in the School of Higher Studies, later called the Faculty of Philosophy and Letters. He soon lost his professorial positions, however, for political reasons.

After 1915, the poetic production of González Martínez increased, and his books of poetry followed one another with a frequency uncommon even among the most prolific poets. Nevertheless, despite his constant dedication to poetry, in 1917, he went back to work for a newspaper, this time as an editorial writer for *El heraldo de México*, while at the same time acting as coeditor of the magazine *Pegaso*.

In 1920, González Martínez began his diplomatic career with an appointment as minister plenipotentiary to Chile; he was transferred to a similar position in Argentina two years later. After another two years, he was appointed minister plenipotentiary for Mexico in Spain and Portugal, and he held this position for six years, until 1931.

The relatively peaceful life of González Martínez suffered two serious disruptions. The first was the death of his wife, Luisa, in 1935, and the second was the death of his son Enrique in 1939. The poet expressed in his poems the sorrow and the solitude that these two deaths caused him.

In 1942, González Martínez was admitted into the Seminary of Mexican Culture. A year later, he was appointed founding member of the important cultural organization the National College of Mexico, and in 1944, he received the Manuel Ávila Camacho Literary Award. In 1949, he presided over the organizing committee of the American Continental Congress of Peace and was nominated for the Nobel Prize in Literature. He died as he was approaching his eighty-first birthday, on February 19, 1952.

Analysis

Placing Enrique González Martínez in the global picture of the movements and tendencies of Hispanic literature is not an easy task. Among the factors contributing to this difficulty is the fact that the poet was active for more than a half century, during which time many styles and techniques succeeded one another. Nevertheless, although González Martínez was influenced by many poets, both from his own epoch and from other eras, he never permitted another poet's idiom to smother his own voice.

González Martínez began to write when the poetic environment in the Hispanic world was dominated by *Modernismo*. The great Nicaraguan poet Rubén Darío had succeeded in imposing his peculiar modality on this movement not only in Latin America but also in Spain. *Modernista* poetry was greatly influenced by the Parnassian and Symbolist schools of French origin, often featuring landscapes of ancient Greece or of eighteenth century France and including all kinds of exotic plants and flowers. The preferred fauna were animals known for their beauty, such as the peacock and the swan—especially the latter, which became a symbol of the movement. Metals and precious stones were used constantly as poetic motifs. The language of the *Modernistas* was musical and richly textured; adjectives were used profusely, and the imagery evoked strange impressions and sensations, synesthesia appearing with extraordinary frequency.

It was only natural that a movement so generalized and powerful as *Modernismo* had an influence on a young poet such as González Martínez, who had an expansive concept of poetry and who was well equipped for artistic creation to the most refined degree. In his poetry can be found Parnassian and Symbolist notes, satyrs and beautiful animals, musically elegant adjectives and synesthesia—everything with the clear desire to produce a refined artistic creation. For these reasons, many would consider González Martínez a member of the *Modernismo* movement.

Nevertheless, González Martínez was never a *Modernista* in the style of Darío. His satyrs and nymphs suffer from a lack of realism, and his fowls and stones—they are not always precious—do not function as mere ornaments in his poetry but contribute to the development of its ideas as well as communicate emotion. Closer connections could be found between González Martínez and *Modernistas* with the tendencies of the Cuban José Martí and the Colombian José Asunción Silva or with Darío in his later years, when his poetry was richer in insight and profundity. In González Martínez, interior concentration, simplicity of expression, and directness of communication are dominant characteristics.

"Wring the Swan's Neck"

For these reasons, González Martínez fits better as a postmodernist. It is true that he was only four years younger than Darío and that he was several years older than the *Modernistas* Leopoldo Lugones, from Argentina, and Julio Herrera y Reissig, from Uruguay. Nevertheless, it must be considered that González Martínez published his first book of poetry in 1903, when he was already thirty-two years old, and that he reached his peak when *Modernismo* was fading and postmodernism was at its apex. In this connection, the sonnet "Tuércele el cuello al cisne" should be mentioned.

This is the famous poem in which González Martínez recommended the death of the swan, the symbol of *Modernismo*, and its replacement by the owl as less ornamental but more wise and thoughtful. The poet himself said that his sonnet was not intended as an attack on Darío and the other first-class *Modernistas*; rather, it was directed against Darío's epigones. Nevertheless, González Martínez's poem was widely regarded as the death blow to *Modernismo* and the beginning of postmodernism. In any case, González Martínez's aesthetic was fundamentally different from that of the *Modernistas*: He was inclined toward meditation and the patient study of the mysteries of life rather than toward verbal brilliance for its own sake.

PRELUDIOS

When González Martínez published his first book of poems, he was already an experienced poet, with perfect technical control. In each poem of his first book, *Preludios*, the formal perfection of a master craftsperson can be observed, although the poet still had not found his direction. In *Preludios*, many different influences can be noted. The strongest is that of the *Modernistas*, which came to the poet through his compatriots Manuel Guitérrez Nájera and Salvador Días Mirón. Other influences were those of Latin poets, such as Horace, and of Mexican traditional poets, such as Manuel José Othon. Some of González Martínez's phrases have all the brilliance and elegance characteristic of *Modernismo*, as in "Ríe" (laugh)—"over the warm ermine of your shoulders,/ your laugh, fair blond, come forth/ as rainy gold"—or in "Baño" (bath), in which he says that the sculptural nude body of a girl is a "volcano of snow in an eruption of roses." His descriptions of nature, and of the love scenes that take place in it, have all the charm and delicacy of the classical or the national poets, as can be seen in the series of sonnets grouped under the title of "Rústica" (rustic).

The presence of these diverse influences and orientations clearly indicates that in *Preludios* the poet was still trying to find his voice and a more profound source of inspiration. The distinctive voice that would later be characteristic of the best of González Martínez's production is heard in only a few poems in *Preludios*, as when in "A una poeta" (to a poet) he exhorts a fictitious colleague to go to nature in search of "an ideal for your longings," telling him: "See the country, look at the sea, contemplate the sky:/ there is beauty there, inspiration and everything!" Likewise, when he talks of the healthy effects of night and silence, he says: "when the angel of the night spreads/ his sweet peace . . . under the blue silence the poet stretches/ his wings towards the world of dreams."

LIRISMOS

Lirismos, the poet's second collection, was a continuation of the search for himself that began in *Preludios*, and an intensification of his desire for formal perfection. The book is composed mostly of sonnets, and the influences of the *Modernistas* and the ancient classics continue, although somewhat mitigated by characteristics of the French Parnassian and Symbolist movements. Upon the appearance of this book, many praised

65

the artistic perfection of its poems and, based on this perfection, considered the book superior to the first one. The poet, however, was not deceived by these opinions and noticed that the Parnassian coldness had frozen his own voice.

Silénter

As a result, in his next book, *Silénter*, with the sonnet of the same title, he seems to advise himself to look for inspiration in self-intimacy, saying, "give forms to your desires, crystallize your idea/ and wait proudly for a distant dawn." In the first tercet of this sonnet, he calls on himself to achieve interior silence, advising himself that "a sacred silence sets you apart from the uproar." In one of the central poems of *Silénter*, which is also one of the poet's best known, "Irás sobre la vida de las cosas . . ." (you will go over the life of things . . .), he persists with his idea of returning to nature and investigating silence. He extols nature—"the soliloquy of the fountain, as well as/ the weak blinking of the star"—and advises "that you refine your soul until you are able to listen to the silence and see the shadow."

In another of his best-known poems, "A veces una hoja desprendida . . ." (sometimes a fallen leaf . . .), González Martínez goes deeper in his understanding of nature, expressing a greater intimacy with it: "that star and I know each other,/ that tree and that flower are my friends." In this poem, his identification with nature becomes complete; the poet exclaims "Divine communion! . . . I finally know what you murmur, clear fountain;/ I finally know what you tell me, errant breeze." In "Soñé con un verso . . ." (I dreamed of a verse . . .), the poet tells of having dreamed of a vibrant, clear, and strong verse; when, after waking, he attempts to relate his dream, he gives a fairly accurate description of his calm and peaceful way of writing poetry: "with mournful crepe my lyre veiled its cords/ and my verse was made of a soft melancholy/ like the steps that glide over the rug." In another poem, "En voz baja" (in a soft voice), the poet tells about his struggle to discover the secret of Nature. He begins by saying, "in all that exists/ I have heard many times your voice, nature"; then, describing his efforts to Nature, a woman, he tells her: "I pursue you and you escape; I adore you and everything is in vain./ Hermetically you hide the clue to the arcanum"; finally he asks when the moment will come in which "devoted lover . . ./ you will tell me in a soft voice the divine secret?"

Los senderos ocultos

In *Los senderos ocultos*, González Martínez continues the process initiated in his preceding books—that is, of trying to understand and identify with nature. Here this process reaches its greatest intensity and achieves the most satisfactory results. Perhaps for this reason, *Los senderos ocultos* has been considered by many to be the poet's best work. In "Busca en todas las cosas . . ." (seek in all things . . .), the author adds "the soul of things" as a new objective of the poet's search. That is why he advises: "seek in all things a soul and a hidden/ meaning," adding later that "you will know little by little how to decipher their language . . ./ Oh divine colloquy of the things and the soul!" In "Renovación" (renovation), the poet continues his search for identification, which now is not with the soul or the life of things, but with life itself, in its more universal and comprehensive sense. That same desire for identification includes the poet's beloved in the poem "A la que va conmigo" (to the one who goes with me), in which he tells her that "we will go through life identified with it" and that the "soul of things will be our own soul."

The pantheistic overtones of "Renovación" are even more evident in "Doux pays" (French for "sweet country"), in which the poet dreams of "a divine marriage between human life/ and the life of the world." Later, these thoughts will be embellished with a kind of Christian sweetness, as, for example, in "Cuando sepas hallar una sonrisa . . ." (when you learn how to find a smile . . .): "when you learn how to find a smile in the drop of water, in the mist,/ in the sun, in the bird, and in the breeze," then "like the Saint of Assisi, you will call brothers/ the tree, the cloud, and the beast"; then "you will reverently take off your sandals/ not to wound the stones in the road." In "Tiendo a la vida el ruego . . ." (I have a request for life . . .), the poet expresses his desire for total possession of and identification with life when he says that he does not ask for "the incomplete gift, but for the totality of life"; in the previously mentioned "Wring the Swan's Neck," he elevates life to the category of a goddess: "adore life intensely/ and let life understand your homage."

In the beautiful and well-known "Como hermana y hermano" (like sister and brother), the poet describes the peaceful way in which he and his beloved are traversing the road of life, and he admits that life has secrets and mysteries that humans cannot discover. When, in the silence of the night, the poet and his beloved hear their hearts beating, he says, "do not fear, there are songs heard/ but we will never know who signs them. . . ." When she, upon feeling a strange sensation, asks if he has kissed her, his answer is, "you will never/ know who gives those kisses." Finally, when she feels a tear sliding down her forehead, she asks him if he is crying, but the poet says, "we will never know who sheds those nocturnal tears."

LA MUERTE DEL CISNE

Although González Martínez maintained his preoccupation with the themes of his early collections, in *La muerte del cisne* (the death of the swan), he began to show a desire for innovation leading to new themes and more varied formal techniques. The result is greater diversity, but also a loss of cohesiveness and the appearance of contradictions. In "Ánima trémula" (trembling soul), the poet aspires to totality and wants to be, at the same time, "the viewer and the spectacle,/ and be the dreamer and the dream." In "A una alma ingenua" (to a simple soul), he shows a preference for what is simple and humble, asking "the soul without ideas," to whom he is talking, to "give me your eyes to see life." In "Iba por un camino" (I was going on a road), the poet shows a powerful desire for life:

"Let's live, let's live, because life is escaping!" In "Hortus conclusus" (Latin for "the enclosed garden"), on the other hand, he chooses to detach himself from life; when life calls, his soul "quietly and taciturnly... has closed the door... and does not answer." A kind of pessimism now appears with some frequency. In "Los días inútiles" (the useless days), the poet, reconstructing his past, feels the awakening of "an immense desire/ to sob by myself and ask for pardon"; in "Mañana los poetas" ("Tomorrow the Poets Will Sing"), he says that the poets of the future, despite all their successes, "will pick up the abandoned lyre from the floor/ and will sing with it our same song."

LATER POETRY

In his subsequent books, González Martínez continued to write his own very personal poetry, meditating in silence on his ideas, in intimate communion with nature, and expressing himself in his direct, simple, and polished language. He was for a long time the most admired poet of Mexico, and several generations of younger poets considered him their guide and inspiration. In his later years, when he was no longer in vogue, his poetry suffered a radical devaluation, and he has never regained his former eminence. Nevertheless, he dominated an entire epoch in his country, and he wrote poems that will not disappear with the passing of time.

OTHER MAJOR WORKS

SHORT FICTION: "Una hembra," 1895; "La chiquilla," 1907; "A vuelo," 1908.

NONFICTION: "Algunos aspectos de la lírica mexicana," 1932; *El hombre del búho*, 1944; *La apacible locura*, 1951.

BIBLIOGRAPHY

Brushwood, John S. *Enrique González Martínez*. New York: Twayne, 1969. An introductory biographical study and critical analysis of selected works by González Martínez. Includes bibliographic references.

Geist, Anthony L., and José B. Monleón, eds. *Modernism and Its Margins: Rescribing Cultural Modernity from Spain and Latin America*. New York: Garland, 1999. A rereading of modernism and the modernist canon from a double distance: geographical and temporal. It is a revision not only from the periphery (Spain and Latin America), but also from this new fin de siècle, a revisiting of modernity and its cultural artifacts from that same postmodernity.

González, Aníbal. *A Companion to Spanish American Modernismo*. Rochester, N.Y.: Tamesis, 2007. This work covers *Modernismo* in various genres, including poetry. Provides context for understanding González Martínez.

Sharman, Adam. *Tradition and Modernity in Spanish American Literature: From Darío to Carpentier*. New York: Palgrave Macmillan, 2006. This survey examines modernism in Spanish American literature and places González Martínez in context.

Tapscott, Stephen, ed. *Twentieth-Century Latin American Poetry: A Bilingual Anthology*. Austin: University of Texas Press, 1996. Provides a brief analysis of the poetry of González Martínez and translations of some of his better-known poems, including "Wring the Swan's Neck" and "Como hermana y hermano."

Washbourne, Kelly, and Sergio Gabriel Waisman, eds. *An Anthology of Spanish American Modernismo: In English Translation, with Spanish Text*. New York: Modern Language Association of America, 2007. Contains translations from the works of González Martínez and provides context for their understanding.

Rogelio A. de la Torre
(including original translations)

JOSÉ HERNÁNDEZ

Born: Chaera de Pueyrredón, Buenos Aires, Argentina; November 10, 1834
Died: Belgrano, Argentina; October 21, 1886

PRINCIPAL POETRY
El gaucho Martín Fierro, 1872 (*The Gaucho Martin Fierro*, 1935)
La vuelta de Martín Fierro, 1879 (*The Return of Martin Fierro*, 1935; included in *The Gaucho Martin Fierro*, 1935)

OTHER LITERARY FORMS

José Hernández (ehr-NON-days) dedicated his life to poetic and prosaic elucidation, illumination, and explanation of all aspects of the lifestyle, politics, and moral values of the Argentine gaucho (a type of cowboy and occasional laborer located in rural Argentina). He wrote many lengthy articles and essays about the political situation of the gauchos in relation to the power struggle between Argentine forces in favor of federalism and those in favor of regional autonomy. Hernández composed many of these works for a sophisticated readership that principally included the well-educated population of Buenos Aires and the provincial capitals of Argentina. While a journalist, he produced various works that depicted the gaucho lifestyle in biographical and instructional prose forms.

ACHIEVEMENTS

Known almost exclusively for his epic poem, *The Gaucho Martin Fierro*, José Hernández received no formal literary awards during his lifetime. However, he is remembered and honored through the Martín Fierro Award, given each year to the most outstanding television and radio productions in Argentina. The small statues that are awarded are in the shape of a gaucho.

BIOGRAPHY

José Rafael Hernández y Pueyrredón was born on the family ranch near San Martín in the province of Buenos Aires, Argentina, on November 10, 1834. By the age of four, he was enrolled in school and was said to have been able to read and write. When he was nine years old, his father (the foreman on the ranches of General Juan Manuel de Rosas) moved the family to the south of the province, where he came into close contact with the rural gaucho lifestyle and customs. It was here that he witnessed at first hand the armed suppression of the Indian population that still occupied much of this part of the province. Hernández received little formal education, but he developed an aptitude for reading, writing, and speaking that impressed his contemporaries. In 1857, he moved to the

José Hernández

city of Paraná, where he met his wife, Carolina. They were married in 1863 and had seven children.

He moved to Buenos Aires in 1863 and began his career as a journalist for the newspaper *El Argentino*. He began to write poetic and prose works and penned articles for the paper *El Eco de Corrientes*. Between 1853 and 1871, he became involved in the Argentine Civil War. He actively participated in the armed rebellion of the gauchos against President Domingo Faustino Sarmiento. The failure of this movement necessitated his self-exile to Brazil in 1871. On his return to Buenos Aires, he began composing his long epic poem, *The Gaucho Martin Fierro*, with the aim of presenting the gaucho lifestyle and mythology to the population of Argentina, at that time still a young country. The first part of the epic poem was published in the newspaper *La Repúblicá*. Shortly thereafter, it was published in book format. Because of his intimate knowledge of the language, culture, and morals of the gaucho people, he was able to create an authentic presentation that became extremely popular with the gauchos as well as various factions of the Argentine population. In 1879, the second part of the work was published.

In 1873, Hernández founded the newspaper *Río de la Plata*, in which he advocated regional autonomy, freedom from conscription of gauchos for the Indian wars, and a country based on agriculture and education. However, the newspaper was soon shut down by political foe and fellow author Sarmiento, who was also the president of Argentina. In his lengthy editorial essays, Hernández expressed disdain for the Europeanized and elitist factions that backed Sarmiento and who considered the gauchos to be unfit as a model for Argentina's future.

Under a new federal administration, Hernández was elected as a congressman in 1879 and a senator from the province of Buenos Aires in 1881. He was still serving in this capacity when he died of cardiac problems on October 21, 1886.

Analysis

José Hernández represents one of the first markedly Latin American voices in literature. That is, his Argentine perspective was based on firsthand knowledge, and he wrote in a style that was not copied or transplanted from a European approach. Hernández lived in a tumultuous time during the nation-forming period of Argentina. The nation was undergoing a struggle between those who wanted to use the gaucho as a national hero and model and those who wished to eliminate the gaucho influence entirely. Hernández favored the incorporation of gaucho values into mainstream Argentine politics and realities. Therefore, he wrote his epic poems to enlighten the educated masses in Buenos Aires, the capital of Argentina.

Hernández's original audience was the educated and urban reader. The author himself had experienced prejudicial treatment during his lifetime in rural, marginalized sections of Argentina, and he believed the gaucho existence was threatened. His goal went beyond education of the urban elites, and he clearly hoped his epic poems would help bring about reconciliation between the urban and rural groups in Argentina. Later, his focus shifted to the gauchos themselves. Hernández was successful in his efforts to accurately describe the gauchos, as can be seen in the fact that his works were immediate best sellers and have continued to be considered essential reading for any serious study of historical and contemporary Argentine values and culture. The author's goal was not limited to describing the lifestyles of the gauchos; he also sought to present their thoughts and values.

The poems address the day-to-day life of the gauchos, relating their social manners and colloquial language. Much like the American Wild West hero, the gaucho is presented as a hardworking, hard-fighting individualist who takes on the corrupt elements of an expanding frontier. Most of the challenges to this individualism result in a physical confrontation, generally a fight between two or more men. Literally all the fights are provoked by women. Unlike the North American counterpart, the gaucho does not win the respect of a woman in the end.

In *The Gaucho Martin Fierro*, the reader finds a determined defense of a marginalized group. The gauchos are presented as unfairly oppressed by a society that cannot or will not treat them fairly. Literally every governmental, military, and legal entity encountered in the poems is presented as corrupt. In this manner, Hernández extorts the reader to empathize with the neglected gaucho. Clearly, one of the goals of the author was to change his society through literature. The concept of the gaucho as a noble example of the new Argentine citizenship was revolutionary at the time of the publication of *The Gaucho Martin Fierro*. Hernández's nemesis, Argentine president Sarmiento, had published *Facundo: Civilización y barbarie—Vida de Juan Facundo Quiroga i aspecto físico, costumbres i habitos de la Republica Argentina* (1845; *Life in the Argentine Republic in the Day of the Tyrants: Or, Civilization and Barbarism*, 1868), a work that portrayed the gauchos as backward and uneducated.

THE GAUCHO MARTIN FIERRO

Hernández used prologues in both parts of *The Gaucho Martin Fierro*. In the part published in 1872, his stated mission was to lament the gauchos' situation, with the goal of demonstrating to an urban audience in Buenos Aires that the preservation of the gaucho lifestyle was a necessary component in the building of an Argentine national identity. Hernández starts by informing the reader that the happy and meaningful life of the gaucho had degenerated into suffering at the hands of indifferent urban intruders. He uses the colloquial speech of the gauchos to emphasize their different culture. They are portrayed as competent speakers, but without much formal education.

Hernández relates how Fierro and his gaucho friend Cruz decide that the only way to escape the injustices heaped on them by an ignorant and corrupt authority system in the evolving frontier lands of Argentina is to flee the society entirely and align themselves with the indigenous culture. This symbolic break with mainstream Argentina was meant to awaken the urban dweller to the injustices that were being wrought with their acquiescence. The problems that Cruz and Fierro endured were not just unfortunate fate, but rather systematic abuse of an entire culture. The two gauchos are presented as universal "others" who are not being noticed by the powers in the distant capital of the nation. Hernández attempts to reconcile the long-standing differences between rural and urban values by exposing the members of the urban segment to his somewhat romanticized but generally accurate descriptions of their rural counterparts.

THE RETURN OF MARTIN FIERRO

The seven years that had passed between the publication of the first and second parts of Hernández's epic poem had produced a markedly different political and social reality in Argentina. By 1879, Hernández had come to back the new Argentine president, who had called for the assimilation of the gauchos into the geopolitical structure of the country. This time, in the prologue to *The Return of Martin Fierro*, the Hernández's intentions are more complex: He intends to give advice to the gaucho himself. Hernández does mention how he educated the urban elites about gaucho culture in the first part of the poem, but his focus in the second part is on instructing gauchos themselves. He encourages good work habits and more education, so that gauchos could become more productive and respected citizens.

Hernández updates the tale of Martín Fierro and Cruz by describing how their sons had integrated themselves into the Argentine national culture by means of productive work and education, as opposed to marginal work efforts and the physical brawling that was portrayed in the first part of the poem. By analogy, the gauchos are advised as to what they must to become more in line with the future needs of the new country. The work reads like a guidebook, instructing the gauchos on how to leave the misery and instability of the past behind.

Numerous examples of education by analogy can be found in the work. One is the speech that Fierro delivers to his sons, in which he relates that the future will not be as easy as the past. It will require productive work, education, and adherence to the concepts of God and country. Another example is found at the end of the poem. A conflict arises that in the 1872 version would have led to a physical fight between the two antagonistic men. Instead, the quarrel is resolved without violence when the men compete to see who is the better singer.

BIBLIOGRAPHY

Foster, David William, and Daniel Altamiranda, eds. *From Romanticism to Modernismo in Latin America*. New York: Garland, 1997. A collection of essays on literary genres in Latin America, including poetry. The introduction is helpful and the work includes a segment on Hernández's *The Gaucho Martin Fierro*. The epic poem is examined from the viewpoint of Romanticism in Latin American poetry. Includes a bibliography.

Hanway, Nancy. *Embodying Argentina: Body, Space, and Nation in Nineteenth Century Narrative*. Jefferson, N.C.: McFarland, 2003. This bilingual anthology is useful for the student who requires information on the history of Argentine nation building in order to understand the importance of Hernández's epic poem. It specifically presents an excerpt from *The Gaucho Martin Fierro*, which deals with the tragedy of the slave ship. The introduction provides a historical summary of Latin American poetry. Includes bibliography and index.

Hernández, José. *The Gaucho Martín Fierro*. Edited by Kate Kavanagh. Albany: State University of New York Press, 1967. Bilingual edition of José Hernández's epic poem with a very useful introduction. Includes bibliography.

Quiroga Lavié, Humberto. *Biografia de José Hernández*. Buenos Aires: Librería

História, 2004. Although written in Spanish, this work is the definitive account of the life, writings and events that gave birth to them in the nineteenth century Argentina of Hernández. It explains the intricate relationship between Hernández and his adversary, Argentine president Sarmiento, himself a recognized author and poet.

Scroggins, Daniel C. *A Concordance of José Hernández's "Martín Fierro."* Columbia: University of Missouri Press, 1971. Easy-to-read edition of the epic poem of Hernández. Includes an introduction to nineteenth century Argentine poetry.

Slatta, Richard W. *Gauchos and the Vanishing Frontier.* Lincoln: University of Nebraska Press, 1992. This excellent history presents the gauchos of nineteenth century Argentina in a cultural perspective that pits them against the evolving modern nation of Argentina. It is valuable for anyone who wants a better understanding of Hernández's portrayal of the gauchos. As with the epic poem, it presents the gaucho as a romanticized character but nonetheless an essential component in the struggle for Argentine nationhood.

Vicuña, Cecilia, and Ernesto Livon-Grosman, eds. *The Oxford Book of Latin American Poetry: A Bilingual Anthology.* New York: Oxford University Press, 2009. This bilingual anthology, considered the best introduction to Latin American poetry, includes an excerpt from Hernández's epic poem. It provides a brief biography and critique of Hernández, biography, and index.

Paul Siegrist

GABRIELA MISTRAL
Lucila Godoy Alcayaga

Born: Vicuña, Chile; April 7, 1889
Died: Hempstead, New York; January 10, 1957

PRINCIPAL POETRY
Desolación, 1922
Ternura, 1924 (enlarged 1945)
Tala, 1938
Antología, 1941
Lagar, 1954
Selected Poems of Gabriela Mistral, 1957
Poesías completas, 1958
Poema de Chile, 1967
A Gabriela Mistral Reader, 1993

OTHER LITERARY FORMS

Although the poems published in the three main collections of Gabriela Mistral (mee-STROL) are the principal source for her recognition, she was active until her death as a contributor of prose to newspapers and journals throughout Latin America. She also wrote for newspapers whenever she was abroad, and her translated articles appeared frequently in the local press. The quality of this extensive and continuous journalistic effort is not consistent, though Mistral's prose style has been recognized for its personal accent and spontaneity. Her articles were extremely varied in theme. Much of what she wrote supported principles espoused in her poetry. Though less introspective, the prose, like the poetry, relates closely to the author's life and derives from episodes that left a profound mark on her. It is combative, direct, and abrupt while revealing her sincerity and ceaseless search for truth and justice.

ACHIEVEMENTS

Latin America's most honored woman poet, Gabriela Mistral was awarded the 1945 Nobel Prize in Literature. The first Latin American writer to be so honored, she was selected as the most characteristic voice of a rich literature that had until then been denied that coveted award. The intrinsic merits of her work, described as lyricism inspired by vigorous emotion, were representative of the idealism of the Hispanic American world.

Mistral's popularity was keen throughout her adult life, during which she received the National Award for Chilean Literature and honorary doctorates from the University of Florence, the University of Chile, the University of California, and Columbia University.

Gabriela Mistral
(Library of Congress)

Neither a disciple of Rubén Darío nor a contributor to the poetic revolution of the vanguard movements (though there are elements of both in her work), Mistral maintained independence from literary groups, preferring to consider herself an outsider. Nevertheless, her personal effort was a ceaseless labor toward unity, in which she pressed her genius into the service of brotherhood among nations, responsibility in professional activity, regard for future generations, appreciation for native American culture, effective education, love for the weak and oppressed, and a yearning for social justice.

All these endeavors are rooted in the principal sentiment of Mistral's poetry—her unsatisfied desire for motherhood. This emotion is in Mistral both a feminine instinct and a religious yearning for fulfillment. She elevates her great feminine anguish to the heights of art; this is her originality.

Biography

Gabriela Mistral was born Lucila Godoy Alcayaga, the child of Chilean parents of Spanish heritage, probably mixed with Indian ancestry. She was said to be part Basque, owing to her mother's last name, and part Jewish, only because her paternal grandmother possessed a Bible and schooled the eager child in its verses. The poet accepted this presumed inheritance, attributing to herself the energy of the Basque, the tenacity of the Jew, and the melancholy of the Indian. When she was three years old, her father left home and never returned. The task of rearing Mistral was shared by her mother and her half sister, Emelina. Both women were teachers and provided the child with primary instruction and a thirst for additional knowledge. Timid and reserved, the young girl had few friends. During her last year of primary instruction, she was falsely accused of wasting classroom materials. Unable to defend herself against this accusation and further victimized when classmates threw stones at her, she was sent home and was taught by Emelina. This first encounter with injustice and human cruelty left a profound impression on the future poet, who became determined to speak out for the rights of the defenseless, the humble, and the poor.

The family moved to La Serena on Chile's coast in 1901. Three years later, the fourteen-year-old Mistral's prose began to appear in local periodicals. These writings seemed somewhat revolutionary in a provincial town and probably accounted for the poet's admission to, and then expulsion from, the normal school. Undeterred, the family continued tutoring her while she finished her studies. In 1905, she began to work as a teacher's assistant. For the next five years, she taught in the primary grades, while nurturing her early work as a writer. This initial poetry possessed a melancholy flavor in tune with poets with whom she was familiar. Certified as an educator in 1910, she began a career as a high school teacher that took her throughout her native country. All during her life, she would characterize herself as a simple rural teacher, and she liked to be remembered as such, more than as a diplomat or a poet. She taught for more than twenty years, assuming the role of spiritual guide for many who approached her. Near the end of her career as an educator, Chile named her Teacher of the Nation. A good portion of her literary work, which has an educational motive, is directed toward young people. Behind the writer is the teacher who desires to encourage moral and spiritual awareness and aesthetic sensitivity.

With the publication of her first book in 1922, the poet's literary name, Gabriela Mistral, definitively replaced her birth name. The name Gabriela was chosen for the archangel Gabriel, one who brings good tidings, and Mistral was chosen for the dry wind that blows in the Mediterranean area of Provence. Also in 1922, Mistral left Chile for Mexico, where she had been invited by José Vasconcelos, secretary of education in Mexico, to participate in a national program of educational reform. Intending at first to stay for six months, she remained in Mexico for two years. This sabbatical began a lifetime of travel during which the poet occupied diplomatic posts, represented her country in international and cultural gatherings, and participated in numerous intellectual endeavors.

In 1932, Mistral became a member of the consular corps of the Chilean government, fulfilling various diplomatic assignments in Spain, Portugal, France, Brazil, and the

United States. At the same time, she continued a life of writing and intellectual pursuits. She taught Latin American literature at the University of Puerto Rico and at several institutions in the United States. In 1953, she became the Chilean delegate to the United Nations, where she served until poor health forced her to retire.

Analysis

Through a poetry that is at times deliberately crude and prosaic, Gabriela Mistral distinguished herself as an artist of tenderness and compassion. Her themes are nourished by her personal sorrow, which she ably elevates to the realm of the universal. Maternity, children, love, God, the fight against instinct, the soul of things, are voiced in anguish and in reverence by this most feminine of poets, whose vigor belies her femininity and whose high concept of morality is always present but never militant.

Mistral's three major collections of poems, *Desolación*, *Tala*, and *Lagar*, were published at sixteen-year intervals. They contain a selection of poems from among the many that the poet produced in newspapers during the intervening years. Each volume comprises material that was written at different times and under changing circumstances; thus, a strict topical unity is not to be expected. Each volume was published in response to an external stimulus that affected the life of the poet.

Desolación

Desolación was compiled through the initiative of Federico de Onís, professor of Spanish at Columbia University and founder of the Hispanic Institute. Onís had selected the poet's work as the theme for a lecture that he gave at the institute in 1921. The participants, primarily Spanish teachers from the United States, were deeply impressed by the depth and beauty of this vigorous new voice in Hispanic American poetry, and when they discovered that the poet had not yet published a book, Onís insisted on publishing the collection under the auspices of the Hispanic Institute.

The unity of the book is the body of moving, impassioned poems that were inspired by two painful experiences in the life of the youthful poet. While a teacher in La Cantera, Mistral became romantically involved with an employee of the railroad company, but because of bitter differences, they ended the relationship. When the young man later committed suicide for reasons unrelated to his association with the poet, Mistral was deeply affected. Several years later, she met a young poet from Santiago with whom she fell passionately in love. When he rejected her in favor of someone from Santiago's wealthy elite, Mistral was crushed. Shortly thereafter, she requested a transfer to Punta Arenas in Chile's inhospitable southland.

Inasmuch as the poems inspired by these devastating episodes do not appear in chronological order, one reads them as if the poet were relating the history of a single painful love. With great lyrical strength, she expresses the awakening of love, the joy and self-consciousness, the boldness, timidity, hope, humiliation, and jealousy. The poems that deal with suicide of the beloved reveal the poet's anguish and her petition to God concerning his salvation. She wonders about his afterlife and expresses her loneliness, remorse, and obsession to be with him still. The poet is pained and in torment, yet in her vigor, she displays jealousy, revenge, and hate, all of which are employed to combat the demanding powers of an enslaving, fateful love. God is petitioned in her own behalf as well. The agony is tempered at intervals by tenderness, her disillusionment nurtured by hope, her pain anointed with pleasure, and the hunger for death soothed by a reverence for life. In her moments of rapture, there is sorrow and loneliness, identified with the agony of Christ, from whom the poet seeks rest and peace in his presence.

The language of these poems is natural, simple, and direct. It is the realism of one who has lived close to the earth, who eschews delicate subtleties in favor of frankness. Mistral's love is expressed with passion and wrath; her words are coarse, bordering on crudity. This is chaste poetry, nevertheless, inasmuch as its fundamental longing for motherhood and the spiritual yearning for God reject the possibility of eroticism or immodesty.

Mistral lifts her spirit up though it is weighed down in anguish. It is suffering that does not destroy, but brings the spirit to life. The lyrical roots of *Desolación* are not a product of imagination: They are a lived tragedy. When Mistral begins to regard her lost youth, foreseeing the seal of fate in her sterility, condemned to perpetual loneliness, she raises a prolonged, sharp moan. Her entire being protests, argues, and begs at the same time. Overcome, the poet mourns her desolation, her martyrdom in not being able to be the mother of a child from the man she loved. This maternal yearning is not simply the impulse toward the preservation of the race. It is the tender cry of one who loves, who lives in agony over the loss of that which is closest to the ultimate joy of her soul.

Mistral's poetry employs a great variety of verse forms. She freely used sonnets, tercets, quatrains, the five-line stanza, sextains, ballads, and other forms, with little regard for the conventional patterns. She favored the Alexandrine, the hendecasyllabic line, and the nine-syllable line, which gradually became her preferred form; the latter seems to blend well with the slow pace of much of her poetry. The poems in *Desolación* do not follow classical models. Mistral toys with new rhymes, in which her consonants are imperfect or are interspersed with assonances. The artist has been accused of an inability to deal properly with metric forms. It is true that she lacked a musical sense. Her images, too, are frequently grotesque, too close to death and violence. Together with poems of rough, unpolished form in *Desolación*, there are others that are flawless in construction. Mistral reworked many of her poems repeatedly, the result generally being a refinement, although at times it was a disappointment. Her major objective was the power of the word rather than the meter of the lines.

Mistral concludes *Desolación* with the request that God forgive her for this bitter book, imploring men who consider life as sweetness to pardon her also. She promises in the future to leave her pain behind and to sing words of hope and love for others.

TALA

Tala fulfilled this promise sixteen years later. She compiled these poems as a concrete gesture to relieve the suffering of the children of Spain who had been uprooted from their homes during the Spanish Civil War (1936-1939). Mistral was disappointed and ashamed that Latin America had not appeared to share her grief for the plight of these homeless children, and the proceeds from the sale of this volume alleviated the difficulties in the children's camps. The title of the book refers to the felling of trees and applies to both the poems themselves and the purpose for which the author compiled them. The limbs are cut from the living trunk and offered as a gift, a part of oneself, a creation. From within the poet who has made her offering, there remains the assumption of the growth of a new forest. *Tala* has its pain (with allusions to the death of the poet's mother), but this volume is more serene than its predecessor. Mistral controls her emotions to a degree, and happiness, hope, and peace flow in her songs. *Tala* speaks of the beauties of America, as the poet humanizes, spiritualizes, and orders the creatures of the continent around the presence of humankind. Mistral gathers all things together, animate and inanimate, nourishes them like children, and sings of them in love, wonder, thanksgiving, and happiness. Far from America, she has felt the nostalgia of the foreigner for home, and she desires to stimulate the youth of her native soil to complete the tasks that are ahead.

Mistral sees Hispanic America as one great people. She employs the sun and the Andes Mountains as elements that bind the nations geographically, and she calls for a similar spiritual kinship. She believed that governments should be born of the needs of nations; they should emphasize education, love, respect for manual labor, and identification with the lower classes. Like José Vasconcelos, she believed that American man has a mission to discover new zones of the spirit that harmonize with the new civilization in which he lives. The poet treats this subject with great enthusiasm, declaring also that there is much in the indigenous past that merits inclusion in the present. She invokes the pre-Columbian past with nostalgia, feeling remorse for the loss of the Indian's inheritance and his acceptance of destiny.

The maternal longing of the poet is the mainspring of Mistral's many lullabies and verses for children that appear in this and other volumes. The other constant, implicitly present in all the poems of *Tala*, is God. She approaches God along paths of suffering, self-discipline, and a deep understanding of the needs of her fellow people. In God, she seeks peace from her suffering, comfort in her loneliness, and perfection. Her ability to humanize all things grows from her desire to find God everywhere. Thus these objects and the wonder derived from them infuse the religious into the poet's creation. Her metaphors and images derive from the contemplation of nature and its relationship with the divine. More objective than the poetry of *Desolación*, this work retains its personal, lyrical quality.

Ternura

Ternura (tenderness) is a collection of Mistral's children's poems. First published in 1924, it consisted of the children's verses that had appeared in *Desolación*. The 1945 edition added more poems for children that the author had written up to that date. The principal emotion is depicted in the title. The poet sings lullabies, rounds, and games, following traditional Spanish verse forms, especially the ballad. The poems generally teach a moral lesson, such as love and respect for others, development of one's sense of right and beauty, reverence for nature, country, and the creations of God. In Mistral's later children's verses, she sought to create a distinctly American atmosphere. Her vocabulary and background reflect regional and local material, drawing generously from Indian culture and beliefs.

The unique relationship between mother and child is felt in Mistral's soft, unhurried lullabies, in which the mother tenderly gives herself to the peace of her offspring, softly engendering in the child a reverence for Earth and all its creatures. She expresses the inner wounds of her heart, but in a tender fashion that does not disturb her baby. The only father in these verses is God, who becomes the source toward whom the yearning mother directs the child.

Lagar

Lagar (wine press) was published less than three years before Mistral's death. Together with the lack of world peace, the years brought new personal tragedies in the suicide of two of Mistral's closest friends and the devastating suicide of her nephew, Juan Miguel Godoy, whom she had reared like a son. Her health declined, and she became preoccupied with thoughts of death. Restless, Mistral moved frequently during this period. *Lagar* tells of the imprint of these experiences on her soul. The wine press of life and death, ever draining her heart, has left her weak and exhausted. In theme, *Lagar* refers back to *Desolación*, though Mistral no longer regards death with the anger of her frustrated youth. She bids it come in silence in its own due time. She is more confident of herself, eliminating the prose glosses that accompanied earlier collections. Her simple, prosaic verses are austere and purified. They beckon to the world beyond the grave in a poetic atmosphere that is as spiritual as it is concrete. Fantasy, hallucination, and dreams all contribute to an ethereal environment governed by imagination and memory.

Like Mistral's other published collections, *Lagar* lacks topical harmony. Mistral delights the reader with playful songs, revels in her creativity, and feels at one with God; yet the pain and weariness of the ever-draining wine press constitute the dominant mood.

The suicide of her nephew, at seventeen, again brought to Mistral's poetry the agony, the terrible emptiness, and the liberation available only when one has renounced earthly life. The young Juan Miguel had been the poet's constant companion, sensitive and helping, the strongest motive for Mistral's own bond with life. With the passing of this last close relative, the poet's will to live became associated more with life beyond the grave than with earthly cares.

Other verses demonstrate the poet's concern with the effects of war. Mistral protests against injustice and identifies with those who suffer through no fault of their own. Religion, not according to a prescribed dogma but rather in a sense of spiritual communication between the living and the dead, along with the ever-present identification with nature, continues as an important theme. In *Lagar*, the fusion of these two motifs is more complete than in the poet's earlier work. Nature is viewed in a spiritual sense. There appears a need to be in contact with the earth and the simplicity of its teaching to maintain spiritual harmony with the divine. This thought comforts the poet, who searches for a spiritual state of knowledge and intelligence. By preceding her nouns with the first-person possessive, she assumes a personal stance not found in her work before, as if she were participating more completely in the process of creation. Indeed, she begins to overuse the adjective, not so much to describe physical attributes as to personify the inanimate and to engender a mood. The mood thus created generally drains or destroys. Past participles used as adjectives (burned, crushed, pierced) fortify this effort, thus strengthening the theme of the title and suggesting the travail of life on Earth as parallel to the crushing of grapes in the wine press.

POEMA DE CHILE

During her last years, Mistral worked intensely on correcting and organizing her numerous unedited and incomplete compositions. Her posthumous *Poema de Chile* is a collection of poems united by one theme, her native country, in which she carries on an imaginary dialogue with a child, "my little one," showing him the geography and the flora and fauna of Chile as they travel together.

BIBLIOGRAPHY

Arce de Vázquez, Margot. *Gabriela Mistral: The Poet and Her Work*. Translated by Helene Masslo Anderson. Ann Arbor: University of Michigan Press, 1990. Biography and critical study of Mistral and her work. Includes bibliographical references.

Castleman, William J. *Beauty and the Mission of the Teacher: The Life of Gabriela Mistral of Chile, Teacher, Poetess, Friend of the Helpless, Nobel Laureate*. Smithtown, N.Y.: Exposition Press, 1982. A biography of Mistral and her life as a teacher, poet, and diplomat. Includes a bibliography of Mistral's writing.

Horan, Elizabeth. *Gabriela Mistral: An Artist and Her People*. Washington, D.C.: Organization of American States, 1994. This biography of Mistral examines her life in Chile and the effect that the social conditions in her native land had on her poetry.

Marchant, Elizabeth. *Critical Acts: Latin American Women and Cultural Criticism*. Gainesville: University Press of Florida, 1999. This refreshing reevaluation of Latin American women writers during the first half of the twentieth century recognizes their overlooked contributions to the public sphere. The critic reconsiders some representative poems, focusing on the dichotomy between Mistral's theories and practices and the female intellectual's alienation from the public sphere. Although Mistral refused a traditional societal role for herself, she advocated it for her readership.

Peña, Karen. *Poetry and the Realm of the Public Intellectual: The Alternative Destinies of Gabriela Mistral, Cecília Meireles, and Rosario Castellanos.* Leeds, England: Legenda, 2007. The author compares and contrasts the poetic works of three Latin American women writers, including Mistral.

Alfred W. Jensen

PABLO NERUDA
Neftalí Ricardo Reyes Basoalto

Born: Parral, Chile; July 12, 1904
Died: Santiago, Chile; September 23, 1973

PRINCIPAL POETRY
Crepusculario, 1923
Veinte poemas de amor y una canción desesperada, 1924 (*Twenty Love Poems and a Song of Despair*, 1969)
Tentativa del hombre infinito, 1926
El hondero entusiasta, 1933
Residencia en la tierra, 1933, 1935, 1947 (3 volumes; *Residence on Earth, and Other Poems*, 1946, 1973)
España en el corazón, 1937 (*Spain in the Heart*, 1946)
Alturas de Macchu Picchu, 1948 (*The Heights of Macchu Picchu*, 1966)
Canto general, 1950 (partial translation in *Let the Rail Splitter Awake, and Other Poems*, 1951; full translation as *Canto General*, 1991)
Los versos del capitán, 1952 (*The Captain's Verses*, 1972)
Odas elementales, 1954 (*The Elemental Odes*, 1961)
Las uvas y el viento, 1954
Nuevas odas elementales, 1956
Tercer libro de odas, 1957
Estravagario, 1958 (*Extravagaria*, 1972)
Cien sonetos de amor, 1959 (*One Hundred Love Sonnets*, 1986)
Navegaciones y regresos, 1959
Canción de gesta, 1960 (*Song of Protest*, 1976)
Cantos ceremoniales, 1961 (*Ceremonial Songs*, 1996)
Las piedras de Chile, 1961 (*The Stones of Chile*, 1986)
Plenos poderes, 1962 (*Fully Empowered*, 1975)
Memorial de Isla Negra, 1964 (5 volumes; *Isla Negra: A Notebook*, 1981)
Arte de pájaros, 1966 (*Art of Birds*, 1985)
Una casa en la arena, 1966 (*The House at Isla Negra: Prose Poems*, 1988)
La barcarola, 1967
Las manos del día, 1968
Aún, 1969 (*Still Another Day*, 1984)
Fin de mundo, 1969 (*World's End*, 2009)
La espada encendida, 1970
Las piedras del cielo, 1970 (*Stones of the Sky*, 1987)

Pablo Neruda
(Library of Congress)

Selected Poems, 1970
Geografía infructuosa, 1972
New Poems, 1968-1970, 1972
Incitación al Nixonicidio y alabanza de la revolución chilena, 1973 (*Incitement to Nixonicide and Praise of the Chilean Revolution*, 1979; also known as *A Call for the Destruction of Nixon and Praise for the Chilean Revolution*, 1980)
El mar y las campanas, 1973 (*The Sea and the Bells*, 1988)
La rosa separada, 1973 (*The Separate Rose*, 1985)
2000, 1974 (English translation, 1992)
El corazón amarillo, 1974 (*The Yellow Heart*, 1990)
Defectos escogidos, 1974
Elegía, 1974 (*Elegy*, 1983)
Jardín de invierno, 1974 (*Winter Garden*, 1986)
Libro de las preguntas, 1974 (*The Book of Questions*, 1991)
El mal y el malo, 1974

Pablo Neruda: Five Decades, a Selection (Poems, 1925-1970), 1974
El río invisible: Poesía y prosa de juventud, 1980
The Poetry of Pablo Neruda, 2003 (Ilan Stavans, editor)

Other literary forms

Pablo Neruda (nay-REW-duh) was an essayist, translator, playwright, and novelist as well as a poet. His memoirs, *Confieso que he vivido: Memorias* (1974; *Memoirs*, 1977), are a lyric evocation of his entire life, its final pages written after the coup that overthrew Salvador Allende. Neruda's translations include works by Rainer Maria Rilke, William Shakespeare, and William Blake. The volume *Para nacer he nacido* (1978; *Passions and Impressions*, 1983) includes prose poems, travel impressions, and the speech that Neruda delivered on his acceptance of the Nobel Prize. He has written a novel, *El habitante y su esperanza* (1926); a poetic drama, *Fulgor y muerte de Joaquín Murieta* (pb. 1967; *Splendor and Death of Joaquin Murieta*, 1972); and essays on Shakespeare, Carlo Levi, Vladimir Mayakovsky, Paul Éluard, and Federico García Lorca, as well as several works of political concern.

Achievements

Winner of the Nobel Prize in 1971, Pablo Neruda is one of the most widely read poets in the world today. His most popular book, *Twenty Love Poems and a Song of Despair*, has more than a million copies in print and, like much of his work, has been translated from Spanish into more than twenty languages. Neruda was so prolific a writer that nine of his collections of poems have been published posthumously.

Neruda's goal was to liberate Spanish poetry from the literary strictures of the nineteenth century and bring it into the twentieth century by returning verse to its popular sources. In *Memoirs*, written just before his death, Neruda congratulates himself for having made poetry a respected profession through his discovery that his own aspirations are representative of those shared by men and women on three continents. Writing on the rugged coast of southern Chile, Neruda found passion and beauty in the harshness of a world that hardens its inhabitants, strengthening but sometimes silencing them. His purpose was to give others the voice they too often lacked.

Biography

Pablo Neruda was born Neftalí Ricardo Reyes Basoalto in the frontier town of Parral in the southern part of Chile on July 12, 1904. His mother died of tuberculosis a few days after his birth, and Neruda lived with his stepmother and father, a railroad conductor, in a tenement house with two other families. Hard work and an early introduction to literature and to the mysteries of manhood distinguished his first seventeen years. In school, the famous Chilean educator and poet Gabriela Mistral, herself a Nobel Prize winner, introduced the young Neruda to the great nineteenth century Russian novelists. In the fall of his sixteenth year, while he was assisting in the wheat harvest, a woman whom he was later unable to identify first introduced the young man to sex. A wide-ranging, voracious appetite for books and the wonders of love are memories to which Neruda continually returns in his work, as well as to the harsh Chilean landscape and the problems of survival that confronted his countrymen.

His father's determination that Neruda should have a profession took the young poet to Santiago, where he intended to study French literature at the university. He had learned French and English in Temuco from his neighbors, many of whom were immigrants. His affiliation as contributor to the journal *Claridad*, with the politically active student group Federación de Estudiantes, and the attractions of life in a large city, where Neruda quickly made friends with many influential people, served to expand his original plans. While living with the widow of a German novelist, Neruda tried repeatedly to gain access to the offices of the Ministry of External Affairs, hoping to obtain a diplomatic post in Europe. More important, he had begun to write his first serious poetry during his evenings alone in a boardinghouse at 513 Maruri Street.

Neruda's hatred of political oppression became firmly established when the students of a right-wing group attacked the officers of *Claridad* and the Santiago police freed the attackers and arrested the editors, one of whom died in jail. Thus, after a year and a half in Santiago, Neruda abandoned his university career and dramatically declared himself a poet and political activist, taking the pen name Pablo Neruda from the Czech writer Jan Neruda (1834-1891) to conceal his activities from his father.

In 1923, to publish his first book of poems, *Crepusculario*, Neruda sold his furniture and borrowed money from his friends; favorable critical reviews validated his decision. The similarity of his verse to that of the Uruguayan poet Sabat Erscaty forced Neruda to turn from inspirational and philosophical themes back to a more intimate poetry based on personal experience. The result in 1924 was *Twenty Love Poems and a Song of Despair*, Neruda's most popular book, in which he sings of the joy and pain of casual affairs with a student from Santiago and the girl he left in Temuco.

Neruda's abandonment of his university career to write for *Claridad* coincided with his moving to Valparaíso. The port city immediately won his favor. He had not abandoned his goal of a diplomatic post, and finally, through the influence of the Bianchi family, he succeeded in meeting the Minister of External Affairs, who was persuaded to allow Neruda to pick his post. Neruda chose the one city available about which he knew nothing: Rangoon, Burma (now Myanmar), then a province of India.

After a short stay in Burma, Neruda obtained a new post in Ceylon (now Sri Lanka), setting the pattern of his life for the next twenty-five years. During this period, Neruda was abroad most of the time, usually under the auspices of the Chilean government—although on occasion he would flee government arrest. Returning to Chile from the Far East, he was quickly off to Argentina, then to Spain (during the Spanish Civil War), then to France, where he had stopped en route to Rangoon and to which he returned a number of times. During the early years of World War II, Neruda held a diplomatic post in Mexico; he resigned in 1943 to return to Chile, where he became active in politics as a member of the Chilean Communist Party.

Neruda's Communist sympathies (which had their origin in the Spanish Civil War) hardened into an uncritical acceptance of Stalinism, which ill accorded with his genuine populist sentiments. He became a frequent visitor to the Eastern bloc in the 1950's and 1960's, even serving on the committee that met annually in Moscow to award the Lenin Peace Prize, which he himself had won in 1950.

From 1960 until his death in 1973, Neruda worked tirelessly, publishing sixteen books of poetry and giving conferences in Venezuela (1959), Eastern Europe (1960), Cuba (1960), the United States (1961, 1966, and 1972), Italy and France (1962), England (1965), Finland (1965), and the Soviet Union (1967). He was named president of the Chilean Writers Association, correspondent of the Department of Romance Languages of Yale University, doctor *honoris causa* at Oxford, and Nobel Prize winner in 1971. In 1969, he was nominated for the presidency of Chile; he rejected the nomination in favor of Salvador Allende, who named Neruda ambassador to France. Neruda's health, however, and his concern about a civil war in Chile, precipitated his return in 1973. His efforts to prevent a coup d'état proved fruitless, and Neruda died a few days after Allende. He had just finished his *Memoirs*, writing that he enjoyed a tranquil conscience and a restless intelligence, a contentment derived from having made poetry a profession from which he could earn an honest living. He had lived, he said, as "an omnivore of sentiments, beings, books, happenings and battles." He would "consume the earth and drink the sea."

ANALYSIS

Pablo Neruda stated in a prologue to one of four editions of *Caballo verde*, a literary review he had founded in 1935 with Manuel Altalaguirre, that the poetry he was seeking would contain the confused impurities that people leave on their tools as they wear them down with the sweat of their hands. He would make poems like buildings, permeated with smoke and garlic and flooded inside and out with the air of men and women who seem always present. Neruda advocated an impure poetry whose subject might be hatred, love, ugliness, or beauty. He sought to bring verse back from the exclusive conclave of select minorities to the turmoil from which words draw their vitality.

CREPUSCULARIO

Neruda's work is divided into three discernible periods, the turning points being the Spanish Civil War and his return to Chile in 1952 after three years of forced exile. During the first phase of his work, from 1923 to 1936, Neruda published six rather experimental collections of verse in which he achieved the poetic strength that carried him through four more decades and more than twenty books. He published *Crepusculario* himself in 1923 while a student at the University of Santiago. *Crepusculario* is a cautious collection of poems reflecting his reading of French poetry. Like the Latin American *Modernistas* who preceded him, he consciously adhered to classical forms and sought the ephemeral effects of musicality and color. The poem that perhaps best captures the message indicated by the title of the book is very brief: "My soul is an empty carousel in the evening light." All the poems in *Crepusculario* express Neruda's ennui and reveal his experimentation with the secondary qualities of language, its potential for the effects of music, painting, and sculpture.

There are several interesting indications of Neruda's future development in *Crepusculario* that distinguish it from similar derivative works. Neruda eventually came to see poetry as work, a profession no less than carpentry, brick masonry, or politics; this conception of poetry is anticipated in the poem "Inicial," in which he writes: "I have gone under Helios who watches me bleeding/ laboring in silence in my absent gardens." Further, in *Crepusculario*, Neruda occasionally breaks logical barriers in a manner that anticipates much of his later Surrealistic verse: "I close and close my lips but in trembling roses/ my voice comes untied, like water in the fountain." Nevertheless, *Crepusculario* is also characterized by a respect for tradition and a humorous familiarity with the sacred that Neruda later abandoned, only to rediscover them again in the third phase of his career, after 1952: "And the 'Our Father' gets lost in the middle of the night/ runs naked across his green lands/ and trembling with pleasure dives into the sea." Linked with this respect for his own traditions is an adulation of European culture, which he also abandoned in his second phase; Neruda did not, however, regain a regard for Western European culture in his mature years, rejecting it in favor of his own American authenticity: "When you are old, my darling (Ronsard has already told you)/ you will recall the verses I spoke to you."

In *Crepusculario*, the first stirrings of Neruda's particular contribution to Spanish poetry are evident—themes that in the early twentieth century were considered unpoetic, such as the ugliness of industrialized cities and the drudgery of bureaucracies. These intrusions of objective reality were the seeds from which his strongest poetry would grow; they reveal Neruda's capacity to empathize with the material world and give it a voice.

Twenty Love Poems and a Song of Despair

One year after the publication of *Crepusculario*, the collection *Twenty Love Poems and a Song of Despair* appeared. It would become the most widely read collection of poems in the Spanish-speaking world. In it, Neruda charts the course of a love affair from passionate attraction to despair and indifference. In these poems, Neruda sees the whole world in terms of the beloved:

> The vastness of pine groves, the sound of beating wings,
> the slow interplay of lights, a solitary bell,
> the evening falling into your eyes, my darling, and in you

> the earth sings.
> Love shadows and timbres your voice in the dying
>   echoing
> afternoon
> just as in those deep hours I have seen
> the field's wheat bend in the mouth of the wind.

Throughout these twenty poems, Neruda's intensity and directness of statement universalize his private experiences, establishing another constant in his work: the effort to create a community of feeling through the expression of common, universal experience.

TENTATIVA DEL HOMBRE INFINITO

In 1926, Neruda published *Tentativa del hombre infinito* (venture of infinite man), his most interesting work from a technical point of view. In this book-length poem, Neruda employed the "automatic writing" espoused by the Surrealists. The poem celebrates Neruda's discovery of the city at night and tests the capacity of his poetic idiom to sound the depths of his subconscious. Ignoring the conventions of sentence structure, syntax, and logic, Neruda fuses form and content.

The poem opens in the third person with a description of the poet asleep in the city of Santiago. It returns to the same image of the sleeping man and the hearth fires of the city three times, changing person from third to second to first, creating a circular or helical structure. The imagery defies conventional associations: "the moon blue spider creeps floods/ an emissary you were moving happily in the afternoon that was falling/ the dusk rolled in extinguishing flowers."

In the opening passages, Neruda explores the realm between wakefulness and sleep, addressing the night as his lover: "take my heart, cross it with your vast pulleys of silence/ when you surround sleep's animals, it's at your feet/ waiting to depart because you place it face to face with/ you, night of black helixes." In this realm between motive and act, Neruda's language refuses to acknowledge distinctions of tense: "a twenty-year-old holds to the frenetic reins, it is that he wanted to follow the night." Also, the limits that words draw between concepts disappear, and thoughts blend like watercolors: "star delayed between the heavy night the days with tall sails."

The poem is a voyage of exploration that leads to a number of discoveries. The poet discovers his own desperation: "the night like wine enters the tunnel/ savage wind, miner of the heavens, let's wail together." He discovers the vastness of the other: "in front of the inaccessible there passes by for you a limitless presence." He discovers his freedom: "prow, mast, leaf in the storm, an abandonment without hope of return impels you/ you show the way like crosses the dead." Most important, he discovers wonder: "the wind leaving its egg strikes my back/ great ships of glowing coals twist their green sails/ planets spin like bobbins." The abstract becomes concrete and hence tractable: "the heart of the world folds and stretches/ with the will of a column and the cold fury of feathers." He discovers joy: "Hurricane night, my happiness bites your ink/ and exasperated, I hold back my heart which dances/ a dancer astonished in the heavy tides which make the dawn rise."

When the poet finds his beloved, he begins to acquire a more logical grasp of objective reality, but when he realizes that he is still dreaming, his joy becomes despair. He gradually awakens; his senses are assaulted by the smell of the timber of his house and the sound of rain falling, and he gazes through the windows at the sky. Interestingly, his dream visions do not abandon him at once but continue to determine his perceptions:

> birds appear like letters in the depths of the sky
> the dawn appears like the peelings of fruit
> the day is made of fire
> the sea is full of green rags which articulate I am the sea
> I am alone in a windowless room
> snails cover the walk
> and time is squared and immobile.

In this experimental work, Neruda mastered the art of tapping his subconscious for associative imagery. Although he never returned to the pure Surrealism of *Tentativa del hombre infinito*, it is the union of strikingly original and often surreal imagery with earthly realism that gives Neruda's mature poetry its distinctive character.

RESIDENCE ON EARTH, AND OTHER POEMS

In the poems of *Residence on Earth, and Other Poems*, Neruda first achieved that mature voice, free of any derivative qualities. One of the greatest poems in this collection, "Galope muerto" ("Dead Gallop"), was written in the same year as *Tentativa del hombre infinito*, 1925, although it was not published in book form until 1933. "Dead Gallop" sets the tone for the collection, in which Neruda repeatedly expresses a passionate desire to assimilate new experiences: "Everything is so fast, so living/ yet immobile, like a mad pulley spinning on itself." Many of the poems in *Residence on Earth, and Other Poems* begin in the same manner, recording those peripheral and secondary sensations that reside on the fringe of consciousness. They work toward the same end, resolving the new into understandable terms. As the poems come into focus, the reader participates in the poet's assimilation of his new world. For example, the significance of his vague memories of saying goodbye to a girl whom he had left in Chile gradually becomes clear in one poem:

> Dusty glances fallen to earth
> or silent leaves which bury themselves.
> Lightless metal in the void
> and the suddenly dead day's departure.
> On high hands the butterfly shines

> its flight's light has no end.
> You kept the light's wake of broken things
> which the abandoned sun in the afternoon throws at the
> > church steps.

Here, one can see Neruda's gift for surreal imagery without the programmatic irrationality and dislocation of the Surrealists.

In *Residence on Earth, and Other Poems*, too, there are magnificent catalogs in the manner of Walt Whitman: "the angel of sleep—the wind moving the wheat, the whistle of a train, a warm place in a bed, the opaque sound of a shadow which falls like a ray of light into infinity, a repetition of distances, a wine of uncertain vintage, the dusty passage of lowing cows."

Like Whitman, Neruda in *Residence on Earth, and Other Poems* opens Spanish poetry to the song of himself: "my symmetrical statue of twinned legs, rises to the stars each morning/ my exile's mouth bites meat and grapes/ my male arms and tattooed chest/ in which the hair penetrates like wire, my white face made for the sun's depth." He presents uncompromising statements of human sensuality; he descends into himself, discovers his authenticity, and begins to build a poetic vision that, although impure, is genuinely human. He manages in these sometimes brutal poems to reconcile the forces of destruction and creation that he had witnessed in India in the material world of buildings, work, people, food, weather, himself, and time.

Although Neruda never achieved a systematic and internally consistent poetic vision, the balance between resignation and celebration that informs *Residence on Earth, and Other Poems* suggests a philosophical acceptance of the world. "Tres cantos materiales" ("Three Material Songs"), "Entrada a la madera" ("Entrance to Wood"), "Apoges del apio" ("Apogee of Celery"), and "Estatuto del vino" ("Ordinance of Wine") were a breakthrough in this respect. In "Entrance to Wood," the poet gives voice to wood, which, though living, is material rather than spiritual. Neruda's discovery of matter is a revelation. He introduces himself into this living, material world as one commencing a funereal journey, carrying his sorrows with him in order to give this world the voice it lacks. His identification with matter alters his language so that the substantives become verbs: "Let us make fire, silence, and noise,/ let us burn, hush and bells."

In "Apogee of Celery," the poet personifies a humble vegetable, as he does later in *The Elemental Odes*. Neruda simply looks closely and with his imagination and humor reveals a personality—how the growth of celery reflects the flight of doves and the brilliance of lightning. In Spanish folklore, celery has humorous though obscene connotations which Neruda unflinchingly incorporates into his poem. The resultant images are bizarre yet perfectly descriptive. Celery tastes like lightning bugs. It knows wonderful secrets of the sea, whence it originates, but perversely insists on being eaten before revealing them.

Popular wisdom also finds its way into the poem "Ordinance of Wine." Neruda's discovery of the wonders of matter and of everyday experience led him to describe the Bacchanalian rites of drunkenness as laws, the inevitable steps of intoxication. In the classical tradition, Neruda compares wine to a pagan god: It opens the door on the melancholy gatherings of the dishonored and disheartened and drops its honey on the tables at the day's edge; in winter, it seeks refuge in bars; it transforms the world of the discouraged and overpowers them so that they sing, spend money freely, and accept the coarseness of one another's company joyfully. The celebrants' laughter turns to weeping over personal tragedies and past happiness, and their tears turn to anger when something falls, breaks, and abruptly ends the magic. Wine the angel turns into a winged Harpy taking flight, spilling the wine, which seeps through the ground in search of the mouths of the dead. Wine's statutes have thus been obeyed, and the visiting god departs.

In "Ordinance of Wine," "Apogee of Celery," and "Entrance to Wood," Neruda reestablished communion between humans and the material world in which they live and work. Since work was the destiny of most of his readers, Neruda directed much of his poetry to this reconciliation between the elemental and the social, seeking to reintroduce wonder into the world of the alienated worker.

Neruda was writing the last poems of *Residence on Earth, and Other Poems* in Madrid when the Spanish Civil War erupted. The catastrophe delayed the publication of the last book of the trilogy by twelve years. More important, the war confirmed Neruda's stance as a defender of oppressed peoples, of the poor. Suddenly, Neruda stopped singing the song of himself and began to direct his verse against the Nationalists besieging Madrid. The war inspired the collection of poems *Spain in the Heart*, a work as popular in Eastern Europe as is *Twenty Love Poems and a Song of Despair* in the West. These poems, such as Neruda's 1942 "Oda a Stalingrad" ("Ode to Stalingrad"), were finally published as part of *Residence on Earth, and Other Poems*. They were written from the defensive point of view of countries fighting against the threat of fascism. In them, the lyric element almost disappears before the onslaught of Neruda's political passion. Indeed, from 1937 to 1947, Neruda's poetry served the greater purpose of political activism and polemics:

> You probably want to know: And where are the lilies?
> the metaphysics covered with poppies?
> And the rain which often struck
> his words filling them
> with holes and birds?
> I'm going to tell you what has happened.
> I lived in a neighborhood in Madrid
> My house was called
> the House of Flowers . . .
> And one evening everything was on fire
> . . . Bandits with planes and with Moors

> bandits with rings and duchesses
> bandits with black friars giving blessings
> came through the sky to kill children.

More than ten years had to pass before Neruda could reaffirm his art above political propaganda.

Canto General

During the 1940's, Neruda worked by plan on his epic history of Latin America, *Canto General*. Beginning with a description of the geography, the flora, and the fauna of the continent, the book progresses from sketches of the heroes of the Inca and Aztec empires through descriptions of conquistadores, the heroes of the Wars of Independence, to the dictators and foreign adventurers in twentieth century Latin America. Neruda interprets the history of the continent as a struggle toward autonomy carried on by many different peoples who have suffered from one kind of oppression or another since the beginnings of their recorded history.

The Captain's Verses

Neruda, however, did not disappear entirely from his work during these years. He anonymously published *The Captain's Verses* to celebrate falling in love with the woman with whom he would spend the rest of his life, Matilde Urrutia. Unlike his previous women, Matilde shared Neruda's origins among the poor of southern Chile as well as his aspirations. These poems are tender, passionate, and direct, free of the despair, melancholy, and disillusionment of *Twenty Love Poems and a Song of Despair* and of *Residence on Earth, and Other Poems*.

Las uvas y el viento

While working in exile for the European Peace Party, Neruda recorded in *Las uvas y el viento* (the grapes and the wind) impressions of new friends and places, of conferences and renewed commitments made during his travels through Hungary, Poland, and Czechoslovakia. Neruda warmly remembers Prague, Berlin, Moscow, Capri, Madame Sun Yat-sen, Ilya Ehrenburg, Paul Éluard, Pablo Picasso, and the Turkish poet Nazim Hikmet. The most interesting works in the collection re-create Neruda's return to cities from which he had been absent for more than thirty years.

The Elemental Odes

Neruda's travels through the East assured his fame. His fiftieth year signaled his return to Chile to fulfill the demand for his work that issued from three continents. In 1954, he built his house on Isla Negra with Matilde Urrutia and published the first of three remarkable collections, *The Elemental Odes*, followed by *Nuevas odas elemen-*

tales (new elemental odes) and *Tercer libro de odas* (third book of odes). In these books, Neruda returned to the discoveries made in the "Material Songs" of *Residence on Earth, and Other Poems*. In the odes, Neruda's poetry again gained ascendancy over politics, although Neruda never ignored his political responsibilities.

The elemental odes reflect no immediately apparent political concern other than to renew and fulfill the search for an impure poetry responsive to the wonder of the everyday world. Neruda writes that earlier poets, himself included, now cause him to laugh because they never see beyond themselves. Poetry traditionally deals only with poets' own feelings and experiences; those of other men and women hardly ever find expression in poetry. The personality of objects, of the material world, never finds a singer, except among writers such as Neruda, who are also workers. Neruda's new purpose is to maintain his anonymity, because now "there are no mysterious shadows/ everyone speaks to me about their families, their work, and what wonderful things they do!"

In the elemental odes, Neruda learns to accept and celebrate the common gift of happiness, "as necessary as the earth, as sustaining as hearth fires, as pure as bread, as musical as water." He urges people to recognize the gifts they already possess. He sings of such humble things as eel stew, in which the flavors of the Chilean land and sea mix to make a paradise for the palate. Against those who envy his work and its unpretentious message of common humanity, Neruda responds that a simple poetry open to common people will live after him because it is as unafraid and healthy as a milkmaid in whose laughter there are enough teeth to ruin the hopes of the envious.

Indeed, the language of the elemental odes is very simple and direct, but, because Neruda writes these poems in such brief, internally rhyming lines, he draws attention to the natural beauty of his Spanish, the measured rhythm of clauses, the symmetry of sentence structure, and the solid virtues of an everyday vocabulary. In the tradition of classical Spanish realism, the elemental odes require neither the magic of verbal pyrotechnics nor incursions into the subconscious to achieve a fullness of poetic vision.

LATER WORK

After the collection *Extravagaria*—in which Neruda redirected his attention inward again, resolving questions of his own mortality and the prospect of never again seeing places and people dear to him—the poet's production doubled to the rate of two lengthy books of poems every year. In response partly to the demand for his work, partly to his increased passion for writing, Neruda's books during the last decade of his life were often carefully planned and systematic. *Navegaciones y regresos* (navigations and returns) alternates a recounting of his travels with odes inspired by remarkable people, places, and events. *One Hundred Love Sonnets* collects one hundred rough-hewn sonnets of love to Matilde Urrutia. *Isla Negra* is an autobiography in verse. *Art of Birds* is a poetic ornithological guide to Chile. *Stones of the Sky, Ceremonial Songs, Fully Em-*

powered, and *The House at Isla Negra* are all-inclusive, totally unsystematic collections unified by Neruda's bold style, a style that wanders aimlessly and confidently like a powerful river cutting designs in stone. *Las manos del día* (the hands of the day) and *La espada encendida* (the sword ignited), written between 1968 and 1970, attest Neruda's responsiveness to new threats against freedom. *Geografía infructuosa* (unfruitful geography) signals Neruda's return again to contemplate the rugged coast of Chile. As Neruda remarks in his *Memoirs* concerning his last decade of work, he gradually developed into a poet with the primitive style characteristic of the monolithic sculptures of Oceania: "I began with the refinements of Praxiteles and end with the massive ruggedness of the statues of Easter Island."

OTHER MAJOR WORKS
LONG FICTION: *El habitante y su esperanza*, 1926.
PLAYS: *Romeo y Juliet*, pb. 1964 (translation of William Shakespeare); *Fulgor y muerte de Joaquín Murieta*, pb. 1967 (*Splendor and Death of Joaquin Murieta*, 1972).
NONFICTION: *Anillos*, 1926 (with Tomás Lago); *Viajes*, 1955; *Comiendo en Hungría*, 1968; *Cartas de amor*, 1974 (letters); *Confieso que he vivido: Memorias*, 1974 (*Memoirs*, 1977); *Lo mejor de Anatole France*, 1976; *Cartas a Laura*, 1978 (letters); *Para nacer he nacido*, 1978 (*Passions and Impressions*, 1983); *Correspondencia durante "Residencia en la tierra,"* 1980 (letters; with Héctor Eandi).

BIBLIOGRAPHY
Agosin, Marjorie. *Pablo Neruda*. Translated by Lorraine Roses. Boston: Twayne, 1986. A basic critical biography of Neruda.
Dawes, Greg. *Verses Against the Darkness: Pablo Neruda's Poetry and Politics*. Lewisburg, Pa.: Bucknell University Press, 2006. Dawes examines how Neruda's poetry was affected by his political views during the Cold War. Examines the moral realism in "España en el corazon" (*Spain in the Heart*).
Feinstein, Adam. *Pablo Neruda: A Passion for Life*. New York: Bloomsbury, 2004. The first authoritative English-language biography of the poet's life. Thoroughly researched and indexed.
Longo, Teresa, ed. *Pablo Neruda and the U.S. Culture Industry*. New York: Routledge, 2002. A collection of essays examining the process by which Neruda's poetry was translated into English and the impact of its dissemination on American and Latino culture.
Méndez-Ramírez, Hugo. *Neruda's Ekphrastic Experience: Mural Art and "Canto General."* Lewisburg, Pa.: Bucknell University Press, 1999. This research focuses on the interplay between verbal and visual elements in Neruda's masterpiece *Canto General*. It demonstrates how mural art, especially that practiced in Mexico, became the source for Neruda's ekphrastic desire, in which his verbal art paints visual elements.

Nolan, James. *Poet-Chief: The Native American Poetics of Walt Whitman and Pablo Neruda*. Albuquerque: University of New Mexico Press, 1994. A comparative study of Whitman and Neruda, and the influence on them of both the theme of Native American culture and the practice of oral poetry.

Sayers Pedén, Margaret. Introduction to *Selected Odes of Pablo Neruda*, by Pablo Neruda. Translated by Sayers Pedén. Berkeley: University of California Press, 2000. Sayers Pedén is among the most highly regarded translators of Latin American poetry. Here her introduction to the translations in this bilingual edition constitutes an excellent critical study as well as providing biographical and bibliographical information.

Teitelboim, Volodia. *Neruda: A Personal Biography*. Translated by Beverly J. DeLong-Tonelli. Austin: University of Texas Press, 1991. A biography written by a close friend and fellow political exile.

Wilson, Jason. *A Companion to Pablo Neruda: Evaluating Neruda's Poetry*. Rochester, N.Y.: Tamesis, 2008. Wilson provides a guidebook to Neruda's numerous poetical works, furthering the readers' understanding.

Woodbridge, Hensley Charles. *Pablo Neruda: An Annotated Bibliography of Biographical and Critical Studies*. New York: Garland, 1988. Reflects the growing interest in Neruda following the translations of his works into English in the 1970's.

Kenneth A. Stackhouse

NICANOR PARRA

Born: San Fabián de Alico, near Chillán, Chile; September 5, 1914

Principal poetry
Cancionero sin nombre, 1937
Poemas y antipoemas, 1954 (*Poems and Antipoems*, 1967)
La cueca larga, 1958
Versos de salón, 1962
Canciones rusas, 1967
Obra gruesa, 1969
Los profesores, 1971
Artefactos, 1972
Emergency Poems, 1972
Antipoems: New and Selected, 1985
Nicanor Parra: Biografia emotiva, 1988
Poemas para combatir la calvicie: Muestra de antipoesia, 1993
Discursos de sobremesa, 1997, 2006 (*After-Dinner Declarations*, 2009; bilingual ed.)
Nicanor Parra en breve, 2001
Antipoems: How to Look Better and Feel Great, 2004

Other literary forms

Nicanor Parra (PAH-rah) and Pablo Neruda coauthored *Pablo Neruda y Nicanor Parra: Discursos* (1962; Pablo Neruda and Nicanor Parra: speeches), which celebrated the appointment of the latter as an honorary member of the faculty of the College of Philosophy and Education of the University of Chile. The volume includes the speech of presentation by Parra, in which he proffers his point of view regarding Neruda's work, and that of acceptance by Neruda. Parra has been active on an international scale in poetry readings, seminars, conferences, and informal gatherings. Many of his poems composed since the publication of *Cancionero sin nombre* (untitled songs) are available in English through the two bilingual volumes published by New Directions—*Poems and Antipoems* and *Emergency Poems*—and one bilingual volume, *After-Dinner Declarations*, published by Host.

Achievements

Nicanor Parra is the originator of the contemporary poetic movement in Latin America known as antipoetry. The antipoet, as this Chilean calls himself, is the absolute antiromantic, debasing all, even himself, while producing verses that are aggressive, wounding, sarcastic, and irritating. He has plowed new terrain in Latin American poetry using a store of methods that traditional poetry rejects or ignores. Parra's work is attacked as boring, disturbing, crude, despairing, ignoble, inconclusive, petulant, and devoid of lyricism. The antipoet generally agrees with these points of criticism, but begs the reader to lay aside what amounts to a nostalgic defense of worn-out traditions and join him in a new experience. Parra has established himself firmly in a prominent position in Hispanic American literature, influencing both his defenders and detractors.

Biography

Nicanor Parra Sandoval, one of eight children in a family plagued by economic insecurity, grew up in Chillán, in the south of Chile. His father was a schoolteacher whose irresponsibility and alcoholism placed considerable strain on the life and order of the family, which was held together by Parra's mother. Parra was in his early teens when his father died. The earlier antipathy he felt toward his father then turned toward his mother, and he left home. He began a process of identification with his father, toward whom he felt both attraction and repulsion, and to whom he attributes the basic elements of his inspiration for antipoetry.

During his youth, Parra composed occasional verses, so that when he went to the University of Chile in Santiago in 1933, he felt that he was a poet in addition to being a student of physics. He associated with the literary leaders at the student residence where he lived, and a year prior to graduating in 1938, he had published his first volume of poetry, *Cancionero sin nombre*.

After completing studies in mathematics and physics at the Pedagogical Institute of the university, Parra taught for five years in secondary schools in Chile. Between 1943 and 1945, he studied advanced mechanics at Brown University in the United States. Returning home in 1948, he was named director of the School of Engineering at the University of Chile. He spent two years in England studying cosmology at Oxford, and upon his return to South America he was appointed professor of theoretical physics at the University of Chile.

The publication of Parra's second collection of poetry, *Poems and Antipoems*, formally introduced the antipoetry with which his name is associated. This new poetry shook the foundation of the theory of the genre in Latin America, winning for its author both condemnation and praise. In 1963, Parra visited the Soviet Union, where he supervised the translation into Spanish of an anthology of Soviet poets, and then traveled to the People's Republic of China. He visited Cuba in 1965, and the following year served as a visiting professor at Louisiana State University, later holding similar positions at New York University, Columbia, and Yale.

Analysis

Nicanor Parra avoids the appearance of didacticism, claiming that he is not a preacher and that he is suspicious of doctrines, yet his purpose is to goad the reader with his corrosive verses, caustic irony, and black humor until the poet's response to human existence is shared. Satiric rather than political, antipoetry's sad, essentially moralizing, verse of hopelessness contains a strange and infinite tenderness toward humanity in its fallen condition. Neither philosophical nor theoretical poetry, it is intended to be an experience that will elicit a reaction and simulate life itself.

Even though he is a mathematician and a physicist, Parra does not consider life to be governed by a logical system of absolutes that, when harnessed, can direct humans toward organization and progress. On the contrary, he believes that the poet's life is absurd and chaotic, and the world is in the process of destruction and decay. Humans either accept this fact, together with their own powerlessness, or they deceive themselves by inventing philosophical theories, moral standards, and political ideologies to which they cling. Parra views his own role as that of obliging humanity to see the falsity of any system that deceives one into believing in these masks that hide the grotesque collective condition in a chaotic universe. Parra makes fun of love, marriage, religion, psychology, political revolutions, art, and other institutions of society. They are rejected as futile dogmas that attempt to ennoble or exalt humans above the reality of their insignificance.

Poetry too comes under attack by this anarchist who claims he has orders to liquidate the genre. As the antipoet, Parra resists defining his own poetic structure, knowing that in such an event it too must be destroyed. Thus, he searches continually for new paths, his own evolution, a revolution.

The prefix notwithstanding, antipoetry, however unconventional, is poetry, and Parra himself willingly explains his concept of the form. It is, he says, traditional poetry enriched by Surrealism. As the word implies, the "antipoem" belongs to that tradition that rejects the established poetic order. In this case, it rebels against the sentimental idealism of Romanticism, the elegance and the superficiality of the *Modernistas*, and the irrationality of the vanguard movement. It is not a poetry of heroes, but of antiheroes, because humans have nothing to sing to or celebrate. Everything is a problem, including the language.

Parra eschews what he considers the abuse of earlier poetic language in favor of a direct, prosaic communication using the familiar speech of everyday life. He desires to free poetry from the domination of figures and tropes destined to accommodate a select group of readers who want to enjoy an experience in poetry that is not possible in life itself. He has declared his intent to write poems that are experiences. He is hostile to metaphors, word games, or any evasive power in language that helps to transpose reality. Parra's task is to speak to everyone and be understood by all. The antipoet re-creates or reproduces slang, jargon, clichés, colloquialisms, words of the street, television commercials, and graffiti. He does not create poetry; he selects and compiles it. The genius of the language is sought in the culture of each country as reflected in the language of life. It is poetry not for literature's sake, but for humanity's sake. Its sentiments are the frustrations and hysteria of modern existence, not the anguish and nostalgia of Romanticism. Inasmuch as poetry is life, Parra also utilizes local or national peculiarities in language to underscore a specific social reality.

The destruction of the traditional poetic language is the first step in stimulating readers to be torn from the sacred myths that soothe them. Parra avoids so-called poetic words or uses them in unfamiliar contexts (the moon, for example, is poison). His images astonish readers with their irreverence, lack of modesty, grotesqueness, and ambiguity. They inherit the oneiric and unusual qualities of the Surrealists. Placed in the context of daily life, they equate the sublime with the ridiculous, the serious with the trivial, the poetic with the prosaic. Comic clichés and flat language are used by the protagonists in the antipoems to express their hurt and despair. The irony thus created by these simultaneous prosaic and tragic elements charges the work with humor and pathos. The reader laughs, though the protagonist, or antihero, suffers. The antihero's ineptitudes, failures, and foolishness are viewed with pity, scorn, and amusement. Parra's placement of familiar language and everyday failures in the life of the antihero, however, catches up with readers and compounds the irony, reducing the initial distance between readers and the protagonist. Readers become uncomfortable as this distance closes, their laughter not far from sadness.

The antihero in Parra's poetry is a rebel, disillusioned with all aspects of life, who suffers and is alone. He is a wanderer, distrustful and doubting, obsessed with suicide and death. Too insignificant, too ridiculous and nihilistic to be a tragic hero, he is merely the caricature of a hero. In need of communication, he undermines himself at every turn, belittling all of his efforts at self-expression. The grotesque inhabitants of the antipoetic world, comedians in an absurd play, unfulfilled in love and in their potentialities, suffer the passage of time, the agonizing problems of aging, and the inevitable confrontation with death. They are incapable of heroic gestures in any realm because their environment, habits, and nature make them ridiculous. The antipoet holds nothing sacred. The serious, the traumatic, is presented in a casual and burlesque fashion. Life is absurd and death is trivial.

The antihero's self-destruction and demoralization are simply mirrors of the malaise of contemporary society. Antipoetry views the world as a sewer in which humans, reduced to the level of vermin, live and multiply. Any effort to alter the situation is destined to failure. Humans nurture their own importance and worth, self-centered creatures obsessed with the need to possess and to consume. Love is false, friendship insincere, and social justice neither exists nor is desired; the environment becomes more and more artificial at the expense of nature and beauty. Political revolutions are deceits that benefit the new leaders but alter nothing. Love is viewed as an egotistical pursuit to fulfill sexual desire; spiritual bonds are denied. Although a few of Parra's poems present women as fragile, innocent beings who are invariably abused by men, the majority of the antipoet's female characters are aggressive rivals who threaten and humiliate men. Yet man, who fears woman, desires and seeks her as a sexual object. Finally, Parra mocks a corrupt Catholic Church; greedy, lascivious priests; a hypocritical pope; and an omni-impotent God.

CANCIONERO SIN NOMBRE

Parra's first collection of poems, *Cancionero sin nombre*, was inspired by the gypsy ballads of Federico García Lorca. The poems are stylized versions of traditional Spanish folkloric ballads, but in Parra's volume the action remains a dreamlike illusion without taking form. This volume had more attackers than defenders, and although some of the elements of his later work are evident, Parra himself calls this work a sin of his youth, better forgotten.

Parra attributes the roots of antipoetry to an independent response to human circumstances, not to any traditions in literature. Nevertheless, he recognizes those writers who have influenced his own literary development. After the publication of his first collection, Parra became enthusiastic about the poetry of Walt Whitman. He delighted in the metric freedom; the relaxed, loose, unconventional language; the narratives and descriptions; and the passionate vehemence that characterized Whitman's verse. When Parra returned to Chile from the United States in 1946, he came to know and appreciate the works of Franz Kafka. Kafka showed Parra the alienation and neurosis of modern culture, the comic deformation, the ironic treatment of the absurd in the human condition, the peculiar importance of atmosphere, the distortions and deformations that entrap the helpless protagonist. Parra was much more comfortable with Kafka's struggling protagonists than with Whitman's heroic vision of humanity. The Chilean's developing poetic style, new to the Spanish-speaking world, was antiromantic, antirhetorical, antiheroic, and antipoetic.

Parra's two-year stay in England beginning in 1949 crystallized this style into that of the antipoet. He was moved by the poetry of John Donne, W. H. Auden, Cecil Day Lewis, Stephen Spender, and especially T. S. Eliot. Parra appreciated Eliot's radical transformation of poetic diction and his inclusion of prosaic and colloquial language in his poems. These English-language poets inspired Parra in their observation of contemporary humanity and of humanity's environment, politics, manners, and religion and the didactic opportunities they exploited in treating these themes.

LA CUECA LARGA AND VERSOS DE SALÓN

Parra's third collection, *La cueca larga* (the *cueca* is a native dance of Chile), exalts wine. Written in the popular tradition of marginal literature, the book is anti-intellectual and vulgar, a frivolous contribution to Chilean folklore akin to antipoetry in preference for the masses and its position on the periphery of established literature.

In *Versos de salón* (salon verses), Parra returns to the antipoetic technique, but with some significant differences. The ironic attack on the establishments of society remains (the collection should be titled "Antisalon Verses"), but these poems are shorter than the earlier ones. They are fragments whose images follow one another in rapid fashion and mirror the absurd chaos of the world. The reader, forced to experience this confusion at first hand, is left searching for a meaning that is not to be found. The chaotic enumeration of the Surrealists, a favorite technique with Parra, abounds, while the anecdotal poetry of *Poems and Antipoems*, with its emphasis on dialogue, all but disappears. The sense of alienation is sharper, the bitterness and disillusion more deeply felt, the humor more pointed. The antihero changes from a victim into an odd creature who flings himself at the world in open confrontation. His introverted suffering is now a metaphysical despair.

CANCIONES RUSAS

Canciones rusas (Russian songs) was a product of the antipoet's visit to the Soviet Union. These poems are gentle, serene, lyrical, serious, a bit optimistic. The caustic spirit of the antipoet is not entirely absent, and the poet is not enthusiastic, but there is an expression of hope. The Soviet experience, not a political doctrine but a hope for underdeveloped nations symbolized by the progress of a people, is responsible for the change in tone. This is visual poetry, simple, stripped of images. The title notwithstanding, however, there is no music in these verses.

ADDRESSING SOCIAL ILLNESSES

In *Obra gruesa* (basic work), Parra returned once again to antipoetry. The Soviet Union is no longer an ideal, and hope for humankind is extinguished. This volume includes all the poetry Parra had published to 1969, with the exception of his first collection. *Los profesores* is a parody of the world of education, in which overly serious teachers fill the minds of their students with worthless information unrelated to human needs. Parra overwhelms the reader with lists of stifling questions, and the pedagogical idiom of the teachers contrasts with the picturesque colloquialisms of the students. *Emergency Poems* is a reprinting of the verses that appeared in "Straight Jacket," a section of *Obra gruesa*, as well as thirty-one new poems. These titles both refer to symptoms of a social illness that is becoming epidemic. A state of emergency is declared (hence the title) as inflation, pollution, and crime increase; wars exist in crisis proportion while people are controlled by the very monsters they invented to protect themselves from reality. Society has placed humans in straight jackets, and the antihero, an old person, is reduced to waiting for death; the sum of the antihero's life equals zero.

Parra's cynicism allows for no program of hope; the symptoms are not accompanied by a proposed remedy. The author uses himself as an example of the critical state of things. These poems enjoy a greater coherence than the author's most recent verses. Anecdotes again begin to appear. Parra's poetry becomes more aggressive and more social, with the appearance of a host of frustrated, unhappy characters, including beggars, drug addicts, and revolutionaries.

Artefactos

In *Artefactos*, Parra moved to a new poetic form. The antipoem had become fashionable in Latin America, and with the imitators came the risk that Parra's creation might become a mere formula. *Artefactos*, not in truth a book but a box of postcards on which each "artifact" appears, along with a brief illustration, approximates antipoetry in purpose and spirit. If some of the lines of poetry from the author's more recent collections were isolated from the poem, they would become artifacts. Indeed, Parra defines them as the result of the explosion of the antipoem, which became so filled with pathos it had to burst. The brief and self-sufficient artifact reduces the antipoem to its essential element, its strength resulting from its brevity and freedom from poetic context. Thus, the once complex antipoem has evolved into the most basic of fragments while still retaining its essence.

After-Dinner Declarations

In *After-Dinner Declarations*, Parra uses the mundane and boring after-dinner speech as the foundation for his poems—what could be more ordinary, more "antipoetic," than an after-dinner speech? The book is made up of five long speech-sequences, each consisting of a number of short poems. In "There Are Different Types of Speeches," he writes " . . . the reader will agree with me/ That all kinds of speeches/ Come down to two possible types:/ Good speeches and bad speeches." The book's translator, David Oliphant, writes in the introduction that Parra's book is a "book of antipoetic homilies, maxims, jeremiads, homages, mathematical puns, and literary histories" that nevertheless take things very seriously, however playful the poet's style and method.

Other major works

NONFICTION: *Pablo Neruda y Nicanor Parra: Discursos*, 1962; *Discursos de sobremesa*, 1997; *Pablo Neruda and Nicanor Parra Face to Face*, 1997.

TRANSLATION: *Lear, Rey and Mendigo*, 2004 (of William Shakespeare's *King Lear*).

MISCELLANEOUS: *Obras completas and algo [más]*, 2006.

Bibliography

Carrasco, Iván. *Para leer a Nicanor Parra*. Santiago, Chile: Editorial Cuarto Propio, 1999. An insightful analysis of the perception of Parra's work as antipoetry. An expert on Parra's work analyzes the evolution of his poetry from its rejection of thematic and syntactic structures to the development of a unique yet mutable voice that responds to its social and political environment. In Spanish.

Neruda, Pablo. *Pablo Neruda and Nicanor Parra Face to Face*. Lewiston, N.Y.: Edwin Mellen Press, 1997. This is a bilingual and critical edition of speeches by both

Neruda and Parra on the occasion of Neruda's appointment to the University of Chile's faculty, with English translations and a useful introduction by Marlene Gottlieb. Bibliographical references.

Parra, Nicanor. *Antipoems: New and Selected*. Translated by Frank MacShane, edited by David Unger. New York: New Directions, 1985. This bilingual anthology focuses on representative antipoems in an attempt to demonstrate how Parra's poetry has revolutionized poetic expression globally as well as within the sphere of Latin American poetry. Notes by the editor enhance understanding for English-speaking readers.

Parrilla Sotomayor, Eduardo E. *Humorismo y sátira en la poesía de Nicanor Parra*. Madrid: Editorial Pliegos, 1997. This study identifies and discusses the elements of humor and satire in Parra's antipoetry. It analyzes the poet's technique as well as unique antirhetorical style and language that creates a direct link to contemporary Latin American society. In Spanish.

Rowe, William. "Latin American Poetry." In *The Cambridge Companion to Modern Latin American Culture*, edited by John King. New York: Cambridge University Press, 2007. Rowe's chapter in this collection on Latin American culture in modern times includes discussion of the life and work of Parra.

Rudman, Mark. "A Garland for Nicanor Parra at Ninety." *New England Review* 26, no. 2 (2005): 204-213. Rudman, in this article celebrating Parra's life at the age of ninety in 2005, remembers meeting the Chilean poet for the first time in 1973. An intimate perspective on Parra and his life and work.

Sarabia, Rosa. *Poetas de la palabra hablada: Un estudio de la poesía hispanoaméricana contemporánea*. London: Tamesis, 1997. This study analyzes the oral nature of the literary production of several representative contemporary Latin American writers with roots in oral literature. In her chapter titled "Nicanor Parra: La antipoesía y sus políticas," the author explores the origins and consequences of antipoetry in its political and social milieus in contemporary Latin America, especially the *Cono Sur*, Chile, and Argentina. In Spanish.

Taylor, John. Review of *After-Dinner Declarations*, by Nicanor Parra, and *Before Saying Any of the Great Words*, by David Huerta. *Antioch Review* 67, no. 3 (Summer, 2009): 594-601. Taylor compares and contrasts the works of these two authors.

Alfred W. Jensen

OCTAVIO PAZ

Born: Mexico City, Mexico; March 31, 1914
Died: Mexico City, Mexico; April 19, 1998

PRINCIPAL POETRY
Luna silvestre, 1933
Bajo tu clara sombra, y otros poemas sobre España, 1937
Raíz del hombre, 1937
Entre la piedra y la flor, 1941
Libertad bajo palabra, 1949, 1960
Águila o sol?, 1951 (*Eagle or Sun?*, 1970)
Semillas para un himno, 1954
Piedra de sol, 1957 (*Sun Stone*, 1963)
La estación violenta, 1958
Agua y viento, 1959
Libertad bajo palabra: Obra poética, 1935-1957, 1960, 1968
Salamandra, 1962 (*Salamander*, 1987)
Selected Poems, 1963
Blanco, 1967 (English translation, 1971)
Discos visuales, 1968
Topoemas, 1968 (*Topoems*, 1987)
La centena, 1969
Ladera este, 1969 (*East Slope*, 1987)
Configurations, 1971
Renga, 1972 (in collaboration with three other poets; *Renga: A Chain of Poems*, 1972)
Early Poems, 1935-1955, 1973
Pasado en claro, 1975 (*A Draft of Shadows, and Other Poems*, 1979)
Vuelta, 1976 (*Return*, 1987)
Poemas, 1979
Selected Poems, 1979
Airborn = Hijos del Aire, 1981 (with Charles Tomlinson)
Arbol adentro, 1987 (*A Tree Within*, 1988)
The Collected Poems of Octavio Paz: 1957-1987, 1987 (includes the translation of several poetry collections)
Obra poetica (1935-1988), 1990
Stanzas for an Imaginary Garden, 1990 (limited edition)
Viento, agua, piedra / Wind, Water, Stone, 1990 (limited edition)

"Snapshots," 1997
A Tale of Two Gardens: Poems from India, 1952-1995, 1997
Figuras y figuraciones, 1999 (*Figures and Figurations*, 2002)

Other Literary Forms

If Octavio Paz (pahz) excelled at poetry, he is no less respected for his writings in a multitude of other humanistic disciplines. Perhaps his best-known prose work is *El laberinto de la soledad: Vida y pensamiento de México* (1950, rev. and enlarged 1959; *The Labyrinth of Solitude: Life and Thought in Mexico*, 1961), which is a discussion of Mexican culture and the Mexican psyche. *El arco y la lira* (1956; *The Bow and the Lyre*, 1971) is an outstanding study in the field of poetics. His literary criticism includes *Los hijos del limo: Del romanticismo a la vanguardia* (1974; *Children of the Mire: Modern Poetry from Romanticism to the Avant-Garde*, 1974); the Charles Eliot Norton lectures for 1971-1972; *The Siren and the Seashell, and Other Essays on Poets and Poetry* (1976); and *Corriento alterna* (1967; *Alternating Current*, 1973). He edited a number of important anthologies, including *Antología poética* (1956; *Anthology of Mexican Poetry*, 1958) and *New Poetry of Mexico* (1970), and he wrote one short play.

Achievements

Octavio Paz was Mexico's outstanding man of letters, the "leading exemplary intellectual of Latin America," as Ivar Ivask notes. His diverse output included poetry, literary criticism, philosophy, anthropology, art history, and cultural, social, and political commentary. As early as the mid-1960's, J. M. Cohen, in his influential study *Poetry of This Age, 1908-1965*, cited Paz with Pablo Neruda as "two of the chief Spanish-American poets." Carlos Fuentes has described Paz as "certainly the greatest living poet of the Spanish language," while Kenneth Rexroth declared Paz to be "without any question the best poet in the Western Hemisphere. There is no writer in English who can compare with him." Although some may disagree with Rexroth, all agree that Paz was one of the finest poets of the twentieth century.

Paz's accomplishments were recognized from the outset of his career. In 1944, he was awarded a Guggenheim Fellowship, which allowed him to study and travel in the United States. In 1963, he received the prestigious Belgian Grand Prix International de Poésie. He gave the Charles Eliot Norton lectures at Harvard during the 1971-1972 academic year. In 1977, three honors were bestowed on him: the Jerusalem Prize, the Premio National de Letras, and the Premio Crítico de Editores de España. The Golden Eagle Prize (Nice, France) followed a year later. The Ollin Yoliztli Prize, Mexico's richest literary honor, was conferred in 1980. The Miguel de Cervantes Prize, "the Spanish-speaking world's highest award," came in 1981. In 1982, Paz was the recipient of the Neustadt International Prize for Literature, one of the literary world's most important awards, often a prelude to the Nobel Prize. Indeed, just eight years later, Paz re-

Octavio Paz
(©The Nobel Foundation)

ceived the 1990 Nobel Prize in Literature. Other accolades included the German Book Trade Peace Prize (1984), the T. S. Eliot Award for Creative Writing (1987), and the Alexis de Tocqueville Prize (1989). The University of Mexico and Boston, Harvard, and New York Universities conferred honorary degrees on Paz.

BIOGRAPHY

Octavio Paz was born on March 31, 1914, in Mexico City. His mother, Josephina Lozano, was of Spanish extraction, while the family of his father, Octavio, was both Mexican and Indian. Paz was a precocious youngster, influenced by his politically active grandfather, a journalist and writer, whose twelve-thousand-volume library provided the necessary material for his intellectual development. Paz's father was a lawyer who joined Emiliano Zapata during the 1910 Mexican Revolution and represented him in America. After secondary school, Paz studied from 1932 to 1937 at the National University of Mexico. In 1931, he founded *Barandal*, the first of his many journals. He also began to publish his poetry, and in 1933, *Luna silvestre*, his first collection, appeared; in the same year, he also founded his second journal, *Cuadernos del valle de Mexico*. In 1937, Paz attended a conference in Spain; after the conference, he decided to remain there for a year. His allegiance was, naturally, to the Republican cause during the Spanish Civil War. In 1938, he passed through Paris, where he met Alejo Carpentier and Robert Desnos; Paz's firsthand encounter with the Surrealists was particularly decisive, and their profound influence on his subsequent work cannot be overestimated.

In 1938, Paz returned to Mexico, where he worked with Spanish political refugees, wrote on political matters for *El popular*, and founded *Taller*. A fourth journal, *El hijo pródigo*, followed in 1943. For these literary periodicals, he translated many French, German, and English works. Receipt of a Guggenheim Fellowship enabled him to spend the 1944-1945 academic year in the United States studying poetry. It was in the United States that he encountered the writings of T. S. Eliot, Ezra Pound, William Carlos Williams, Wallace Stevens, and E. E. Cummings, poets whose impact on Paz's work equaled that of the Surrealists some years before. When he ran out of money in New York in 1946, he decided to join the Mexican diplomatic service; he was sent to Paris, where he met Jean-Paul Sartre, Albert Camus, Jules Supervielle, and many other writers. During the next twenty-three years, his diplomatic work allowed him to spend extended periods in many countries, including Switzerland, the United States, Japan, and India. Asia opened a new world to Paz, and after his first trip in 1952, his writings begin to display many Asian characteristics. He then returned to Mexico and spent the period from 1953 to 1958 writing in his usual prolific fashion.

In 1962, Paz was appointed Mexico's ambassador to India, and it was there that he met Marie-José Tramini, whom he married in 1964; they had one daughter. Although Paz's political interests had waned over the years, he resigned his ambassadorship in 1968 in protest against the Mexican government's overreaction to the student riots. During the 1970-1971 academic year, Paz was the Simón Bolívar Professor of Latin American Studies at Cambridge University, and during the following academic year, he held the Charles Eliot Norton Professorship of Poetry at Harvard. He also taught at the universities of Texas, Pittsburgh, and California, San Diego. In 1971, he founded yet another journal, *Plural*, a political and literary review, which lasted until 1976, when he founded his last literary-cultural periodical, *Vuelta*. Early in 1982, King Juan Carlos of Spain presented Paz with the Miguel de Cervantes Prize, and some months later, he received the Neustadt International Prize for Literature at the University of Oklahoma. The Nobel Prize in Literature followed in 1990. He died in Mexico City on April 19, 1998.

ANALYSIS

Any poet whose worldview has a chance to develop and mature over an extended period of time will create different types of poetry. Eliot, for example, began with short lyrics, moved toward longer and deeper pieces such as *The Waste Land* (1922), and concluded with the powerfully philosophical *Four Quartets* (1943). Eliot provides an especially germane analogue, since Octavio Paz was influenced by his work and is often compared to him thematically and stylistically; as J. M. Cohen remarked, "With the exception of

T. S. Eliot, Octavio Paz is the only contemporary poet capable of feeling his metaphysics, and calling them to life."

Paz, too, began his career writing short lyrics, advanced to longer, surrealistic pieces, reworked the prose poem, and finally, after more than a quarter of a century of creative activity, began to experiment with collagelike texts and assemblages that bear little relation to poetry as traditionally defined. Such experiments follow the logic of Paz's stylistic evolution; he has always been a self-conscious poet and he has written many poems about poetry and the nature of the creative process. Indeed, Paz's conception of poetry is philosophical: Poetry alone permits humans to comprehend their place in the universe.

"Poetry"

In "Poesía" ("Poetry"), for example, Paz personifies this power of language to engage reality: "you burn my tongue with your lips, this pulp,/ and you awaken the rages, the delights,/ the endless anguish. . . ." The creative act is perceived as a struggle and the poet as a vehicle through whom words are spoken, comparable to a Greek oracle: "You rise from the furthest depth in me. . . ." Paz's references to images as "babblings" and to "prophets of my eyes" confirm the implication of oracular utterance. The poet is a seer, and only his articulation can defeat the ubiquitous silence of the universe.

"The Bird"

It is silence against which Paz battled most consistently, beginning with his early lyric pieces. Silence can be neutral, but it also represents Camus's indifferent cosmos, offering neither help nor solace. "El Pájaro" ("The Bird") presents the neutral form of silence, a natural scene broken by a bird's song. Ironically, articulation is not a palliative; here, it merely reminds the poet of his mortality. There is the silence of lovers, the silence of solitude, and the silence of death—silences that can be broken only by the poet. Other thematic threads that run through Paz's poetry—recurring images and motifs such as light, lightning, women, transparency, mirrors, time, language, mysticism, cycles, the urban wasteland, and various mythic perceptions—all can be related to his conception of the nature of poetry.

"Stars and Cricket"

Many of Paz's poems fall within traditional lengths, ranging from roughly ten to thirty lines, but he has not hesitated to publish the briefest haiku-like outbursts. Consider "Estrellas y grillo" ("Stars and Cricket") in its cryptic entirety:

> The sky's big.
> Up there, worlds scatter.
> Persistent,

> Unfazed by such a night,
> Cricket:
> Brace and bit.

SUN STONE

At the same time, Paz also experimented with the long poem. His *Sun Stone* consists of 584 eleven-syllable lines of abstruse rumination:

> I search without finding, I write alone,
> there's no one here, and the day falls,
> the year falls, I fall with the moment,
> I fall to the depths, invisible path
> over mirrors repeating my shattered image. . . .

"INTERRUPTED ELEGY"

One of Paz's most moving poems is "Elegía interrumpida" ("Interrupted Elegy"), a philosophical description of a number of people whose deaths affected the poet. Each of the poem's five stanzas begins with the same incantation: "Now I remember the dead of my own house." From this point, Paz muses on first impressions, those who take their leave quickly, those who linger, those who are forgotten—and all this in subdued, sparsely imagistic language. The poem itself is a metaphysical quest, and the dead whom it memorializes are brought to life. Despite the cathartic nature of the elegy, however, Paz's concluding couplet is despairing: "The world is a circular desert,/ heaven is closed and hell is empty."

EAGLE OR SUN?

Eagle or Sun?, a collection of short prose poems, the first book of its kind in Spanish, has been extremely influential. Part 1, "Trabajos del poeta" ("The Poet's Works"), consists of sixteen brief sections, each of which elaborates a narrative line, but usually in strongly imagistic and even surrealistic language. The surface concerns of these poems mask Paz's underlying interest: the poet's relationship with his creation. This is not allegory, which is read on one level and interpreted on another: Here, the reader perceives the two levels simultaneously. The ubiquitous silence is interrupted by a tapping ("it is the sound of horses' hooves galloping on a field of stone . . ."); these are the words appearing, demanding articulation. They pour out uncontrollably, this "vomit of words":

> The thistle whistles, bristles, buckles with chuckles. Broth of moths, charts of farts, all together, ball of syllables of waste matter, ball of snot splatter, ball of the viscera of syllable sibyls, chatter, deaf chatter. I flap, I swing, smashdunguided I flap.

Here, Paz conveys what it is like to be an artist, always at the mercy of competing inner voices, of spontaneous creative demands.

The second part of *Eagle or Sun?*, "Arenas movedizas" ("Shifting Sands"), consists of nine sections; each is a self-contained account couched in mundane, imageless prose with occasional dialogue interspersed. Some of the sections, such as "El ramo azul" ("The Blue Bouquet"), recall the manner of Jorge Luis Borges; others, such as "Un aprendizaje difícil" ("A Difficult Apprenticeship"), are Kafkaesque; still others, such as "Mi vida con la ola" ("My Life with the Wave"), have the flavor of André Breton: Together, they resemble a collection of very short stories more than they do a series of prose poems.

The concluding part of *Eagle or Sun?*, the title section, contains twenty-one pieces. Divided between investigations into the poetics of creation and metaphysical narratives—Paz thus attempts to combine the methodologies developed in parts 1 and 2—these pieces are abstract and are therefore less accessible than the earlier ones in the volume, but they are not meant to be hermetic conundrums. The opening sentences of "Mayúscula" ("Capital") exemplify this final mode:

> The screaming crest of dawn flames. First egg, first peck, decapitation and delight! Feathers fly, wings spread, sails swell, and wing-oars dip in the sunrise. Oh unreined light, first light rearing.

It is clear that *Eagle or Sun?* is a multifaceted volume, the three parts of which are tenuously connected only through their formal similarities, with each part functioning autonomously.

Surrealistic imagery

One of the most pervasive stylistic elements in Paz's poetry is a finely controlled Surrealism. Unlike many programmatic Surrealists, Paz never allows his work to degenerate into a series of unrelated, bizarre images. Rather, he inserts potent incongruities into his lyric or metaphysical sequences, where they are most effective. Consider "Semillas para un himno" ("Seeds for a Psalm"), a relatively traditional fifty-four-line poem, imagistic to be sure, but in a subdued and striking fashion, as in the line "Even the blind decipher the whip's writing." This, however, is followed immediately by "Clusters of beggars are hanging from the cities." The power of this image—by far the most radical in the poem—derives precisely from the fact that it is not merely another in a string of bizarre, surreal tropes.

If surrealistic imagery is Paz's most pervasive rhetorical device, mythic experience is his favored structuring principle. Indeed, Paz believes that in the modern age, poetry has supplanted myth as a redemptive force, a revealer of truth as the poet perceives it. Rachel Phillips has observed that what she terms the mythic mode allows Paz "to clothe his epistemological anxieties in comfortingly familiar garb. . . ." This is certainly true for the traditional mythology with which most Western readers are acquainted, but many readers of Paz's work, even Latin Americans, will be confused and at times alienated by the complex indigenous Mexican myths that play such an important role in some of his poetry, especially in "Salamandra" ("Salamander") and the long and difficult *Sun Stone*, to which Cohen refers as "one of the last important poems to be published in the Western world. . . ." The same caveat obtains for Paz's poems that revolve around the history, philosophy, and myths of India.

BLANCO

Here and there throughout his oeuvre, Paz has experimented with unusual poetic forms. Until the mid-1960's, this tendency was generally limited to eccentric page layout and syntactical sparsity; *Blanco* is the epitome of this phase. Here, the poem emerges from a multifaceted layout and, in its original publication, in the format of a scroll; one is reminded of *Un Coup de dés jamais n'abolira le hasard* (1897; *A Dice-Throw*, 1958; also as *Dice Thrown Never Will Annul Chance*, 1965) by Stéphane Mallarmé, a poet whose influence on Paz is often noted. An extremely complex poem with its three simultaneous lines, *Blanco* has met with a mixed critical response: Rachel Phillips calls it a masterpiece, while poet-translator Robert Bly regards the poem as a disaster.

DISCOS VISUALES AND RENGA

Paz followed *Blanco* with more extreme formal experiments. In *Discos visuales*, for example, sets of concentric and overlapping disks spin on axes; as the top disk revolves, different words appear in its little windows. One thus "creates" a variety of poems by turning the upper disk. Another of Paz's forays into the unconventional is the collaborative *Renga*, a poem in which the four stanzas of each section have been individually composed by four different poets in four different languages.

"SNAPSHOTS"

In 1997, a year before he died, Paz published "Snapshots" in a literary review. These eleven disconnected couplets are prosaic, metaphorical, surreal, and progressive. They are the desperate and sometimes depressing thoughts of an old man who may already be aware that he is ill: Reminiscences, premonitions, and recollections scrupulously articulated indicate that Paz never stopped observing, thinking, and experimenting. This powerful echo of the past concludes,

>swarm of reflections on the page, yesterday confused
>   with today, the seen,
>entwined with the half-seen, inventions of memory,
>   gaps of reason;
>
>encounters, farewells, ghosts of the eye, incarnations
>   of touch unnamed
>presences, seeds of time: at the wrong time.

Paz's work is a fecund source of inspiration for his readers. His thematic and structural diversity, linguistic mastery, and philosophical commitment have produced an astonishing and replete body of poetry and prose. He drew on both indigenous and international material to provide readers with a universally comprehensible message: Plurality and diversity are positive objectives. The result is that Paz was the premiere man of letters in Mexico and Hispanic America and one of the outstanding literary and cultural figures of the twentieth century.

OTHER MAJOR WORKS

PLAY: *La hija de Rappaccini*, pb. 1990 (dramatization of a Nathaniel Hawthorne story; *Rappacini's Daughter*, 1996).

NONFICTION: *Voces de España*, 1938; *Laurel*, 1941; *El laberinto de la soledad: Vida y pensamiento de México*, 1950, 1959 (*The Labyrinth of Solitude: Life and Thought in Mexico*, 1961); *El arco y la lira*, 1956 (*The Bow and the Lyre*, 1971); *Las peras del olmo*, 1957; *Rufino Tamayo*, 1959 (*Rufino Tamayo: Myth and Magic*, 1979); *Magia de la risa*, 1962; *Cuatro poetas contemporáneos de Suecia*, 1963; *Cuadrivio*, 1965; *Poesía en movimiento*, 1966 (*New Poetry of Mexico*, 1970; translated and edited by Mark Strand); *Puertas al campo*, 1966; *Remedios Varo*, 1966; *Claude Lévi-Strauss: O, El nuevo festín de Esopo*, 1967 (*Claude Lévi-Strauss: An Introduction*, 1970); *Corriento alterna*, 1967 (*Alternating Current*, 1973); *Marcel Duchamp*, 1968 (*Marcel Duchamp: Or, The Castle of Purity*, 1970); *Conjunciones y disyunciones*, 1969 (*Conjunctions and Disjunctions*, 1974); *México: La última década*, 1969; *Posdata*, 1970 (*The Other Mexico: Critique of the Pyramid*, 1972); *Las cosas en su sitio*, 1971; *Los signos en rotación y otros ensayos*, 1971; *Traducción: Literatura y literalidad*, 1971; *Apariencia desnuda: La obra de Marcel Duchamp*, 1973 (*Marcel Duchamp: Appearance Stripped Bare*, 1978); *El signo y el garabato*, 1973; *Solo a dos voces*, 1973; *La búsqueda del comienzo*, 1974; *Los hijos del limo: Del romanticismo a la vanguardia*, 1974 (*Children of the Mire: Modern Poetry from Romanticism to the Avant-Garde*, 1974); *El mono gramático*, 1974 (*The Monkey Grammarian*, 1981); *Teatro de signos/transparencias*, 1974; *Versiones y diversiones*, 1974; *The Siren and the Seashell, and Other Essays on Poets and Poetry*, 1976; *Xavier Villaurrutia en persona y en obra*, 1978; *In/mediaciones*, 1979; *México en la obra de Octavio Paz*, 1979, expanded 1987; *El ogro filantrópico: Historia y politica 1971-1978*, 1979 (*The Philanthropic Ogre*, 1985); *Sor Juana Inés de la Cruz: O, Las trampas de la fé*, 1982 (*Sor Juana: Or, The Traps of Faith*, 1989); *Sombras de obras: Arte y literatura*, 1983; *Tiempo nublado*, 1983 (*One Earth, Four or Five Worlds: Reflections on Contemporary History*, 1985); *Hombres en su siglo y otros ensayos*, 1984; *On Poets and Others*, 1986; *Convergences: Essays on Art and Literature*, 1987; *Primeras letras, 1931-1943*, 1988 (Enrico Mario Santi, editor); *Poesía, mito, revolución*, 1989; *La búsqueda del presente/In Search of the Present: Nobel Lecture, 1990*, 1990; *La otra voz: Poesía y fin de siglo*, 1990 (*The Other Voice: Essays on Modern Poetry*, 1991); *Pequeña crónica de grandes días*, 1990; *Convergencias*, 1991; *Al paso*, 1992; *One Word to the Other*, 1992; *Essays on Mexican Art*, 1993; *Itinerario*, 1993 (*Itinerary: An Intellectual Journey*, 1999); *La llama doble: Amor y erotismo*, 1993 (*The Double Flame: Love and Eroticism*, 1995); *Un más allá erótico: Sade*, 1993 (*An Erotic Beyond: Sade*, 1998); *Vislumbres de la India*, 1995 (*In Light of India*, 1997).

EDITED TEXTS: *Antología poética*, 1956 (*Anthology of Mexican Poetry*, 1958; Samuel Beckett, translator); *New Poetry of Mexico*, 1970.

MISCELLANEOUS: *Lo mejor de Octavio Paz: El fuego de cada día*, 1989; *Obras completas de Octavio Paz*, 1994; *Blanco*, 1995 (facsimiles of manuscript fragments and letters).

BIBLIOGRAPHY

Bloom, Harold, ed. *Octavio Paz*. Philadelphia: Chelsea House, 2002. A collection of essays examining the poetry of Paz, looking at motifs and Surrealistic aspects, among other topics.

Chiles, Frances. *Octavio Paz: The Mythic Dimension*. New York: Peter Lang, 1987. Discusses the use of myth in Paz's poetry.

Durán, Manuel. "Remembering Octavio Paz." *World Literature Today* 73, no. 1 (Winter, 1999): 101-103. A reminiscence and critical commentary on Paz's work. Tributes to, critical essays on, and an interview with Paz. (Reprinted with additions from *Books Abroad*, Autumn, 1972.)

Fein, John M. *Toward Octavio Paz: A Reading of His Major Poems, 1957-1986*. Lexington: University Press of Kentucky, 1986. A critical analysis of six of the longer works.

Grenier, Yvon. *From Art to Politics: Octavio Paz and the Pursuit of Freedom*. Lanham, Md.: Rowman & Littlefield, 2001. Focuses on the ways in which Paz's social and political views surface in his poetry.

Hozven, Roberto, ed. *Otras voces: Sobre la poesía y prosa de Octavio Paz*. Riverside: University of California Press, 1996. A collection of critical essays in both English and Spanish. Includes bibliographical references.

Lutes, Todd Oakley. *Shipwreck and Deliverance: Politics, Culture, and Modernity in the Works of Octavio Paz, Gabriel García Márquez, and Mario Vargas Llosa*. Lanham, Md.: University Press of America, 2003. A comparative study of modernism in three Latin American authors.

Quiroga, José. *Understanding Octavio Paz*. Columbia: University of South Carolina Press, 1999. A critical study of selected poems by Paz. Includes a bibliography of the author's works, an index, and bibliographical references.

Underwood, Leticia Iliana. *Octavio Paz and the Language of Poetry: A Psycholinguistic Approach*. New York: Peter Lang, 1992. Includes illustrations and bibliographical references.

Williamson, Rodney. *The Writing in the Stars: A Jungian Reading of the Poetry of Octavio Paz.* Toronto, Ont.: University of Toronto Press, 2007. Williamson interprets Paz's poetry through the lens of the thought of Carl Jung, paying attention in particular to the concept of the archetype.

Wilson, Jason. *Octavio Paz.* Boston: Twayne, 1986. A solid introduction in Twayne's World Authors series. Contains a bibliography and an index.

Robert Hauptman

ALFONSO REYES

Born: Monterrey, Mexico; May 17, 1889
Died: Mexico City, Mexico; December 27, 1959

PRINCIPAL POETRY
Huellas, 1923
Ifigenia cruel, 1924
Pausa, 1926
Cinco casi sonetos, 1931
Romances del Rio de Enero, 1933
A la memoria de Ricardo Güiraldes, 1934
Golfo de Mexico, 1934 (*Gulf of Mexico*, 1949)
Yerbas del Tarahumara, 1934 (*Tarahumara Herbs*, 1949)
Infancia, 1935
Minuta, 1935
Otra voz, 1936
Cantata en la tumba de Federico García Lorca, 1937
Poema del Cid, 1938 (modern version of *Cantar de mío Cid*)
Villa de Unión, 1940
Algunos poemas, 1941
Romances y afines, 1945
La vega y el soto, 1946
Cortesía, 1948
Homero en Cuernavaca, 1949
Obra poética, 1952

OTHER LITERARY FORMS

Alfonso Reyes (RAY-yays) was an essayist, short-story writer, and critic as well as a poet. Indeed, the bulk of the more than twenty volumes of his *Obras completas* (1955-1967; complete works)—an ongoing project undertaken by the Mexican Fondo de Cultura Económica to make accessible the seemingly inexhaustible archive of manuscripts and papers that he left behind—is criticism rather than poetry. Spanning cultures and disciplines, the breadth of his knowledge was truly astounding. His *Grata compañía* (1948; pleasing company), for example, includes essays on Robert Louis Stevenson, G. K. Chesterton, Marcel Proust, Jean-Jacques Rousseau, René Descartes, Jakob Burckhardt, José Maria de Eça de Queiróz, Hermann Alexander Keyserling, Graça Aranha, Leopoldo Lugones, Miguel de Unamuno y Jugo, Antonio Caso, and Pedro Henríquez Ureña. In the fourteen issues of his personal newsletter, *Monterrey*, sent from Rio de Janeiro and Buenos Aires, he particularly liked to focus on the relationship of great European intellectual figures to the American experience: Johann Wolfgang von Goethe and the United States, Giuseppe Garibaldi and Cuba, Ramón María del Valle-Inclán and Mexico, Luis de Góngora y Argote and New Spain, Paul Morand and Brazil, and so on.

Reyes's masterpiece, *Visión de Anáhuac* (1917; *Vision of Anáhuac*, 1950)—its title referring to the Aztec name for the Valley of Mexico, the site of the mighty Aztec capital, Tenochtitlán (later Mexico City)—written in Madrid in 1915, is a brilliant prose poem of some twenty-five pages depicting the Indian civilization on the eve of the Spanish conquest. *Cartones de Madrid* (1917; sketches of Madrid) is a collection of impressionistic essays. Reyes's essays are always lyric—even when they treat philosophical themes—and are often laced with humor. Some of his finest short stories, such as "La cena" (the dinner) and "La mano del comandante Aranda" ("Major Aranda's Hand"), blend a lyric realism with supernatural or fantastic elements, while others, such as "El testimonio de Juan Peña" (the testimony of Juan Peña) and "Silueta del indio Jesús" (silhouette of the Indian Jesus), treat indigenous themes. Among his best literary criticism are the essays of *La experiencia literaria* (1942; literary experience) and "Sobre la estética de Góngora" (on the aesthetics of Góngora), an essay which contributed significantly to the modern reappraisal of the Baroque poet. In *El deslinde: Prolegómenos a la teoría literaria* (1944; the boundary line: prolegomenon to literary theory), he addressed a wide range of aesthetic questions, drawing on semantics, philology, and the philosophy of language.

Reyes was an avid translator. He rendered several of Chesterton's works, including a volume of his detective stories, *El candor de Padre Brown* (1921), into Spanish. He also translated *Olalla* (1922), by Stevenson, and *A Sentimental Journey* (1768), by Laurence Sterne (*Viaje sentimental por Francia e Italia*, 1919). Reyes's translation of the first nine books of Homer's *Iliad* (c. 750 B.C.E.; English translation, 1611) as *La Ilíada de Homero* is considered the best available in Spanish, and he also produced a modern prose version of the *Cantar de mío Cid* (early thirteenth century) as *Poema del Cid*. He translated poems by Stéphane Mallarmé, José-Maria de Heredia, Robert Browning, Oliver Goldsmith, Dante, and Goethe, and, in conjunction with N. Tasin, a story by Anton Chekhov. Finally, Reyes produced Spanish versions of C. M. Bowra's *Ancient Greek Literature* (1933) as *Historia de la literatura griega* (1948), and Gilbert Murray's *Euripides and His Age* (1913) as *Eurípides y su época* (1949).

Achievements

Alfonso Reyes strove indefatigably to draw the literature and culture of Latin America into the Latin cultural sphere of Spain, France, and Italy, and to effect a reconciliation between Spain and its former colonies. Indeed, his cosmopolitan spirit did much to internationalize a hitherto parochial Latin American literature. In his own country, he cast the light of Vergil and Goethe upon the Mexican landscape. Reyes assimilated a great deal from contemporary French writers such as André Gide, Paul Valéry, and Valery Larbaud, and he maintained lifelong friendships and correspondences with the most influential Spanish intellectuals of his time—Unamuno, Valle-Inclán, José Ortega y Gasset, Juan Ramón Jiménez, and Ramón Gómez de la Serna. Reyes, by his own example, was able to disprove to the Spaniards the widely held opinion that Spanish American writers were capable of nothing more inspired than exaggerated stylistic flourishes. As Mexican ambassador to Brazil, he worked to improve cultural relations between the Spanish-speaking countries and Brazil. He opened so many channels of communication with the outside world that Octavio Paz (quoting a phrase used in another context by Reyes himself) called him "the horseman of the air," and Xavier Villaurrutía dubbed him "the man of the roads."

Considering the unique nature of Reyes's literary contributions, he has neither direct antecedents nor direct successors in the Hispanic tradition, yet many have learned from his example. Paz has cited *La experiencia literaria* and *El deslinde* as works of particular value to him. Gabriela Mistral described *Vision of Anáhuac* as the best single piece of Latin American prose, and Larbaud and Juan José Domenchina have suggested that the work exercised an influence on the *Anabase* (1924; *Anabasis*, 1930) of Saint-John Perse.

In the realm of poetry, Reyes stands out as one of the first Latin American writers to incorporate into Spanish verse the casual tradition of the English lyric, with its alternations of delicacy with diversion and seriousness with whimsy. As a critic working under the tutelage of Ramón Menéndez Pidal, Reyes wrote important analyses of past writers; in particular, he was instrumental in refurbishing the image of the seventeenth century poet Góngora, a rediscovery of great importance to Spanish literature.

The University of California, the University of Michoácan, and the University of Mexico, as well as Tulane University, Havana University, Harvard University, and Princeton University, awarded honorary degrees to Reyes. He received the Premio Nacional de Ciencias y Artes (National Prize for Arts and Sciences) in 1945 and was named president of the Mexican Academy in 1957, after having been a member for nearly forty years.

Biography

Alfonso Reyes Ochoa was born in Monterrey, Nuevo León, Mexico, the ninth of twelve children born to General Bernardo Reyes and Aurelia Ochoa, both of whom were from the environs of Guadalajara in the state of Jalisco. General Reyes, the author of an array of military manuals, brochures, and histories, was an enlightened and efficient governor of the state of Nuevo León and was largely responsible for the progressive spirit which obtains in Monterrey even in the twenty-first century. Of his early years, Reyes wrote in "Sol de Monterrey" ("Monterrey Sun"), "I knew no shadow in my childhood,/ only the brilliance of the sun"; a sun that followed at his heels "like a Pekinese." Reyes entered the Escuela Nacional Preparatoria in Mexico City in 1905, and went on to the Escuela Nacional de Altos Estudios. Mexico at that time was in the tight grip of the dictator Porfirio Díaz, and although the positivist milieu that Díaz encouraged was not favorable to the study of the humanities, Reyes immersed himself in the study of the classics.

Reyes married Manela Mota in 1911, and their only child, Alfonso, was born in 1912. The following year, Reyes received a law degree from the University of Mexico. He became the youngest member of the Centennial Generation (which included Pedro Henríquez Ureña, Antonio Caso, and José Vasconcelos), a group dedicated to changing the official modes of thought in Mexico. Reyes also helped found the Ateneo de la Juventud (Athenaeum of Youth), an institution for young intellectuals that flourished until 1940.

When Díaz was ousted by Francisco Madero in 1910, Mexico was thrown into a welter of revolt and banditry. Before dawn on February 9, 1913, rebel troops tried to install General Reyes, long viewed as Díaz's successor, as head of state. General Reyes was shot to death in street fighting at the Zocalo in Mexico City; seventeen years later, his son honored his father—that "tower of a man"—in a prose elegy, "Oración del 9 de febrero de 1913" ("Prayer of the Ninth of February"), giving Reyes the opportunity to observe in himself a "presentiment of an obscure equivocation in the moral clockwork of our world." There is also a four-stanza poem on the same subject, "+9 de febrero de 1913," in which the poet asks, "Where are you, man of seven wounds,/ blood spurting at midday?" and proceeds to promise that "if I have continued to live since that day,/ it is because I carry you with me, where you are inviolable."

In August of 1913, Reyes went to Paris as second secretary of the Mexican legation. The following year, he gravitated to Madrid, where he earned a meager living from journalism. He soon became associated with the famous Center of Historical Studies in Madrid, directed by Pidal, and made valuable contributions to the *Revista de filología española*. He worked in the company of such scholars as Américo Castro, Federico de Onís, Tomás Navarro Tomás, and Antonio Solalinde, all of whom Reyes called "the princes of Spanish philology" and into whose society he was readily admitted. Reminiscing years later about those days in Madrid, Reyes wrote that literature had been everywhere—in the air, in the cafés, and in the streets.

In 1927, Reyes returned to Mexico and became the Mexican ambassador to Argentina, where he remained until 1930, when he went to Rio de Janeiro as ambassador to Brazil. In 1939, he returned to Mexico to stay, after nearly twenty-five years of almost continuous diplomatic service. He proceeded to establish two great educational institutions: the group of scholars called El Colegio Nacional and the graduate school of the humanities, El Colegio de México. His home in Mexico City included a magnificent library that became for Reyes a sanctuary of the muses; the library was dubbed "Capilla

Alfonsina" (Alfonsine Chapel) by his friend, Enrique Díez-Canedo, a Spanish poet.

At the age of seventy, Reyes succumbed to the last of a series of heart attacks and was buried in the Rotonda de los Hombres Ilustres in the Panteón Civil de Dolores in Mexico City. His wife was killed in an accident in 1965, and their granddaughter, Alicia Reyes, directs the Alfonsine Chapel, used as a research center and sponsored by the Mexican government.

Analysis

Like his contemporaries, the Argentine Ricardo Güiraldes, the Chilean Pedro Prado, and the Colombian José Eustasio Rivera, Alfonso Reyes was above all a writer of prose, yet at no time in his life did he cease to write poetry. He began to write verse at an early age, and his first poems appeared in print when he was sixteen. The poems reflect his love for ancient Greece and for the sculptures of Phidias and Praxiteles. Reyes's first book of verse, *Huellas* (footprints), containing pieces from the years 1906 to 1919, appeared in 1923. These poems reveal a Parnassian influence evident in the works of other Latin American poets of the time, yet they already showed some of Reyes's characteristic variety of subject matter, mood, and style. Later, he would make use of realism (especially in his descriptions of Mexico) and Surrealism in *Gulf of Mexico*.

There is something of the dilettante about Reyes the poet; chatting with or about his friends, musing over feminine beauty, worrying about death, reworking the *ubi sunt* commonplace, or simply delighting in intellectual silliness. "I prefer to be promiscuous/ in literature," Reyes wrote in the poem "Teoría prosaica" ("Prose Theory"), claiming further that he preferred the antiquated measurements of the *almud*, the *vara*, and the *cuarterón* to the metric system. Reyes kept his poetic sanity by alternating "the popular ballad/ of my neighbor/ with the rare quintessence/ of Góngora and Mallarmé."

Exhaustive vocabulary

A traveler and an explorer in different worlds, Reyes made use of everyday speech, the Greek chorus, the monologue of Mallarmé, the Spanish of the Golden Age, and names from the Tarahumara pharmacopoeia. Reyes exhausted all sources of Spanish vocabulary. In his poems, there are Latin expressions, Greek words, and obscure Arabisms not normally used in conversational language—*alcatraz* (cornucopia), *almirez* (brass mortar), *alquitara* (still)—yet none of these occurs in such profusion or within such complicated syntax as to overwhelm the reader. Reyes delighted in place-names, in words peculiar to certain countries that gave his work local color—*ñañigo* (member of a secret Cuban society of blacks), *tamanco* (Brazilian sandal)—and in chatty words—*corretón* (gadding about), *copetín* (little goblet). He frequently repeated synonymous or near-synonymous words in the same line, as if searching for maximum precision—*curuja, buho* (both meaning "owl"); *alfónsigo, pistacho* (both meaning "pistachio"); and *tierra, terrena, terruño* (all meaning "land").

Epithets

Reyes was also fond of epithets. His father is the "ruddy lion," Benito Juárez is the "master of the bow" whose arrows "fastened in the heavens' red meteors," and the American Hispanist Sylvanus Griswold Morley is the "California Quijote." Occasionally, Reyes embedded in his poetry significant lines from Dante or Mallarmé in the original Italian or French. Nothing was alien to Reyes, and the world that he inhabited is "our" world rather than "the" world. The statue of David in Florence is "my" David, the street in Rio de Janeiro where he lived is "my" rua de Laranjeiras, and his native city, Monterrey, was so much his that he marveled at why he had never attached its name to his own. He sometimes spoke of himself as Alfonso in his poems and especially delighted in words or neologisms that resembled his name, such as *alfónsigo* (pistachio), *alfonsecuente* (on the model of *consecuente*, coherent, or "Alfonso-coherent").

Hellenism

Reyes considered even the humblest subject matter worthy of poetry, and much of his charm stems from his ability to popularize intellectual material. He demonstrated his love of Greek mythology and Hellenism in his verse play, *Ifigenia cruel* (cruel Iphigenia), which is crafted in the simplest language. Here, he converted the Euripidean heroine into a formidable Amazon torn between her career as a sacrificial priestess and her desire for her home. Eventually, she opts for the former; as Barbara Bockus Aponte observes, the Iphigenia who prefers her liberty to the tradition of her home in Greece is the Reyes who left behind the strife of Mexico and abjured thoughts of vengeance in the search for his own freedom.

Reyes's Hellenism is evident as well in *Homero en Cuernavaca* (Homer in Cuernavaca), comprising thirty sonnets that are sometimes romantic but just as often satirical (as in "De Helena"). In these poems, as well as in *Ifigenia cruel*, the language is kept simple.

"Jacob" and "Lamentación de Navidad"

While the Bible did not inspire Reyes as much as did the *Iliad*, a biblical influence is nevertheless apparent in his poetry. His "Lamentación de Navidad" (Christmas lament) ends with a prayer that the poet be given works to accomplish or be made to fly like the seeds to settle eventually on fertile ground. He utilized the theme of Jacob wrestling with the angel (his "white enemy") in "Jacob," which Reyes narrates in the first person, and this poem, too, ends with a prayer that the angel win the match. Reyes used the same theme in his essay "Jacob o la idea de la poesía" (Jacob or the idea of poetry), in which he describes the artistic process as a struggle with "lo inefable" (the unutterable).

"Sopa"

Typical of Reyes's mixture of learning and playfulness are his poems titled *Minuta* (menu)—poems about such "unpoetic" subjects as soup, bread, salad, a plate of almonds. His two-stanza poem "Sopa" (soup), for example, is introduced by an epigraph from Saint Theresa ("between the soup pots walks the Lord"). In a simple four-line poem, Reyes honored the aperitif: "Exquisite collaboration/ of host and hostess;/ the ice of the visit is broken/ in the glass that brings good cheer." Elsewhere, Reyes reminded his readers that gastronomic concerns have always occupied an important place in Hispanic literary tradition, citing Fernando de Rojas's play *Comedia de Calisto y Melibea* (1499; commonly known as *La Celestina*; *Celestina*, 1631), Miguel de Cervantes's *El ingenioso hidalgo don Quixote de la Mancha* (1605, 1615; *The History of the Valorous and Wittie Knight-Errant, Don Quixote of the Mancha*, 1612-1620; better known as *Don Quixote de la Mancha*), and Francisco Delicado's *Retrato de la loçana andaluza* (1528; *Portrait of Lozana: The Lusty Andalusian Woman*, 1987).

Reyes was clearly one of the most brilliant and versatile writers in modern Spanish, yet his great gifts never produced the masterpieces that his readers expected from him. His most lasting contribution to Latin American culture lies in his example as an international man of letters, a lover of literature, and a tireless cultural activist.

OTHER MAJOR WORKS

SHORT FICTION: *El plano oblicuo*, 1920; *Quince presencias*, 1955; *Alfonso Reyes: Prosa y poesía*, 1977 (includes "Major Aranda's Hand," "Silueta del indio Jesús," and "El testimonio de Juan Peña").

NONFICTION: *Cuestiones estéticas*, 1911; *Cartones de Madrid*, 1917; *Visión de Anáhuac*, 1917 (*Vision of Anáhuac*, 1950); *Retratos reales e imaginarios*, 1920; *Simpatías y diferencias*, 1921-1926; *Cuestiones gongorinas*, 1927; *Discurso por Virgilio*, 1933; *Capítulos de literatura española*, 1939; *La crítica en la edad ateniense*, 1941; *La experiencia literaria*, 1942; *Ultima Thule*, 1942; *El deslinde: Prolegómenos a la teoría literaria*, 1944; *Grata compañía*, 1948; *The Position of America, and Other Essays*, 1950 (includes *Vision of Anáhuac*); *Arbol de pólvora*, 1953; *Parentalia: Primer libro de recuerdos*, 1954; *Albores: Segundo libro de recuerdos*, 1960; *Mexico in a Nutshell, and Other Essays*, 1964.

TRANSLATIONS: *Viaje sentimental por Francia e Italia*, 1919 (of Laurence Sterne's *A Sentimental Journey*); *El candor de Padre Brown*, 1921 (of G. K. Chesterton's detective stories); *Olalla*, 1922 (of Robert Louis Stevenson's stories); *Historia de la literatura griega*, 1948 (of C. M. Bowra's *Ancient Greek Literature*); *Eurípides y su época*, 1949 (of Gilbert Murray's *Euripides and His Age*); *La Ilíada de Homero*, 1951 (of Homer's *Iliad*).

MISCELLANEOUS: *Obras completas*, 1955-1967.

BIBLIOGRAPHY

Aponte, Barbara Bockus. *Alfonso Reyes and Spain: His Dialogue with Unamuno, Valle-Inclán, Ortega y Gasset, Jiménez, and Gómez de la Serna*. Austin: University of Texas Press, 1972. The author explores the dialogues that Reyes maintained with Spanish literary contemporaries. Their correspondence sheds light upon the lives and works of all these writers. Reyes relied upon this form of communication to maintain friendships and share ideas. As a member of the Mexican intellectual elite, Reyes recognized that his Spanish contacts were vital to his literary development.

Carter, Sheila. *The Literary Experience*. Mona, Jamaica: Savacou, 1985. A critical analysis of *El deslinde*, with bibliographic references.

Conn, Robert T. *The Politics of Philology: Alfonso Reyes and the Invention of the Latin American Literary Tradition*. Lewisburg, Pa.: Bucknell University Press, 2002. Conn examines Reyes and his legacy in the context of Latin American and Spanish intellectual life.

Robb, James W. "Alfonso Reyes." In *Latin American Writers*, edited by Carlos A. Solé. Vol. 2. New York: Charles Scribner's Sons, 1989. A thorough article from the Scribner writers series.

_____. *Patterns of Image and Structure*. New York: AMS Press, 1969. Critical analysis of the essays of Reyes.

Jack Shreve

CÉSAR VALLEJO

Born: Santiago de Chuco, Peru; March 16, 1892
Died: Paris, France; April 15, 1938

PRINCIPAL POETRY
Los heraldos negros, 1918 (*The Black Heralds*, 1990)
Trilce, 1922 (English translation, 1973)
España, aparta de mí este cáliz, 1939 (*Spain, Take This Cup from Me*, 1974)
Poemas en prosa, 1939 (*Prose Poems*, 1978)
Poemas humanos, 1939 (*Human Poems*, 1968)
Obra poética completa, 1968
César Vallejo: The Complete Posthumous Poetry, 1978
Poesía completa, 1978
Selected Poems, 1981
The Complete Poetry: A Bilingual Edition, 2007 (Clayton Eshleman, editor)

OTHER LITERARY FORMS

César Vallejo (vah-YAY-hoh) wrote fiction, plays, and essays, as well as lyric poetry, although his achievement as a poet far outstrips that in any other genre. His short stories—many of them extremely brief—may be found in *Escalas melografiadas* (1923; musical scales). A longer short story, "Fabla salvaje" (1923; primitive parlance), is a tragic idyll of two rustic lovers, and *Hacia el reino de los Sciris* (1967; toward the kingdom of the Sciris) is set in the time of the Incas. *El tungsteno* (1931; *Tungsten*, 1988), is a proletarian novel with an Andean setting that was written in 1931, the year Vallejo joined the Communist Party. Another story, *Paco Yunque* (1969), is about the mistreatment of a servant's son by a classmate who happens to be the master's son.

Vallejo became interested in the theater around 1930, but he destroyed his first play, "Mampar." Three others, *Entre las dos orillas corre el río* (pb. 1979; the river flows between two banks); *Lock-Out* (pb. 1979), and *Colacho hermanos: O, presidentes de América* (pb. 1979; Colacho brothers), never published during the poet's lifetime, are now available in *Teatro completo* (1979; complete theatrical work). His long essay, *Rusia en 1931: Reflexiones al pie del Kremlin* (1931; reissued in 1965), was followed by *Rusia ante el segundo plan quinquenal* (1965); *Contra el secreto profesional* (1973); and *El arte y la revolución* (1973). His master's thesis, *El romanticismo en la poesía castellana*, was published in 1954.

Achievements

Finding an authentic language in which to write has always represented a fundamental problem for Latin American writers, since it became evident that the language inherited from the Spanish conquerors could not match Latin American reality. The problem of finding such a language goes hand in hand with that of forging a separate cultural identity. An important attempt at renovating poetic language was made by the Spanish American *Modernistas* around the turn of the century, but their verse forms, imagery, and often exotic subject matter were also becoming obsolete by the time César Vallejo reached maturity. It was thus up to him and his contemporaries to find a language that could deal with contemporary concerns involving war, depression, isolation, and alienation. Although hardly recognized in his lifetime, Vallejo did more than perhaps any other poet of his generation to provide an idiom that would at once reflect the Spanish tradition, his own Peruvian heritage, and the contemporary world. Aware of his heritage from Spain's great writers of the past, he blended traditional poetic vocabulary and tropes with homely Peruvian idioms and even the language of children. Where the result was still inadequate, he made up new words, changed the function of old ones, and incorporated a lexicon never before seen in poetry, often savaging poetic convention.

Vallejo's gradual conversion to Marxism and Communism is of great interest to those attempting to understand how collectivist ideals may shape poetry. The evolution of his ideology continues to be studied intensively by many individuals committed to bettering the conditions of poverty and alienation about which Vallejo wrote so eloquently—conditions that still exist in Latin America and other parts of the world. His unflinchingly honest search for both linguistic and moral solutions to the existential anguish of modern human beings gives his poems universal validity, while their density and complexity challenge critics of the most antithetical modes.

Biography

César Abraham Vallejo was born in Santiago de Chuco, a primitive "city" of some fourteen thousand inhabitants in Peru's northern mountains that could only be reached by a rail trip and then several days ride on mule or horseback. Both of his grandfathers had been Spanish priests and both of his grandmothers native Peruvians of Chimu Indian stock. His parents were literate and of modest means; his father was a notary who became a subprefect in the district. Francisco de Paula Vallejo and María de los Santos Mendoza were an upright and religious pair whose marriage produced twelve offspring and who were already middle-aged when their youngest child, César, was born. In his writings, Vallejo was often to remember the security and warmth of his childhood home—games with three of his older siblings, and particularly with his mother, who might have been especially indulgent with her sensitive youngest child.

At age thirteen, Vallejo left Santiago de Chuco to attend high school in Huamachuco, another mountain village, where he received an introduction to literature and began scribbling verses. Economic difficulties prevented him from continuing the university studies that he had begun in the larger coastal cities of Trujillo and Lima in 1911. The young man first went to work in a nearby tungsten mine—an experience that he would later draw upon for his Socialist Realist novel *Tungsten*—and then on a coastal sugar plantation. While there, he observed the tightly structured hierarchy that kept workers in misery while the middle class, to which he himself belonged, served the needs of the elite. In 1913, he returned to the University of Trujillo and graduated two years later, having written a master's thesis titled *El romanticismo en la poesía castellana*. For the next few years, he studied law in Trujillo, supporting himself by becoming a first-grade teacher. One of his pupils, Ciro Alegría, later to become an important novelist, described Vallejo in those days as lean, sallow, solemn, and dark skinned, with abundant straight black hair worn somewhat long, brilliant dark eyes, a gentle manner, and an air of sadness.

During these years, Vallejo became familiar with the writings of Ralph Waldo Emerson, José Rodó, Friedrich Nietzsche, Miguel de Unamuno y Jugo, Walt Whitman, and Juan Ramón Jiménez. Vallejo also read the poems of two of the leading Spanish American *Modernistas*, Rubén Darío and Julio Herrera y Reissig, as well as those of Peruvian poets of the day. Vallejo declaimed his own poems—mostly occasional verse—at various public ceremonies, and some of them appeared in Trujillo's newspapers. Critical reception of them ranged from the cool to the hostile, since they were considered to be exaggerated and strange in that highly traditional ambience. Vallejo fell in love with a young Trujillo girl, Zoila Rosa Cuadro, the subject of several poems included in *The Black Heralds*. The breakup of this relationship provided one motive for his departure, after he had obtained a law degree, for Lima in 1918. There he found a position teaching in one of the best elementary schools and began to put the finishing touches on his first volume of poems.

Vallejo was soon in love with the sister-in-law of one of his colleagues, a woman identified only as "Otilia." A number of the *Trilce* poems, which he was writing at the time, deal with this affair. It ended when the poet refused to marry the woman, resulting in the loss of his job. This crisis was compounded by the death of his mother, a symbol of stability whose loss made him feel like an orphan. For some time, Vallejo had thought of going to Paris, but he decided to return first to his childhood home in Santiago de Chuco. During a national holiday, he was falsely accused of having been the instigator of a civil disturbance and was later seized and imprisoned for 112 days despite the public protests of many Peruvian intellectuals. The experience affected him profoundly, and the poems that he wrote about it (later published in *Trilce*) testify to the feeling of solidarity with the oppressed that he voiced for the first time. While in prison, he also wrote a number of the sketches to appear in *Escalas melografiadas*. In 1923, he sailed for Europe, never again to return to Peru.

While Vallejo's days in Lima had often been marked by personal problems, in Paris, he experienced actual penury, sometimes being forced to sleep in the subway. Eventually, he found employment in a press agency but only after a serious illness. He began to contribute articles to Lima newspapers, made friends with a number of avant-garde artists, and journeyed several times to Spain, where he was awarded a grant for further study. Increasingly concerned with injustice in the world, he made his first trip to Russia in 1928 with the intention of staying. Instead, he returned within three weeks, living soon afterward with a Frenchwoman, Georgette de Philippart, who was later to become his wife. With some money that had come to her, the pair set out on a tour by train through Eastern Europe, spending two weeks in Moscow and returning by way of Rome. As Vallejo's enthusiasm for Marxism became increasingly apparent in his newspaper articles, he found them no longer welcome in Lima, and in 1930, he was ordered to leave France because of his political activity. Once again in Spain, he wrote several plays and the novel *Tungsten* and published *Rusia en 1931*, the only one of his books to sell well. No publisher could be found for several other works. After a third and final visit to Russia as a delegate to the International Congress of Writers, he wrote *Rusia ante el segundo plan quinquenal* (Russia facing the second five-year plan) and officially joined the Communist Party.

In 1932, Vallejo was permitted to return to Paris, where he tried unsuccessfully to publish some new poems. In 1936, the Spanish Civil War broke out, and Vallejo became an active supporter of the Republic, traveling to Barcelona and Madrid to attend the Second International Congress for the Defense of Culture. He visited the battlefront and learned at first hand of the horrors suffered by the Spanish people in the war. Returning to Paris for the last time, he poured his feelings into his last work, *Spain, Take This Cup from Me*. In March, 1938, he became ill. Doctors were unable to diagnose his illness, and Vallejo died a month later on Good Friday, the day before the troops of Francisco Franco won a decisive victory in Spain.

Analysis

One of the unique qualities of César Vallejo's poetry—one that makes his work almost impossible to confuse with that of any other poet writing in the Spanish language—is his ability to speak with the voice and sensibility of a child, whether as an individual orphaned by the breakup of a family or as a symbol of deprived and alienated human beings everywhere. Always, however, this child's voice, full of expectation and hope, is implicitly counterposed by the adult's ironic awareness of change and despair. Inseparable from these elements is the poet's forging of a language capable of reflecting the register and the peculiarly elliptical reasoning of a child and, at the same time, revealing the Hermetic complexity of the adult intellectual's quest for security in the form of truth. The poetry that is Vallejo's own answer to these problems is some of the most poignant and original ever produced.

The Black Heralds

The lines of Vallejo's subsequent development are already evident in his first volume, *The Black Heralds*, a collection of sixty-nine poems grouped under various subtitles. As critics have observed, many of these poems reflect his involvement with Romantic and *Modernista* poetry. They are conspicuous in many cases for their descriptions of idyllic scenes in a manner that juxtaposes words of the Peruvian Sierra and the vocabulary of Symbolism, including religious and erotic elements. Vallejo did not emphasize rhyme and rhythm to the extent that some *Modernistas* did, but most of these early poems are framed in verse forms favored by the latter, such as the Alexandrine sonnet and the *silva*. While demonstrating his impressive mastery of styles already worked out by others, he was also finding his own voice.

This originality is perhaps most evident in the last group of poems in *The Black Heralds*, titled "Canciones de Hogar" ("Home Songs"), poems dealing with the beginning of Vallejo's sense of orphanhood. In "A mi hermano Miguel in memoriam" ("To My Brother Miguel in Memoriam"), the poet relives a moment of the childhood game of hide-and-seek that he used to play with his "twin heart." Speaking to his brother, Vallejo announces his own presence in the part of the family home from which one of the two always ran away to hide from the other. He goes on to remind his playmate of one day on which the latter went away to hide, sad instead of laughing as he usually was, and could not be found again. The poem ends with a request to the brother to please come out so as not to worry "mama." It is remarkable in that past and present alternate from one line to the next. The language of childhood, as well as the poet's assumed presence at the site of the events, lends a dramatic immediacy to the scene. At the same time, the language used in the descriptive passages is clearly that of the adult who is now the poet. Yet in the last verse, the adult chooses to accept literally the explanation that the brother has remained in hiding and may finally respond and come out, which would presumably alleviate the mother's anxiety and make everything right once more. The knowledge that the poet is unable (or refuses) to face the permanent alteration of his past may elicit feelings of tragic pathos in the reader.

"Los pasos lejanos" ("The Distant Steps") recalls the poet's childhood home in which his parents, now aged, are alone—the father sleeping and the mother walking in the orchards. Here, the only bitterness is that of the poet himself, because he is now far away from them. He in turn is haunted by a vision of his parents as two old, white, and bent roads along which his heart walks. In "Enereida," he imagines that his father has died, leading to a regression in time so that the father can once again laugh at his small children, including the poet himself, who is again a schoolboy under the tutelage of the village priest.

Many of the poems in *The Black Heralds* deal with existential themes. While religious imagery is pervasive, it is apparent that the poet employs it to describe profane experiences. Jean Franco has shown that in speaking of "the soul's Christs" and "Marías who leave" and of Communions and Passions, Vallejo trivializes religious language rather than attempting to inflate the importance of his own experiences by describing them in religious terms. As well as having lost the security and plenitude of his childhood home, the poet has lost the childhood faith that enabled him to refer in words to the infinite.

In the title poem, "Los heraldos negros" ("The Black Heralds"), Vallejo laments life's hard blows, harder sometimes than humans can stand. He concludes that these blows come from the hatred of God, that they may be the black heralds sent by Death. In "Los dados eternos" ("The Eternal Dice"), God is a gambler throwing dice and may as easily cast death as life. In fact, Earth itself is his die. Now worn to roundness, it will come to rest only within the sepulchre. Profane love is all that is left; while the beloved may now be pure, she will not continue to be so if she yields to the poet's erotic impulses. Love thus becomes "a sinning Christ," because humankind's nature is irrevocably physical. Several poems allude to the poet's ideal of redeeming himself through brotherly love, a thematic constant in Vallejo's work, yet such redemption becomes difficult if not impossible if a person is lonely and alienated. In "Agape," the poet speaks of being alone and forgotten and of having been unable therefore to "die" for his brother. "La cena miserable" ("The Wretched Supper") tells of the enigma of existence in which humans are seen, as in "Agape," as waiting endlessly for spiritual nurture, or at least for some answer concerning the meaning of life. Here, God becomes no more than a "black spoon" full of bitter human essence, even less able than humans to provide needed answers. The lives of humans are thus meaningless, since they are always separated from what they most desire—whether this be the fullness of the past, physical love, God's love, or brotherly love.

Even in the poems most laden with the trappings of *Modernismo*, Vallejo provides unusual images. In "El poeta a su amada" ("The Poet to His Beloved"), he suggests that his kiss is "two curved branches" on which his beloved has been "crucified." Religious imagery is used with such frequency that it sometimes verges on parody, and critics agree that in playing with language in this way Vallejo is seeking to highlight its essential ambiguity, something he continues to do in *Trilce* and *Human Poems*, even while totally abandoning the imagery of *Modernismo*. Such stripping away of excess baggage is already visible in *The Black Heralds*. Antitheses, oxymorons, and occasional neologisms are also to be noted. While the great majority of the poems are elegantly correct in terms of syntax—in marked contrast to what is to become the norm in *Trilce*—there are some instances of linguistic experimentation, as when nouns are used as adjectives. In "The Distant Steps," for example, the mother is described as being "so soft, so wing, so departure, so love." Another device favored by the poet in all his later poems—enumeration—is also present. Finally, traditional patterns of meter and rhyme are abandoned in "Home Songs," with the poetic emotion being allowed to determine the form.

TRILCE

Despite these formal adumbrations and although *The Black Heralds* is not a particularly transparent work, there is little in it to prepare the reader for the destruction of language in the Hermetic density of *Trilce*, which came along only three years later. These were difficult years for the poet, in which he lost his mother, separated from Otilia, and spent what he was later to refer to as the gravest moments of his life in the Trujillo jail. All the anguish of these events was poured into the seventy-seven free-verse poems of his second major work. If he suffered existentially in *The Black Heralds* and expressed this suffering in writing, it was done with respect for traditional verse forms and sentence structure, which hinted at an order beyond the chaos of the poet's interior world. In *Trilce*, this order falls. Language, on which "logical assumptions" about the world are based, is used in such a way as to reveal its hollowness: It is cut loose and orphaned. Abrupt shifts from one metaphorical sphere to another make the poems' internal logic often problematic.

A hint of what is to come is given in the title, a neologism usually taken to be a hybrid of *tres* (three) and *dulce* (sweet), an interpretation that is in accord with the poet's concern about the ideal number expressed in several poems. It is not known, however, what, if any, concrete meaning the poet had in mind when he coined the word; it has become a puzzle for readers and critics to solve. It is notable that in "interpreting" the *Trilce* poems, critics often work out explications that seem internally consistent but that turn out to be related to a system diametrically opposed to the explication and system of some other critic. It is possible, however, to say with certainty that these poems deal with a struggle to do something, bridge something, and say something. Physical limits such as the human body, time, space, and numbers often render the struggle futile.

Two of the thematic sets of *Trilce* for which it is easiest to establish concrete referents are those dealing with the poet-as-child and those dealing with his imprisonment. In poem III, the poet once again speaks in the voice of a child left at home by the adults of the family. It is getting dark, and he asks when the grown-ups will be back, adding that "Mama said she wouldn't be gone long." In the third stanza, an ironic double vision of years full of agonizing memories intrudes. As in "To My Brother Miguel in Memoriam," the poet chooses to retain the child's faith, urging his brothers and sisters to be good and obey in letter and spirit the instructions left by the mother. In the end, it is seen that the "leaving" is without remedy, a function of time itself; it eventually results in the poet's complete solitude without even the comfort of his siblings. In poem XXIII, the mother, the only symbol of total plenitude, is seen as the "warm oven" of the cookies described as "rich hosts of time." The nourishment provided by the mother was given freely and naturally, taken away from no one and given without the child's being obliged. Still, the process of nurturing leads to growing up and to individuation and alienation. Several poems mythicize the process of birth but shift so abruptly to demythicize human existence that the result is at first humorous. In poem XLVII, a candle is lighted to protect the mother while she gives birth, along with another for the babe who, God willing, will grow up to be bishop, pope, saint, "or perhaps only a columnary headache." Later, in *Human Poems*, there is a Word Incarnate whose bones agree in number and gender as it sinks into the bathtub ("Lomo de las sagradas escrituras"/ "Spine of the Scriptures").

In poem XVIII, the poet surveys the four walls of the cell, implacably closed. He calls up a vision of the "loving keeper of innumerable keys," the mother, who would liberate him if she could. He imagines the two longer walls as mothers and the shorter ones as the children each of them is leading by the hand. The poet is alone with only his two hands, struggling to find a third to help him in his useless adulthood. In poem LVIII, the solid walls of the cell seem to bend at the corners, suggesting that the poet is dozing as a series of jumbled thoughts produce scenes in his mind that follow no easy logical principle of association. The poet sees himself helping the naked and the ragged, then dismounting from a panting horse that he also attempts to help. The cell is now liquid, and he becomes aware of the companions who may be worse off than he. Guilt suddenly overwhelms him, and he is moved to promise to laugh no more when his mother arises early to pray for the sick, the poor, and the prisoners. He also promises to treat his little friends better at play, in both word and deed. The cell is now boundless gas, growing as it condenses. Ambiguously, at the end, he poses the question, "Who stumbles outside?" The openness of the poem is similar to that of many others in *Trilce*, and it is difficult to say what kind of threat to the poet's resolutions is posed by the figure outside. Again, the poetic voice has become that of a child seeking to make all that is wrong in the world right once more by promising to be "a good boy." Of course, he is not a child at all, as the figure outside may be intended to remind both him and the reader. The result is once again a remarkable note of pathos tinged with poignant irony.

Many of *Trilce*'s poems deal with physical love and even the sexual act itself. "Two" seems to be the ideal number, but "two" has "propensities of trinity." Clearly, the poet has no wish to bring a child into the world, and sex becomes merely an act of organs that provides no solution to anything. While the poet seems to appreciate the maternal acts performed by his lover, he fails to find any transcendental satisfaction in the physical relationship, even though he is sad when it is over.

An important theme that emerges in *Trilce* and is developed more fully in *Human Poems* and *Spain, Take This Cup from Me* is that of the body as text. In poem LXV, the house to which the poet returns in Santiago seems to be his mother's body. Parts of the body—the back, face, shoulder, eyes, hands, lips, eyelashes, bones, feet, knees, fingers, heart, arms, breasts, soles of the feet, eyelids, ears, ribs—appear in poem after poem, reminding the reader of human and earthly functions and the limitations of human beings.

In many ways, *Trilce* resembles the poetry of such avant-garde movements as Surrealism, Ultraism, and Creationism in the boldness of its images, its unconventional vocabulary, and its experimentation with graphics. Vallejo did have very limited exposure to some of this poetry after he reached Lima; his critics, however, generally agree that

Trilce was produced independently. While Vallejo may have been encouraged to experiment by his knowledge of European literary currents, his work coincides with them as an original contribution.

HUMAN POEMS

As far as is known, the poems after *Trilce* were written in Europe; with very few exceptions, none was published until 1939, a year after the poet's death, when they appeared under the title *Human Poems*. While Vallejo's life in Peru was far from affluent, it must have seemed easy in comparison with the years in Paris, where he often barely subsisted and suffered several illnesses. In addition, while he did see a new edition of *Trilce* published through the intervention of friends in 1931 and his *Rusia en 1931* did go into three editions during his lifetime, he could never count on having his writings accepted for publication.

Human Poems, considered separately from *Spain, Take This Cup from Me*, is far from being a homogeneous volume, and its final configuration might have been different had it been Vallejo who prepared the final edition rather than his widow. Generally speaking, the poems that it includes deal with ontological anguish whose cause seems related to physical suffering, the passage of time, and the impossibility of believing that life has any meaning. In fact, *Human Poems* examines suffering and pain, with their corollaries, poverty, hunger, illness, and death, with a thoroughness that few other works can match. At times, the anguish seems to belong only to the poet, now not only the orphan of *Trilce* but alienated from other people as well. In "Altura y pelos" ("Height and Hair"), the poet poses questions: "Who doesn't own a blue suit?/ Who doesn't eat lunch and board the streetcar . . . ?/ Who is not called Carlos or any other thing?/ Who to the kitty doesn't say kitty kitty?" The final answer given is "Aie? I who alone was solely born." At least two kinds of irony seem to be involved here. The activities mentioned are obviously trivial, but neither is it easy to be alone. In the well-known "Los nueve monstruos" ("The Nine Monsters"), the poet laments the abundance of pain in the world: "Never, human men/ was there so *much* pain in the chest, in the lapel, in the wallet/ in the glass, in the butcher-shop, in arithmetic!" and "never/ . . . did the migraine extract so much forehead from the forehead!" Pain drives people crazy "in the movies,/ nails us into the gramophones,/ denails us in bed . . ." The poem concludes that the "Secretary of Health" can do nothing because there is simply "too much to do."

"The Nine Monsters" is representative of several features of *Human Poems*. The language is extremely concrete, denoting things that are inseparable from everyday existence. Much of the poem consists of lists, continuing a device for which the poet had already shown a disposition in his first work. Finally, the logic of the systems represented by the items named is hard to pin down, so that it is somewhat reminiscent of child logic in its eccentricity. Again and again, Vallejo's remarkable sensibility is demonstrated beyond any preciosity or mere posturing.

One reason for the poet's alienation is that he sees people as engaged in trivial occupations and as being hardly more advanced on the evolutionary scale than pachyderms or kangaroos, whereas he himself aspires to rise above his limitations. In "Intensidad y altura" ("Intensity and Height"), he tells of his desire to write being stifled by his feeling "like a puma," so that he might as well go and eat grass. He concludes, "let's go, raven, and fecundate your rook." He thus sees himself condemned not to rise above the purely mundane. Religion offers no hope at all. In "Acaba de pasar el que vendrá..." ("He Has Just Passed By, the One Who Will Come..."), the poet suggests that "the one who will come"—presumably the Messiah—has already passed by but has changed nothing, being as vague and ineffectually human as anyone else.

While the majority of these posthumously published poems convey utter despair, not all of them do. Although the exact dates of their composition are generally unknown, it is natural to associate those that demonstrate growing concern for others with Vallejo's conversion to Marxist thought and eventually to Communism. In "Considerando en frío..." ("Considering Coldly..."), speaking as an attorney at a trial, the poetic voice first summarizes the problems and weaknesses of humanity (he "is sad, coughs and, nevertheless,/ takes pleasure in his reddened chest/... he is a gloomy mammal and combs his hair...") Then, however, he announces his love for humanity. Denying it immediately, he nevertheless concludes, "I signal him,/ he comes,/ I embrace him, moved./ So what! Moved... Moved...." Compassion thus nullifies "objectivity." In "La rueda del hambriento" ("The Hungry Man's Wheel"), the poet speaks as a man so miserable that his own organs are pulled out of him through his mouth. He begs only for a stone on which to sit and a little bread. Apparently ignored, aware that he is being importunate, he continues to ask, disoriented and hardly able to recognize his own body. In "Traspié entre dos estrellas" ("Stumble Between Two Stars"), the poet expresses pity for the wretched but goes on to parody bitterly Christ's Sermon on the Mount ("Beloved be the one with bedbugs,/ the one who wears a torn shoe in the rain"), ending with a "beloved" for one thing and then for its opposite, as if calling special attention to the emptiness of mere words. It is possible to say that in these poems the orphan has finally recognized that he is not alone in his orphanhood.

SPAIN, TAKE THIS CUP FROM ME

Although first published as part of *Human Poems*, *Spain, Take This Cup from Me* actually forms a separate, unified work very different in tone from most of the other posthumous poems—a tone of hope, although, especially in the title poem, the poet seems to suspect that the cause he has believed in so passionately may be lost. In this poem, perhaps the last that Vallejo wrote, the orphan—now all human children—has found a mother. This mother is Spain, symbol of a new revolutionary order in which oppression may be ended. The children are urged not to let their mother die; nevertheless, even should this happen, they have a recourse: to continue struggling and to go out and find a new mother.

Another contrast is found in the odes to several heroes of the Civil War. Whereas, in *Human Poems*, humans are captives of their bodies and hardly more intelligent than the lower animals, *Spain, Take This Cup from Me* finds people capable of true transcendence through solidarity with others and the will to fight injustice. A number of poems commemorate the battles of the war: Talavera, Guernica, Málaga. Spain thus becomes a text—a book that sprouts from the bodies of an anonymous soldier. The poet insists again and again that he himself is nothing, that his stature is "tiny," and that his actions rather than his words constitute the real text. This may be seen to represent a greatly evolved negation of poetic authority, first seen in *The Black Heralds* with the repeated cry, "I don't know!"

Nevertheless, *Spain, Take This Cup from Me* rings with a biblical tone, and the poet sometimes sounds like a prophet. James Higgins has pointed out certain images that recall the Passion of Christ and the New Jerusalem, although religious terminology, as in all Vallejo's poetry, is applied to humans rather than to divinity. While Vallejo continues to use techniques of enumeration—which are often chaotic—and to use concrete nouns (including many referring to the body), he also employs abstract terms such as peace, hope, martyrdom, harmony, eternity, and greatness. The sense of garments, utensils, and the body's organs stifling the soul is gone and is replaced by limitless space. In Vallejo's longest poem, "Himno a los voluntarios de la República" ("Hymn to the Volunteers for the Republic"), a panegyric note is struck.

One of Vallejo's most immediately accessible poems, "Masa" ("Mass"), tells almost a parable of a dead combatant who was asked by one man not to die, then by two, and finally by millions. The corpse kept dying until surrounded by all the inhabitants of Earth. The corpse, moved, sat up and embraced the first man and then began to walk. The simplicity of the story and of its narration recalls the child's voice in *Trilce*, promising to cease tormenting his playmates in order to atone for the world's guilt. In this piece, as well as in all Vallejo's last group of poems, however, the irony is gone.

Poetic cycle

It is thus possible to see the completion of a cycle in the four works. Disillusionment grows in *The Black Heralds*, and then alienation works its way into the language itself in *Trilce*. *Human Poems* is somewhat less Hermetic than *Trilce*, but life is an anguished nightmare in which the soul is constrained by the ever-present body that seems to be always wracked with pain. Only in *Spain, Take This Cup from Me*, with the realization that men are brothers who can end their common alienation and suffering by collective action, does the poet regain his lost faith and embark upon a positive course. The orphan relocates the lost mother, whom he now sees to be the mother of all, since all men are brothers. The true significance of Vallejo's poetry, however, lies in his honesty in questioning all established rules of poetic expression, as well as the tradition of poetic authority, in order to put poetry fully in touch with the existential prison house of twentieth century humanity.

OTHER MAJOR WORKS

LONG FICTION: *Fábula salvaje*, 1923 (novella); *El tungsteno*, 1931 (*Tungsten*, 1988).

SHORT FICTION: *Escalas melografiadas*, 1923; *Hacia el reino de los Sciris*, 1967; *Paco Yunque*, 1969.

PLAYS: *Colacho hermanos: O, presidentes de América*, pb. 1979; *Entre las dos orillas corre el río*, pb. 1979; *La piedra cansada*, pb. 1979; *Lock-Out*, pb. 1979; *Teatro completo*, 1979.

NONFICTION: *Rusia en 1931: Reflexiones al pie del Kremlin*, 1931, 1965; *El romanticismo en la poesía castellana*, 1954; *Rusia ante el segundo plan quinquenal*, 1965; *Contra el secreto profesional*, 1973; *El arte y la revolución*, 1973.

BIBLIOGRAPHY

Britton, R. K. "Love, Alienation, and the Absurd: Three Principal Themes in César Vallejo's *Trilce*." *Modern Language Review* 87 (July, 1992): 603-615. Demonstrates how Vallejo's poetry expresses the anguished conviction that humankind is simply a form of animal life subject to the laws of a random, absurd universe.

Dove, Patrick. *The Catastrophe of Modernity: Tragedy and the Nation in Latin American Literature*. Lewisburg, Pa.: Bucknell University Press, 2004. This discussion of the theme of modernity as a catastrophe contains a chapter on Vallejo's *Trilce*.

Hart, Stephen M. *Stumbling Between Forty-six Stars: Essays on César Vallejo*. London: Centre of César Vallejo Studies, 2007. A collection of essays on various aspects of the poet.

Hart, Stephen M., and Jorge Cornejo Polar. *César Vallejo: A Critical Bibliography of Research*. Rochester, N.Y.: Boydell and Brewer, 2002. A bibliography collecting works of Vallejo. Invaluable for researchers.

Hedrick, Tace Megan. "Mi andina y dulce Rita: Women, Indigenism, and the Avant-Garde in César Vallejo." In *Primitivism and Identity in Latin America: Essays on Art, Literature, and Culture*, edited by Erik Camayd-Freixas and José Eduardo González. Tucson: University of Arizona Press, 2000. Relates the indigenism of "Dead Idylls" from *The Black Heralds* to the "avant-garde concerns and practices" of *Trilce*, often considered Vallejo's most brilliant work.

Higgins, James. *The Poet in Peru: Alienation and the Quest for a Super-Reality*. Liverpool, England: Cairns, 1982. Contains a good overview of the main themes of Vallejo's poetry.

Lambie, George. "Poetry and Politics: The Spanish Civil War Poetry of César Vallejo." *Bulletin of Hispanic Studies* 69, no. 2 (April, 1992): 153-170. Analyzes the presence of faith and Marxism in *Spain, Take This Cup from Me*.

Niebylski, Dianna C. *The Poem on the Edge of the Word: The Limits of Language and the Uses of Silence in the Poetry of Mallarmé, Rilke, and Vallejo*. New York: Peter

Lang, 1993. In the context of the language "crisis" of modern poetry and the poet's dilemma in choosing language or silence, Niebylski examines the themes of time and death in Vallejo's *Human Poems*.

Sharman, Adam, ed. *The Poetry and Poetics of César Vallejo: The Fourth Angle of the Circle*. Lewiston, N.Y.: Edwin Mellen Press, 1997. Collection of essays examining Vallejo's work from the perspectives of Marxism, history, the theme of the absent mother, and postcolonial theory.

Lee Hunt Dowling

DAISY ZAMORA

Born: Managua, Nicaragua; June 20, 1950

Principal poetry

La violenta espuma, 1981 (*The Violent Foam: New and Selected Poems*, 2002)
En limpio se escribe la vida, 1988 (*Riverbed of Memory*, 1992)
Clean Slate: New and Selected Poems, 1993 (bilingual edition)
A cada quién la vida, 1989-1992, 1994 (*Life for Each*, 1994; bilingual edition)
Tierra de nadie, tierra de todos, 2007 (*No-Man's Land, Everybody's Land*, 2007)

Other literary forms

Daisy Zamora (zah-MOH-rah) is primarily known for her poetry. Her words played an important role during her participation in the Sandinista Revolution in Nicaragua, when she was program director for clandestine Radio Sandino during the final 1979 Sandinista offensive.

Achievements

Daisy Zamora is a prominent Latin American poet. Her uncompromising stance on human rights, culture, women's issues, revolution, history, and art is presented in a manner that beckons to the average reader and motivates him or her to join in her unquenchable search for justice via the poetic voice. Her works have been translated into Bulgarian, Chinese, Czech, Dutch, English, Flemish, French, German, Italian, Russian, Slovak, Spanish, Swedish, and Vietnamese. Her poems, essays, and articles have been published in magazines and literary newspapers throughout Latin America, the Caribbean, Canada, Europe, and the United States. *The Oxford Book of Latin American Poetry: A Bilingual Anthology* (2009) includes her work.

Zamora received the Mariano Fiallos Gil National Poetry Prize from the University of Nicaragua in 1977. In 1995, she was featured in Bill Moyer's Public Broadcasting Service series *The Language of Life*. In 2002, the California Arts Council awarded her a fellowship for poetry, and the Nicaraguan Writers Center gave her an award for her valuable contributions to Nicaraguan literature. The National Association of Artists in Nicaragua named her writer of the year in 2006. Zamora has given numerous lectures and conducted many workshops in poetry at prestigious universities in the United States and Europe.

Biography

Daisy Zamora was born in Managua, Nicaragua, on June 20, 1950. She grew up in a wealthy and politically active family. She received her primary education in Roman

Catholic convent schools. Later, she attended Universidad Centroamericana in Nicaragua and received a degree in psychology. She earned a postgraduate degree at the Instituto Centroamericano de Administracion de Empresas (INCAE), a Central American branch of Harvard University. Zamora has also studied at the Academia Dante Alighieri and the Escuela Nacional de Bellas Artes. During the struggle against the regime of Anastasio Somoza Debayle in the 1970's, she joined the Sandinista National Liberation Front (FSLN) in 1973 and was exiled, living in Honduras, Panama, and Costa Rica. During the final Sandinista offensive in 1979, she served as program director for the clandestine Radio Sandino. After the Sandinista victory against Somoza, she served as the vice minister of culture and the executive director of the Institute of Economic and Social Research of Nicaragua. In addition to her political work, Zamora has fought for women's rights all her adult life.

Zamora has taught poetry workshops at various universities and lectured in the Latin American and Latino studies department at the University of California, Santa Cruz. She married the American author George Evans; the couple has three children. She has been spending part of the year in San Francisco and part in Managua.

Analysis

Daisy Zamora writes about common, ordinary women, her lovers, and revolutionaries—both those whom she encountered in her active role in the Nicaraguan revolution and lesser-known revolutionaries. The focus of her poems is not the repressive elite but rather the proletariat masses. Zamora's work discusses marginal groups in a manner that implores the reader to consciously or unconsciously participate in a form of identity construction of these diverse factions.

The structure, style, and method of Zamora's poetry is an amalgamation of simplicity and eloquence. Using almost simplistic Nicaraguan Spanish, she creates easily understandable and condensed lines that straightforwardly present her eloquent and sensualistic understanding of the issue being presented. The poems seem to be written not just about everyday Nicaraguan citizens, but also for them. Her poems relate the day-to-day activities and experiences of her fellow Nicaraguans and are accessible to the average person. They project an imagery that reflects the passion, emotions, thoughts, and ideas of life and love. She excels in the treatment of women and their issues.

Although they are highly accessible, Zamora's poems are not superficial. The syntactic and symmetrically uncomplicated text presents a gamut of social, gender, and political dilemmas in a manner that is unique to Zamora, a manner that gives the reader pause and permits, even demands, further consideration. Zamora's works are widely read and often memorized and recited in many Spanish-speaking countries, including countries with high rates of poverty, disease, illiteracy, inadequate housing, and domestic violence—the very groups Zamora is seeking to reach with her work. Her works are welcomed in Latin American countries where the reading of poetry and the honoring of poets is much more a part of everyday life than in the more literate, developed world. Zamora's poetry has also found an audience in academic circles and institutions in the United States and Europe, which attests to her poetry's depth.

Zamora writes with a revolutionary zeal. The approachability of her poetry does not, in any manner, limit her impassioned defense of women's causes. She does not hesitate to rail against the poor treatment of women in Nicaragua and other countries. She pulls no punches in her denunciation of the situations in which many women in Latin America find themselves. Zamora not only movingly exposes the tragic consequences for women trapped in dysfunctional marriages, underpaid and dehumanizing jobs, and other potential-limiting situations, but she also reveals and excoriates the macho cultures that produce and promote limited cultural expectations for women and other disenfranchised groups.

In her poetry, Zamora pays extreme attention to detail. She accentuates seemingly insignificant details in the everyday lives of women and others. Mundane actions such as washing clothes reveal the monotonous toll of the laundrywoman's job. The sensuality of a woman is revealed by means of elaborate depictions of flowers. She uses uncomplicated but detailed images to solicit introspection on the part of the reader in complicated dilemmas.

THE VIOLENT FOAM

Zamora's husband, Evans, translated her first collection, *The Violent Foam*, into English. In this collection, Zamora writes of the struggles of her country and her gender. She compares the realities of the Nicaraguan Revolution to the realities of the fight for women's rights. Her poems often relate to a more subtle but real revolution fought within the bounds of everyday life in Latin America. She includes many astute references to women caught in mundane work and stifling marriages. The women of these poems are captive within a society that limits not only their possibilities, but also their right to express their angst and hopelessness. Her themes include the monotony of life for Nicaraguan women. For example, Zamora describes the tedious world of a seamstress, whose nights are spent dreaming of endless stitching and of repetitive, mindless work that does not allow time for interaction with men. The seamstress laments to her son that his father has ruined her chances to the point where she cannot even imagine what might otherwise have been. In the era in which these poems were penned, many felt the Nicaraguan Revolution was ongoing. Regardless, it is obvious that Zamora felt that the uprising of women in response to the confining patriarchal culture of Nicaragua was an inevitable and ongoing process.

CLEAN SLATE

In *Clean Slate*, Zamora directly and eloquently challenges the patriarchal hegemony of her geographical and temporal space. With a determined but fair approach, she takes on reproduction, family, daily housework, the dual role of woman as angel and whore, work equality, and macho-related issues as they relate to Nicaraguan women. Zamora's unique point of view—that of a woman who actively participated in the Nicaraguan Revolution that eventually brought down the Somoza dynasty, one of the most entrenched and male-dominated regimes in Latin America—is evident in the poems. However, her themes go beyond critiquing the lack of balance between the masculine and feminine in Latin America and embrace the natural physical alliance between the sexes. Her scorn for arrogant male dominance does not preclude the simple but profound exposition of the inherent values of the female body and existence. Zamora embraces the capacity for affection as expressed by both genders. She states that being born a woman in Latin America necessitates unjust and unwarranted devotion to others in terms of service and dedication. Her poems embody a uniquely Nicaraguan feminism, often without the North American and European fervor in opposition to all things male. In "Vision of Your Body," she succinctly articulates how the sight of a lover's body can evoke sentiments as strong as the earth itself being ripped apart.

OTHER MAJOR WORK
EDITED TEXT: *La mujer nicaragüense en la poesía: Anthología*, 1992.

BIBLIOGRAPHY
Balderston, Daniel, and Mike Gonzalez, eds. *Encyclopedia of Latin American and Caribbean Literature, 1900-2003*. New York: Routledge, 2004. Contains a short biographical entry on Zamora. Also contains an introduction that places Zamora in context.
Bowen, Kevin. *Writing Between the Lines: An Anthology on War and Its Social Consequences*. Amherst: University of Massachusetts Press, 1997. This anthology includes an analysis of several of Zamora's poems, including "Surreptitious Encounter with Joaquin Pasos," "Urgent Message to My Mother," and "Testimony: Death of a Guatemalan Village." Includes index and bibliography.
Dawes, Greg. *Aesthetics and Revolution: Nicaraguan Poetry, 1979-1990*. Minneapolis: University of Minnesota Press, 1993. Contains a chapter on feminist and feminine self-representation that features a section on Zamora. Dawes finds her to be a realist rather than an avant-garde poet.
Gioseffi, Daniela, ed. *Women on War: An International Anthology of Writings from Antiquity to the Present*. 2d ed. New York: Feminist Press at the City University of New York, 2003. Contains a brief biography of Zamora and her poems "Song of Hope" and "When We Go Home Again." Gioseffi's introduction provides perspective on Zamora's writings.
Jason, Philip K., ed. *Masterplots II: Poetry Series*. Rev. ed. Pasadena, Calif.: Salem Press, 2002. Contains an in-depth analysis of Zamora's poem "Dear Aunt Chofi."

Zamora, Daisy. "Daisy Zamora." Interview by Margaret Randell. In *Sandino's Daughters: Testimonies of Nicaraguan Women in Struggle*. Rev. ed. New Brunswick, N.J.: Rutgers University Press, 1995. First published in 1981, this work is based on a series of interviews Randell conducted with women involved in the Sandinista Revolution. In the Zamora interview, written like a memoir, she describes her life before, during, and after the war; her political beliefs; and her poetry. Includes a few poems.

———. "'I Am Looking for the Women of My House': Daisy Zamora." Interview by Margaret Randell. In *Sandino's Daughters Revisited: Feminism in Nicaragua*. New Brunswick, N.J.: Rutgers University Press, 1994. In this interview, Zamora talks about her background, her work during the war, and women's rights in Nicaragua.

Paul Siegrist

CHECKLIST FOR EXPLICATING A POEM

I. The Initial Readings

A. Before reading the poem, the reader should:
1. Notice its form and length.
2. Consider the title, determining, if possible, whether it might function as an allusion, symbol, or poetic image.
3. Notice the date of composition or publication, and identify the general era of the poet.

B. The poem should be read intuitively and emotionally and be allowed to "happen" as much as possible.

C. In order to establish the rhythmic flow, the poem should be reread. A note should be made as to where the irregular spots (if any) are located.

II. Explicating the Poem

A. *Dramatic situation*. Studying the poem line by line helps the reader discover the dramatic situation. All elements of the dramatic situation are interrelated and should be viewed as reflecting and affecting one another. The dramatic situation serves a particular function in the poem, adding realism, surrealism, or absurdity; drawing attention to certain parts of the poem; and changing to reinforce other aspects of the poem. All points should be considered. The following questions are particularly helpful to ask in determining dramatic situation:
1. What, if any, is the narrative action in the poem?
2. How many personae appear in the poem? What part do they take in the action?
3. What is the relationship between characters?
4. What is the setting (time and location) of the poem?

B. *Point of view*. An understanding of the poem's point of view is a major step toward comprehending the poet's intended meaning. The reader should ask:
1. Who is the speaker? Is he or she addressing someone else or the reader?
2. Is the narrator able to understand or see everything happening to him or her, or does the reader know things that the narrator does not?
3. Is the narrator reliable?
4. Do point of view and dramatic situation seem consistent? If not, the inconsistencies may provide clues to the poem's meaning.

C. *Images and metaphors.* Images and metaphors are often the most intricately crafted vehicles of the poem for relaying the poet's message. Realizing that the images and metaphors work in harmony with the dramatic situation and point of view will help the reader to see the poem as a whole, rather than as disassociated elements.
   1. The reader should identify the concrete images (that is, those that are formed from objects that can be touched, smelled, seen, felt, or tasted). Is the image projected by the poet consistent with the physical object?
   2. If the image is abstract, or so different from natural imagery that it cannot be associated with a real object, then what are the properties of the image?
   3. To what extent is the reader asked to form his or her own images?
   4. Is any image repeated in the poem? If so, how has it been changed? Is there a controlling image?
   5. Are any images compared to each other? Do they reinforce one another?
   6. Is there any difference between the way the reader perceives the image and the way the narrator sees it?
   7. What seems to be the narrator's or persona's attitude toward the image?

D. *Words.* Every substantial word in a poem may have more than one intended meaning, as used by the author. Because of this, the reader should look up many of these words in the dictionary and:
   1. Note all definitions that have the slightest connection with the poem.
   2. Note any changes in syntactical patterns in the poem.
   3. In particular, note those words that could possibly function as symbols or allusions, and refer to any appropriate sources for further information.

E. *Meter, rhyme, structure, and tone.* In scanning the poem, all elements of prosody should be noted by the reader. These elements are often used by a poet to manipulate the reader's emotions, and therefore they should be examined closely to arrive at the poet's specific intention.
   1. Does the basic meter follow a traditional pattern such as those found in nursery rhymes or folk songs?
   2. Are there any variations in the base meter? Such changes or substitutions are important thematically and should be identified.
   3. Are the rhyme schemes traditional or innovative, and what might their form mean to the poem?
   4. What devices has the poet used to create sound patterns (such as assonance and alliteration)?
   5. Is the stanza form a traditional or innovative one?
   6. If the poem is composed of verse paragraphs rather than stanzas, how do they affect the progression of the poem?

7. After examining the above elements, is the resultant tone of the poem casual or formal, pleasant, harsh, emotional, authoritative?

F. *Historical context.* The reader should attempt to place the poem into historical context, checking on events at the time of composition. Archaic language, expressions, images, or symbols should also be looked up.

G. *Themes and motifs.* By seeing the poem as a composite of emotion, intellect, craftsmanship, and tradition, the reader should be able to determine the themes and motifs (smaller recurring ideas) presented in the work. He or she should ask the following questions to help pinpoint these main ideas:
1. Is the poet trying to advocate social, moral, or religious change?
2. Does the poet seem sure of his or her position?
3. Does the poem appeal primarily to the emotions, to the intellect, or to both?
4. Is the poem relying on any particular devices for effect (such as imagery, allusion, paradox, hyperbole, or irony)?

BIBLIOGRAPHY

GENERAL REFERENCE SOURCES

BIOGRAPHICAL SOURCES
Colby, Vineta, ed. *World Authors, 1975-1980*. Wilson Authors Series. New York: H. W. Wilson, 1985.
_____. *World Authors, 1980-1985*. Wilson Authors Series. New York: H. W. Wilson, 1991.
_____. *World Authors, 1985-1990*. Wilson Authors Series. New York: H. W. Wilson, 1995.
Cyclopedia of World Authors. 4th rev. ed. 5 vols. Pasadena, Calif.: Salem Press, 2003.
Dictionary of Literary Biography. 254 vols. Detroit: Gale Research, 1978- .
International Who's Who in Poetry and Poets' Encyclopaedia. Cambridge, England: International Biographical Centre, 1993.
Seymour-Smith, Martin, and Andrew C. Kimmens, eds. *World Authors, 1900-1950*. Wilson Authors Series. 4 vols. New York: H. W. Wilson, 1996.
Thompson, Clifford, ed. *World Authors, 1990-1995*. Wilson Authors Series. New York: H. W. Wilson, 1999.
Wakeman, John, ed. *World Authors, 1950-1970*. New York: H. W. Wilson, 1975.
_____. *World Authors, 1970-1975*. Wilson Authors Series. New York: H. W. Wilson, 1991.
Willhardt, Mark, and Alan Michael Parker, eds. *Who's Who in Twentieth Century World Poetry*. New York: Routledge, 2000.

CRITICISM
Brooks, Cleanth, and Robert Penn Warren. *Understanding Poetry*. 4th ed. Reprint. Fort Worth, Tex.: Heinle & Heinle, 2003.
Classical and Medieval Literature Criticism. Detroit: Gale Research, 1988- .
Contemporary Literary Criticism. Detroit: Gale Research, 1973- .
Day, Gary. *Literary Criticism: A New History*. Edinburgh, Scotland: Edinburgh University Press, 2008.
Draper, James P., ed. *World Literature Criticism 1500 to the Present: A Selection of Major Authors from Gale's Literary Criticism Series*. 6 vols. Detroit: Gale Research, 1992.
Habib, M. A. R. *A History of Literary Criticism: From Plato to the Present*. Malden, Mass.: Wiley-Blackwell, 2005.
Jason, Philip K., ed. *Masterplots II: Poetry Series, Revised Edition*. 8 vols. Pasadena, Calif.: Salem Press, 2002.
Literature Criticism from 1400 to 1800. Detroit: Gale Research, 1984- .

Lodge, David, and Nigel Wood. *Modern Criticism and Theory*. 3d ed. New York: Longman, 2008.

Magill, Frank N., ed. *Magill's Bibliography of Literary Criticism*. 4 vols. Englewood Cliffs, N.J.: Salem Press, 1979.

MLA International Bibliography. New York: Modern Language Association of America, 1922- .

Nineteenth-Century Literature Criticism. Detroit: Gale Research, 1981- .

Twentieth-Century Literary Criticism. Detroit: Gale Research, 1978- .

Vedder, Polly, ed. *World Literature Criticism Supplement: A Selection of Major Authors from Gale's Literary Criticism Series*. 2 vols. Detroit: Gale Research, 1997.

Young, Robyn V., ed. *Poetry Criticism: Excerpts from Criticism of the Works of the Most Significant and Widely Studied Poets of World Literature*. 29 vols. Detroit: Gale Research, 1991.

POETRY DICTIONARIES AND HANDBOOKS

Carey, Gary, and Mary Ellen Snodgrass. *A Multicultural Dictionary of Literary Terms*. Jefferson, N.C.: McFarland, 1999.

Deutsch, Babette. *Poetry Handbook: A Dictionary of Terms*. 4th ed. New York: Funk & Wagnalls, 1974.

Drury, John. *The Poetry Dictionary*. Cincinnati, Ohio: Story Press, 1995.

Kinzie, Mary. *A Poet's Guide to Poetry*. Chicago: University of Chicago Press, 1999.

Lennard, John. *The Poetry Handbook: A Guide to Reading Poetry for Pleasure and Practical Criticism*. New York: Oxford University Press, 1996.

Matterson, Stephen, and Darryl Jones. *Studying Poetry*. New York: Oxford University Press, 2000.

Packard, William. *The Poet's Dictionary: A Handbook of Prosody and Poetic Devices*. New York: Harper & Row, 1989.

Preminger, Alex, et al., eds. *The New Princeton Encyclopedia of Poetry and Poetics*. 3d rev. ed. Princeton, N.J.: Princeton University Press, 1993.

Shipley, Joseph Twadell, ed. *Dictionary of World Literary Terms, Forms, Technique, Criticism*. Rev. ed. Boston: George Allen and Unwin, 1979.

INDEXES OF PRIMARY WORKS

Frankovich, Nicholas, ed. *The Columbia Granger's Index to Poetry in Anthologies*. 11th ed. New York: Columbia University Press, 1997.

_____. *The Columbia Granger's Index to Poetry in Collected and Selected Works*. New York: Columbia University Press, 1997.

Guy, Patricia. *A Women's Poetry Index*. Phoenix, Ariz.: Oryx Press, 1985.

Hazen, Edith P., ed. *Columbia Granger's Index to Poetry*. 10th ed. New York: Columbia University Press, 1994.

Hoffman, Herbert H., and Rita Ludwig Hoffman, comps. *International Index to Recorded Poetry*. New York: H. W. Wilson, 1983.

Kline, Victoria. *Last Lines: An Index to the Last Lines of Poetry*. 2 vols. New York: Facts On File, 1991.

Marcan, Peter. *Poetry Themes: A Bibliographical Index to Subject Anthologies and Related Criticisms in the English Language, 1875-1975*. Hamden, Conn.: Linnet Books, 1977.

Poem Finder. Great Neck, N.Y.: Roth, 2000.

POETICS, POETIC FORMS, AND GENRES

Attridge, Derek. *Poetic Rhythm: An Introduction*. New York: Cambridge University Press, 1995.

Brogan, T. V. F. *Verseform: A Comparative Bibliography*. Baltimore: Johns Hopkins University Press, 1989.

Fussell, Paul. *Poetic Meter and Poetic Form*. Rev. ed. New York: McGraw-Hill, 1979.

Hollander, John. *Rhyme's Reason*. 3d ed. New Haven, Conn.: Yale University Press, 2001.

Jackson, Guida M. *Traditional Epics: A Literary Companion*. New York: Oxford University Press, 1995.

Padgett, Ron, ed. *The Teachers and Writers Handbook of Poetic Forms*. 2d ed. New York: Teachers & Writers Collaborative, 2000.

Pinsky, Robert. *The Sounds of Poetry: A Brief Guide*. New York: Farrar, Straus and Giroux, 1998.

Preminger, Alex, and T. V. F. Brogan, eds. *New Princeton Encyclopedia of Poetry and Poetics*. 3d ed. Princeton, N.J.: Princeton University Press, 1993.

Spiller, Michael R. G. *The Sonnet Sequence: A Study of Its Strategies*. Studies in Literary Themes and Genres 13. New York: Twayne, 1997.

Turco, Lewis. *The New Book of Forms: A Handbook of Poetics*. Hanover, N.H.: University Press of New England, 1986.

Williams, Miller. *Patterns of Poetry: An Encyclopedia of Forms*. Baton Rouge: Louisiana State University Press, 1986.

LATIN AMERICAN POETRY

GENERAL

Bleznick, Donald William. *A Sourcebook for Hispanic Literature and Language: A Selected, Annotated Guide to Spanish, Spanish-American, and United States Hispanic Bibliography, Literature, Linguistics, Journals, and Other Source Materials*. 3d ed. Lanham, Md.: Scarecrow Press, 1995.

Newmark, Maxim. *Dictionary of Spanish Literature.* Westport, Conn.: Greenwood Press, 1972.

Sefami, Jacobo, comp. *Contemporary Spanish American Poets: A Bibliography of Primary and Secondary Sources.* Bibliographies and Indexes in World Literature 33. Westport, Conn.: Greenwood Press, 1992.

Woodbridge, Hensley Charles. *Guide to Reference Works for the Study of the Spanish Language and Literature and Spanish American Literature.* 2d ed. New York: Modern Language Association of America, 1997.

CARIBBEAN

Brown, Stewart, and Mark McWatt, eds. *The Oxford Book of Caribbean Verse.* New York: Oxford University Press, 2005.

Fenwick, M. J. *Writers of the Caribbean and Central America: A Bibliography.* Garland Reference Library of the Humanities 1244. New York: Garland, 1992.

James, Conrad, and John Perivolaris, eds. *The Cultures of the Hispanic Caribbean.* Gainesville: University Press of Florida, 2000.

Martinez, Julia A., ed. *Dictionary of Twentieth-Century Cuban Literature.* Westport, Conn.: Greenwood Press, 1990.

MEXICO AND CENTRAL AMERICA

Agosín, Marjorie, and Roberta Gordenstein, eds. *Miriam's Daughters: Jewish Latin American Women Poets.* Foreword by Agosín. Santa Fe, N.Mex.: Sherman Asher, 2001.

Cortes, Eladio. *Dictionary of Mexican Literature.* Westport, Conn.: Greenwood Press, 1992.

Dauster, Frank N. *The Double Strand: Five Contemporary Mexican Poets.* Louisville: University Press of Kentucky, 1987.

Foster, David William. *Mexican Literature: A Bibliography of Secondary Sources.* 2d ed. Metuchen, N.J.: Scarecrow Press, 1992.

_____, ed. *Mexican Literature: A History.* Austin: University of Texas Press, 1994.

González Peña, Carlos. *History of Mexican Literature.* Translated by Gusta Barfield Nance and Florence Johnson Dunstan. 3d rev. ed. Dallas: Southern Methodist University Press, 1968.

Nicholson, Irene. *A Guide to Mexican Poetry, Ancient and Modern.* Mexico: Editorial Minutiae Mexicana, 1968.

Vicuña, Cecilia, and Ernesto Livon-Grosman, eds. *The Oxford Book of Latin American Poetry: A Bilingual Anthology.* New York: Oxford University Press, 2009.

Washbourne, Kelly, ed. *An Anthology of Spanish American Modernismo: In English Translation, with Spanish Text.* Translated by Washbourne with Sergio Waisman. New York: Modern Language Association of America, 2007.

SOUTH AMERICA

Agosín, Marjorie, and Roberta Gordenstein, eds. *Miriam's Daughters: Jewish Latin American Women Poets*. Foreword by Agosín. Santa Fe, N.Mex.: Sherman Asher, 2001.

Brotherston, Gordon. *Latin American Poetry: Origins and Presence*. New York: Cambridge University Press, 1975.

Perrone, Charles A. *Seven Faces: Brazilian Poetry Since Modernism*. Durham, N.C.: Duke University Press, 1996.

Rowe, William. *Poets of Contemporary Latin America: History and the Inner Life*. New York: Oxford University Press, 2000.

Smith, Verity, ed. *Encyclopedia of Latin American Literature*. Chicago: Fitzroy Dearborn, 1997.

Stern, Irwin, ed. *Dictionary of Brazilian Literature*. Westport, Conn.: Greenwood Press, 1988.

Vicuña, Cecilia, and Ernesto Livon-Grosman, eds. *The Oxford Book of Latin American Poetry: A Bilingual Anthology*. New York: Oxford University Press, 2009.

Washbourne, Kelly, ed. *An Anthology of Spanish American Modernismo: In English Translation, with Spanish Text*. Translated by Washbourne with Sergio Waisman. New York: Modern Language Association of America, 2007.

GUIDE TO ONLINE RESOURCES
WEB SITES

The following sites were visited by the editors of Salem Press in 2010. Because URLs frequently change, the accuracy of these addresses cannot be guaranteed; however, long-standing sites, such as those of colleges and universities, national organizations, and government agencies, generally maintain links when their sites are moved.

LitWeb
http://litweb.net

LitWeb provides biographies of hundreds of world authors throughout history that can be accessed through an alphabetical listing. The pages about each writer contain a list of his or her works, suggestions for further reading, and illustrations. The site also offers information about past and present winners of major literary prizes.

Poetry in Translation
http://poetryintranslation.com

This independent resource provides modern translations of classic texts by famous poets and also provides original poetry and critical works. Visitors can choose from several languages, including English, Spanish, Chinese, Russian, Italian, and Greek. Original text is available as well. Also includes links to further literary resources.

Poetry International Web
http://international.poetryinternationalweb.org

Poetry International Web features information on poets from countries such as Indonesia, Zimbabwe, Iceland, India, Slovenia, Morocco, Albania, Afghanistan, Russia, and Brazil. The site offers news, essays, interviews and discussion, and hundreds of poems, both in their original languages and in English translation.

Poet's Corner
http://theotherpages.org/poems

The Poet's Corner, one of the oldest text resources on the Web, provides access to about seven thousand works of poetry by several hundred different poets from around the world. Indexes are arranged and searchable by title, name of poet, or subject. The site also offers its own resources, including "Faces of the Poets"—a gallery of portraits—and "Lives of the Poets"—a growing collection of biographies.

Voice of the Shuttle
http://vos.ucsb.edu

One of the most complete and authoritative places for online information about literature, Voice of the Shuttle is maintained by professors and students in the English Department at the University of California, Santa Barbara. The site provides countless links to electronic books, academic journals, literary association Web sites, sites created by university professors, and many other resources.

Electronic Databases

Electronic databases usually do not have their own URLs. Instead, public, college, and university libraries subscribe to these databases, provide links to them on their Web sites, and make them available to library card holders or other specified patrons. Readers can visit library Web sites or ask reference librarians to check on availability.

Canadian Literary Centre

Produced by EBSCO, the Canadian Literary Centre database contains full-text content from ECW Press, a Toronto-based publisher, including the titles in the publisher's Canadian fiction studies, Canadian biography, and Canadian writers and their works series; *ECW's Biographical Guide to Canadian Novelists*; and *George Woodcock's Introduction to Canadian Fiction*. Author biographies, essays and literary criticism, and book reviews are among the database's offerings.

Literary Reference Center

EBSCO's Literary Reference Center (LRC) is a comprehensive full-text database designed primarily to help high school and undergraduate students in English and the humanities with homework and research assignments about literature. The database contains massive amounts of information from reference works, books, literary journals, and other materials, including more than 31,000 plot summaries, synopses, and overviews of literary works; almost 100,000 essays and articles of literary criticism; about 140,000 author biographies; more than 605,000 book reviews; and more than 5,200 author interviews. It contains the entire contents of Salem Press's MagillOnLiterature Plus. Users can retrieve information by browsing a list of authors' names or titles of literary works; they can also use an advanced search engine to access information by numerous categories, including author name, gender, cultural identity, national identity, and the years in which he or she lived, or by literary title, character, locale, genre, and publication date. The Literary Reference Center also features a literary-historical time line, an encyclopedia of literature, and a glossary of literary terms.

MagillOnLiterature Plus

MagillOnLiterature Plus is a comprehensive, integrated literature database produced by Salem Press and available on the EBSCOhost platform. The database contains the full text of essays in Salem's many literature-related reference works, including *Masterplots, Cyclopedia of World Authors, Cyclopedia of Literary Characters, Cyclopedia of Literary Places, Critical Survey of Poetry, Critical Survey of Long Fiction, Critical Survey of Short Fiction, World Philosophers and Their Works, Magill's Literary Annual,* and *Magill's Book Reviews.* Among its contents are articles on more than 35,000 literary works and more than 8,500 poets, writers, dramatists, essayists, and philosophers; more than 1,000 images; and a glossary of more than 1,300 literary terms. The biographical essays include lists of authors' works and secondary bibliographies, and hundreds of overview essays examine and discuss literary genres, time periods, and national literatures.

Rebecca Kuzins; updated by Desiree Dreeuws

GEOGRAPHICAL INDEX

ARGENTINA
    Borges, Jorge Luis, 17
    Hernández, José, 70

BRAZIL
    Drummond de Andrade, Carlos, 48

CHILE
    Mistral, Gabriela, 76
    Neruda, Pablo, 85
    Parra, Nicanor, 99

EL SALVADOR
    Alegría, Claribel, 9

MEXICO
    Cruz, Sor Juana Inés de la, 31
    González Martínez, Enrique, 60
    Paz, Octavio, 107
    Reyes, Alfonso, 118

NICARAGUA
    Alegría, Claribel, 9
    Cardenal, Ernesto, 24
    Darío, Rubén, 40
    Zamora, Daisy, 139

PERU
    Vallejo, César, 126

CATEGORY INDEX

AVANT-GARDE POETS
    Vallejo, César, 126

BALLADS
    Cruz, Sor Juana Inés de la, 31

CHILDREN'S/YOUNG ADULT POETRY
    Mistral, Gabriela, 76

CLASSICISM: TWENTIETH CENTURY
    Reyes, Alfonso, 118

EPICS
    Cardenal, Ernesto, 24
    Hernández, José, 70
    Neruda, Pablo, 85

EPIGRAMS
    Cardenal, Ernesto, 24

EXPERIMENTAL POETS
    Darío, Rubén, 40
    Parra, Nicanor, 99
    Paz, Octavio, 107

FEMINIST POETS
    Alegría, Claribel, 9
    Cruz, Sor Juana Inés de la, 31
    Zamora, Daisy, 139

LOVE POETRY
    Alegría, Claribel, 9
    Cruz, Sor Juana Inés de la, 31
    Neruda, Pablo, 85
    Vallejo, César, 126

LYRIC POETRY
    Cardenal, Ernesto, 24
    Cruz, Sor Juana Inés de la, 31
    Darío, Rubén, 40

    Mistral, Gabriela, 76
    Neruda, Pablo, 85
    Vallejo, César, 126

METAPHYSICAL POETS
    Cruz, Sor Juana Inés de la, 31

MODERNISM
    Cardenal, Ernesto, 24
    Neruda, Pablo, 85
    Paz, Octavio, 107

MODERNISMO
    Darío, Rubén, 40
    Drummond de Andrade, Carlos, 48
    González Martínez, Enrique, 60

NARRATIVE POETRY
    Drummond de Andrade, Carlos, 48

OCCASIONAL VERSE
    Cruz, Sor Juana Inés de la, 31

ODES
    Neruda, Pablo, 85

POLITICAL POETS
    Alegría, Claribel, 9
    Cardenal, Ernesto, 24
    Darío, Rubén, 40
    Hernández, José, 70
    Neruda, Pablo, 85
    Zamora, Daisy, 139

POSTMODERNISM
    Cardenal, Ernesto, 24
    González Martínez, Enrique, 60
    Parra, Nicanor, 99
    Paz, Octavio, 107

PROSE POETRY
  Borges, Jorge Luis, 17
  Paz, Octavio, 107

RELIGIOUS POETRY
  Cardenal, Ernesto, 24
  Cruz, Sor Juana Inés de la, 31

SATIRIC POETRY
  Parra, Nicanor, 99
SONNETS
  Cruz, Sor Juana Inés de la, 31
  González Martínez, Enrique, 60
  Mistral, Gabriela, 76
  Neruda, Pablo, 85
SURREALIST POETS
  Neruda, Pablo, 85

  Vallejo, César, 126
SYMBOLIST POETS
  Borges, Jorge Luis, 17

ULTRAISM
  Neruda, Pablo, 85
  Vallejo, César, 126

VISIONARY POETRY
  Darío, Rubén, 40
  Neruda, Pablo, 85

WOMEN POETS
  Alegría, Claribel, 9
  Cruz, Sor Juana Inés de la, 31
  Mistral, Gabriela, 76
  Zamora, Daisy, 139

SUBJECT INDEX

"A Víctor Hugo," 43
After-Dinner Declarations (Parra), 105
Águila o sol? See Eagle or Sun?
Alcayaga, Lucila Godoy. *See* Mistral, Gabriela
Alegría, Claribel, 9-16
    Casting Off, 14
    Flores del volcán/Flowers from the Volcano, 11
    Fugues, 13
    Luisa in Realityland, 12
    Sorrow, 14
    Woman of the River, 12
Alguma poesia (Drummond de Andrade), 53
Andrade, Carlos Drummond de. *See* Drummond de Andrade, Carlos
"Año lírico, El" (Darío), 44
Artefactos (Parra), 105
Azul (Darío), 44

Basoalto, Neftalí Ricardo Reyes. *See* Neruda, Pablo
"Bird, The" (Paz), 111
Black Heralds, The (Vallejo), 130
Blanco (Paz), 114
"Blazon" (Darío), 45
Boitempo (Drummond de Andrade), 57
Borges, Jorge Luis, 17-23
    Dream Tigers, 21
    Fervor de Buenos Aires, 20
    The Gold of Tigers, 21
Bustos Domecq, H. *See* Borges, Jorge Luis
Bustos, F. *See* Borges, Jorge Luis

Cancionero sin nombre (Parra), 103
Canciones rusas (Parra), 104

Cántico cósmico. See Music of the Spheres, The
Canto General (Neruda), 95
Cantos de vida y esperanza, los cisnes, y otros poemas (Darío), 46
Captain's Verses, The (Neruda), 95
Cardenal, Ernesto, 24-30
    "Marilyn Monroe," 28
    The Music of the Spheres, 28
    "Zero Hour," 27
Casting Off (Alegría), 14
Claro enigma (Drummond de Andrade), 56
Clean Slate (Zamora), 141
Cosmic Canticle. See Music of the Spheres, The
Creacionismo, 4
Crepusculario (Neruda), 89
Cruz, Sor Juana Inés de la, 1, 31-39
    "Esta tarde, mi bien," 34
    First Dream, 36
    "Hombres necios," 35
Cueca larga, La (Parra), 103

Darío, Rubén, 2, 40-47
    "A Víctor Hugo," 43
    "El Año lírico," 44
    Azul, 44
    "Blazon," 45
    Cantos de vida y esperanza, los cisnes, y otros poemas, 46
    Prosas Profanas, and Other Poems, 45
    "To Roosevelt," 46
Desolación (Mistral), 79
Discos visuales (Paz), 114
Discursos de sobremesa. See After-Dinner Declarations

159

Domecq, H. Bustos. *See* Borges, Jorge Luis
Dream Tigers (Borges), 21
Drummond de Andrade, Carlos, 48-59
   Alguma poesia, 53
   Boitempo, 57
   Claro enigma, 56
   Fazendeiro do ar, 56
   "In the Middle of the Road," 53
   "Isso é aquilo," 57
   Lição de coisas, 57
   "Poem of Seven Faces," 54
   "Residue," 55
   A rosa do povo, 55
   "Search for Poetry," 55
   Sentimento do mundo, 55
   "Song to the Man of the People C. C.," 55

Eagle or Sun? (Paz), 112
Elemental Odes, The (Neruda), 95
España. See Spain, Take This Cup from Me
"Esta tarde, mi bien" (Cruz), 34
Exteriorismo (poetic technique), 5

Fazendeiro do ar (Drummond de Andrade), 56
Feminist poets, 6
Fervor de Buenos Aires (Borges), 20
First Dream (Cruz), 36
Flores del volcán/Flowers from the Volcano (Alegría), 11
Fugues (Alegría), 13

Gaucho Martin Fierro, The (Hernández), 73
Gold of Tigers, The (Borges), 21
González Martínez, Enrique, 60-69
   Lirismos, 65
   La muerte del cisne, 67
   Preludios, 65
   Los senderos ocultos, 66
   Silénter, 66
   "Wring the Swan's Neck," 64

Hacedor, El. See Dream Tigers
Heraldos negros, Los. See Black Heralds, The
Hernández, José, 2, 70-75
   The Gaucho Martin Fierro, 73
   The Return of Martin Fierro, 73
"Hombres necios" (Cruz), 35
"Hora cero, La." *See* "Zero Hour"
Human Poems (Vallejo), 134

"In the Middle of the Road" (Drummond de Andrade), 53
"Interrupted Elegy" (Paz), 112
Inés de la Cruz, Sor Juana. *See* Cruz, Sor Juana Inés de la
"Isso é aquilo" (Drummond de Andrade), 57

"Jacob" (Reyes), 123
Juana, Sor. *See* Cruz, Sor Juana Inés de la

Lagar (Mistral), 82
"Lamentación de Navidad" (Reyes), 123
Latin American poetry, 1-8
Lirismos (González Martínez), 65
Lição de coisas (Drummond de Andrade), 57
Luisa in Realityland (Alegría), 12
Lynch, B. Suárez. *See* Borges, Jorge Luis

"Marilyn Monroe" (Cardenal), 28
Martínez, Enrique González. *See* González Martínez, Enrique
Martínez, Ernesto Cardenal. *See* Cardenal, Ernesto
Mistral, Gabriela, 76-84
   Desolación, 79
   Lagar, 82
   Poema de Chile, 83
   Tala, 81
   Ternura, 82
Modernismo, 2, 42, 53, 64
Muerte del cisne, La (González Martínez), 67